BEST REMEMBERED

☆

A HUNDRED STARS

of

YESTERYEAR

Acknowledgements

Thanks to Charles Oliver who so expertly verified the text
and to Barbara Adkins for her proofreading.
The cartoon strip on page 113 was originally published in *Jane at War*
and re-produced here by courtesy of *The Mirror.*

Eric Midwinter has written, to date, over 40 books on a variety of topics.
Those relevant to the subjects covered in *Best Remembered* include:
From Third Age Press ~
A Voyage of rediscovery: a guide to writing your life story (2nd edition 2001)
Encore: a guide to planning a celebration of your life (1993)
The Rhubarb People (1993)
Getting to know me (1996)
From other publishers ~
Make 'em laugh: famous comedians and their worlds (1979)
The lost seasons: cricket in wartime 1939 - 1945 (1987)
Brylcreem Summer: the 1947 cricket season (1991)
Yesterdays: the way we were: 1919 - 1939 (1998)
Yesterdays: the way we were: 1939 - 1953 (2001)

Rufus Segar worked for The Economist Group for 30 years. For the past dozen
years he has illustrated many books — two each of Eric Midwinter's and
H B Gibson's for Third Age Press — and many topographical books:
Hythe 1992, and *Hungerford 2000* being the longest ones.
Working on *Best Remembered* has made him realise how much he has been
indebted to John Hassall: 1886 - 1956 (Albert, qv. here)
and Dudley D Watkins: 1907 - 1967 (Desperate Dan, qv. here).

BEST REMEMBERED

A HUNDRED STARS

of

YESTERYEAR

Eric Midwinter

Illustrations by Rufus Segar

Third Age Press

Third Age Press

ISBN 1 898576 18 1
First edition

Third Age Press Ltd, 2002
Third Age Press, 6 Parkside Gardens
London SW19 5EY
Managing Editor Dianne Norton

Illustrations © by Rufus Segar
Cover design by Rufus Segar

Layout design by Dianne Norton
Printed and bound in Great Britain
by Intype

CONTENTS

Introduction

The BBC first broadcast in 1922 and became a public corporation in 1927. In that same year Al Jolson's *the Jazz Singer*, the first-ever 'talkie' film, was screened. For a quarter of a century sound radio and sound cinema reigned supreme as conveyors of popular culture. Although dance halls, sports stadia and variety theatres remained crowded and welcoming, and although there was a large growth of interest in records, many people relied on the radio and the cinema for entertainment, not least for light, usually dance, music, as well as 'wireless' sports commentaries and sport as covered on cinema newscasts. Then television began to claim dominance, a threat to practically every other entertainment sector. The televising of the Coronation in 1953 is normally regarded as the breakthrough point. Many people remember this as the occasion when the first TV set was bought or rented. There were about 5m sets at that juncture — by 1971 over 90% of families had one. The Coronation was watched by 2m people on the streets; 12m listening on radio; and 20.5m watching in often quite large groups round the telly.

That period from about 1927 to 1953 covers the formative years of many of those now in or approaching the Third Age, that is, in the 55-80 age-bands. It is a 25 or 26-year phase that covered some or all of the childhood, adolescence and young adulthood of this age-group. The cultural icons of that quarter century are the ones that its members will recall most vividly, with admiration, affection, even passion, for each star inspired his or her devotees when at their most impressionable. There are two interfacing reasons for offering tastes of the appropriate popular culture of the time. On the one side, there is the straightforward case for nostalgia, the simple delight of being reminded of a past pleasure. On the other hand, there is the positive case for reminiscence, the belief that, in recollecting those enjoyments of yesteryear, older people might well find ways of confidently putting their own life into perspective, finding some sense of self-identity in the process.

It is well-recognised that, in so far as either nostalgia or reminiscence does have, for many, this robust and supportive attribute, the use of 'triggers' to ignite or 'hooks' upon which to hang memories is an extremely useful tool. Thus this gallery of a hundred famous names from the everyday leisure pursuits of that age might combine the business of active reminiscence with the pleasure of plain enjoyment.

For the decent sake of coherence, it seems proper to delineate a beginning and an end, a threshold and a bar, for this venture into the popular culture of yesterday. 'The golden age of radio', coupled with the movie boom — 30m tickets sold each week at the 1940s peak — provides that coherence. Together they created a new and, for the first time, immediate national consciousness that was to prevail, proudly and intact, until it was successfully challenged by the current national art-form, television. In a mechanical sense, what TV did was to combine the pictures of the cinema with the sounds of the radio and offer the nation the equivalent of an Odeon in every sitting-room.

Radio and cinema, with their off-shoot of records, completed the shift, begun about 1870, to a national cultural format from a much more localised sets of cultures with localised heroes and heroines; in particular, the spread of popular music on a countrywide basis is a fine example of this trend. Indeed, the era we are reviewing also covers the principal impact of dance band tunes as the pop music of its day. Drawing off the rag-time tradition, and with the introduction of the fox-trot into Britain just after the end of World War I, the dance band phenomenon was scarcely to be challenged until the brash arrival of Rock'n'Roll in the early 1950s.

There was still a lot of live entertainment. The years in question witnessed the heyday of variety, that colourfully mixed bag of performers which grew out of the old-time music hall during the 1920s and more or less vanished in the 1950s under the pressure of television. This same period also saw the setting for the frothy revue, borrowing strenuously from both the music hall sketch and musical comedy song and dance disciplines. A miscellany of items, often threaded together by a wispy theme, it had had its origins in France and its very lightness, even its superficiality, appealed to many, especially in those rather nervous and frenetic inter-wars years. The exclusive clubs, hotels and restaurants were also the locus for intimate revue-style cabaret entertainment, and they also offered a comfortable billet to the top dance bands of the age. Thousands of others flocked to their local dance hall or 'palais'.

Then there was, of course, live sport, especially football, cricket and horse racing, all of which continued to have immense followings, certainly until after World War II. In fact, another marker for the end of our period might well be the slump in large 'gates' at many of such sporting fixtures as the 1950s progressed. Once more, the lure of the telly was held to be responsible, along with other counter-attractions like the desire to enjoy an outing in the family car — private motoring was to see a huge increase about this time. Although sports fans had long delighted in reading of the exploits of their heroes in the national press, this pre- to post-war period was also notable for the technical presentation of sport via radio and film, particularly the ubiquitous news-reel, which never failed to show high-lights of the big race or the dramatic boxing-match. Radio was soon adept at its regular 'outside broadcasting' of all kinds of popular sport, with sports commentators soon as well-known as those whose activities they described. Such technological advance meant that overseas sports stars, like overseas film stars, could also be brought to the British public's avid attention, whilst faster liner travel and, eventually, air transport brought some of these foreign heroes — and heroines — to our very doors.

From these broad bands of popular culture a hundred of the 'best remembered' of such personalities have been selected and their brief profiles included for the delectation of the reader. Obviously, several could quite as easily turn up in one section as in another, as comedian, for instance, or singer or film star, but, on balance, an attempt has been made to include each little biography in the section where the person concerned made premier impact. In approximate terms, there are seventy idols from the fields of comedy, popular song, dance music, radio, the 'light' stage and both British and American movies. That leaves room for 20 sportsmen and women,

neatly divided home and away, Britain and elsewhere, plus what we hope will prove an intriguing collection of fictional names of the time, invented characters who, on radio or through some other medium, became extremely famous.

Those now in late middle or older age are among the first generations to enjoy this all-encompassing national culture, one which, because it was artificially processed, was shared instantly — we listened to the same radio programme and watched the same film and danced to the same melody together. Thus the advent of radio and sound film and the coming of television build reasonable gateways down memory lane. Between them lie some 25 or so years of chronological mileage; along that section of memory lane strolled and performed great stars across a wide range of entertainment.

'Then shall our names', our famed hundred might add, after the manner of Shakespeare's Henry V at Agincourt, 'familiar in his mouth as household words . . . be in their flowing cups freshly remembered'.

Using *Best Remembered* for reminiscence purposes

First and foremost, this is a book to be enjoyed in its own right, but we are aware that, in households, among friends and in groups, it will give rise to considerable discussion. Here are one or two simple tips for those who might wish to use these hundred profiles for discussion or in a more structured way.

Readers, either as individuals or in groups, might be invited to consider the listings and content, first, to see what memories are generated by the names.

☆ How many of the hundred or of each group of ten do I remember?

☆ How many do I recall vividly, as opposed to just vaguely?

☆ When or at what age did I first watch/hear/become aware of X?

☆ Who was I with and what were the circumstances?

Next, there might be some friendly argument over the weightings in these judgements.

☆ How do I remember them?

☆ How accurate are the attempts to paint these hundred pen-pictures?

☆ Do I recall them as being as good as, worse than or even better than the writer's opinion?

Then there are two very important questions.

☆ On the one hand, to what extent have I changed my mind about these stars; do I like them more or less than when I was younger; how far have tastes changed and how would they fare in the modern spotlight?

☆ On the other hand, are there 'absentees'?

☆ Which others, using the school-room word of that era, would you like to mark 'present'?

☆ For each group of ten, suggest the additions you would make to the list — or, for that, matter who might you omit?

As a follow-up to that, another idea might be to arrange each ten in order of impact or brilliance.

☆ How would I rate these ten artistes or performers, one to ten, assessing them as a critic of their particular art-form?

A final thought is that readers/users might be invited to follow the example of recent practice, in which, around the start of the Millennium, everyone was busily reporting their hundred best films, their hundred best songs, their hundred best cricketers and so on. You might like to arrange these hundred icons in numerical sequence, in terms of their overall influence on or contribution to the popular culture of their times. In either case, ten or a hundred, if you are working with a group, why not end your discussion with a vote along these lines?

For more formal group-work, one might take each section on a weekly or fortnightly basis, possibly using the kind of questions raised here, and thereby providing a ten-session course. Obviously, there are opportunities for those who wish to do some writing or taping. This might be descriptive or critical in character of the stars listed here. Depending on the section, there is a substantial amount of CD, tape and video footage available to stimulate such discussion. Contributors may well have pictures, tapes or records, as well as memories.

Don't forget to use the general introduction and the scene-setting prefaces to each section. These talk about the social context in which these hundred big names operated. They might give rise to questions like:

☆   What was it like going to the cinema in those days?

☆   How many of these entertainments could my family or myself afford?

☆   What was the experience like of going to a league football match?

☆   How did I make out at the dance hall?

☆   What were my favourite radio programmes? . . . and many other similar questions.

Then again, there might be scope for less formal and more entertaining times. For instance, quizzes based on the information in the book might be popular and, for starters, you'll find one at the back of this book. There might be good opportunities for a rousing or sentimental sing-song; or for trying out again some of those war-time recipes, if you want to vary the type of refreshments offered; or, indeed, for some dressing up and acting out the culture of those days.

In a home or a group where there are residents who spent their formative years in other countries, these discussions should give ample opportunities for them to share their heroes with you.

Now for every example quoted above about how to use these pen-pictures, there is in each case a further possibility. That is the opportunity they afford for intergenerational activity. With children or with young adults, or with the 'middle' generation, the sons and daughters of the thirdagers, there are many chances for sharing these reminiscences. The younger generations could comment on the comedians or singers or sportspersons they have found to be the heroes and heroines for their peer-group, leading to discussion and other activities comparing and contrasting the then with the now. Who do they think will be remembered in 50 or more years time?   Above all, enjoy . . .

Rita Hayworth in Gilda in 1946

Shirley Temple in 1934

Claude Rains and Humphrey Bogart in *Casablanca*, 1943
Claude Rains had made his first film in Hollywood, *The Invisible Man* in 193?

Al Jolson in *The Jazz Singer*, 1927

Fred Astaire and Ginger Rogers in *Top Hat* in 1935

Charles Laughton as Captain Kidd in 1948

Greta Garbo in *Queen Christina* in 1933

Errol Flynn running through the Marx Brothers to get to
Basil Rathbone as Guy de Gisbourne in *The Adventures of Robin Hood*, 1938

Judy Garland in *The Wizard of Oz* in 1939

Catching a Movie ~ Hollywood Glamour
Ten American Film Stars

The cinema was the first and probably the most persuasive of major American influences on British life. It is often said now that what the United States does today we follow suit tomorrow — films were both an example of this and a conduit for other American influences, like dress and music and language. By the coming of 'talkies' in 1927 cinemagoing was well-established, but poor old Britain had taken a back-seat. The home film industry had practically closed down during the 1914-1918 war and was extremely slow to recover, and Hollywood seized the initiative with gusto.

In 1927 a quota 'protection' system was introduced, whereby a certain number of British films had to be shown, but, until the later 1930s and into the war years, it never genuinely challenged the Hollywood domination. Some critics say this led to even worse home-grown films, as producers sought to make inexpensive 'quota-quickies'. Later on, directors like Alexander Korda (*The Private Life of Henry VIII*, with a memorable Charles Laughton in the lead) and Alfred Hitchcock (with films like *The 39 Steps*, with Robert Donat, and *The Lady Vanishes*, before he, too, vanished to Hollywood) began to prosper.

The mothers of the present older generation raved over Rudolph Valentino (born Rodolpho d'Antonguolla), he of the staring eye, flared nostril and sensual lip. Their fathers just wished they might adopt his sheikh-like image. His funeral, following his sudden death in 1926, aged barely 31, was a huge national occasion, accompanied by shrieks, swoonings and suicides. The impact of such broodingly and necessarily silent romantic idols was emphatic. Indeed, it has been claimed that Hollywood film taught the British lessons in romance, assisting them in courtship and even in the techniques of kissing. It is certainly true that the raven-dark of the cinema offered a warm niche for innocent cuddling. Some cinemas even obliged its more romantically-inclined clients by providing double seats, although that charitable thought was soon dispelled when puritanical usherettes shone their glaring torches censoriously on canoodling couples.

The broader mood was, however, one of escape from an often laborious and impoverished existence into a couple of hours of luxurious or spectacular life. In part for this reason, some in the upper brackets of society found the cinema vulgar and it was to be some time before it was widely recognised, like the legitimate theatre, as an art-form. Curiously, given its largely American character, the one abiding genius to emerge from the early cinema was Lambeth-born Charlie Chaplin. An example of such moral suspicions about the films was the trouble over Sunday showings. Some 90 local authorities had extended the licences of the cinemas in their domain to embrace Sunday opening, usually with a somewhat inferior brand of film. In 1930 a pious common informer invoked the 1782 Sunday Observance Act in an attempt to halt such scandalous activity. It was decided that the existing local authorities might continue in their desperate and sinful conduct, but that, elsewhere, local plebiscites must be held to determine the issue. In effect, few areas bothered, until the social pressures of World War II triggered a widespread move towards Sunday cinema, always on the understanding that a proportion of the take had to go to locally agreed charities.

In the event, the churches, no less the pubs, had some cause for concern, for cinema-going eclipsed both in some degree. Among the lower middle and aspiring working classes the cinema proved really popular. It was a family thing, and a liberator of wives and mothers. The basic fashion of 'going out', of taking people from their houses for a while, was in itself important. More and more men took their family to the cinema on a Saturday night and stayed out of — or delayed their visit to — the public house, where the presence of women was still often frowned upon, as it still was at the football match or boxing booth. Similarly, this kind of family outing started to replace the family procession to church on Sunday morning.

The cinema took on the role of the church architecturally. An equally recognisable temple was created in the 'Odeon-style' picture palaces, some of them of immense size, all of them with a quite definable air of imposing majesty, with their extravagant Art Deco interiors. They were, beyond a doubt, very much more comfortable than churches — and they often had organs as well. These were mighty electrical jobs, often Wurlitzers, that rose from the bowels of the stage, with the seated organist already smiling and playing away. Sometimes there would be lyrics on screen for customers to sing along with, the sharpened spotlight bobbing from word to word. The organists had begun to drive out the legendary piano-players, those adept musicians who had so cleverly adjusted tempo and melody to the changing fortunes of the silent film melodrama. One estimate has it that 80% of British musicians found work in the silent cinema, where there was frequently a mix of film and variety acts for which musical support was also required. Within three years of the first 'talkies', all silent film had just about vanished, with mass unemployment among musicians, but the organists hung on in there.

Hollywood, it has been said, 'concocted fantasies to enliven the grey round' and a further criticism was that, as well as a somewhat shallow escapism, cinema was about watching passively rather than being active. Nonetheless, A J P Taylor has opined that 'the cinema was the greatest educative force of the early 20th century'. It is a formidable view, but the sheer energy and invention of American film, ranging over comedy, musical spectacle, the western genre, and a series of other species of film-making, had undeniable appeal and effect. Where many serious British actors remained a trifle snooty about film-making, leaving the medium more to musical comedy and music hall stars, like Gracie Fields, Will Hay, George Formby and Jessie Matthews, to all intents and purposes, at least from an English stance, the top-billing stars of the USA flocked to Hollywood and readily climbed in front of the cameras. It has been quite a task to choose just ten representatives of the glamorous and charismatic stars from Hollywood's golden age, but here they are.

 AL JOLSON (c.1885-1950, born Snrednicke, Lithuania, before emigrating to Washington DC, USA)

Al Jolson (Asa Joelson) brought together two distinctive traditions, then added a third savoury ingredient. The tuneful son of a Jewish cantor, with the profound sense of the sung prayer instilled into him, he was inducted in 1908 — after a rather varied show-biz initiation — into the jaunty but limited regime of the 'black-up' minstrel show, with the Lew Dockstader combine. (Such troupes, incidentally, had reached Britain as early as the 1860s, with the Christy's Minstrels especially notable. Many thirdagers will better recall the Kentucky Minstrels on radio in the 1930s and 1940s, with their mix of Stephen Foster melodies and breezy if innocuous cross-talk, while TV's Black and White Minstrels were a bright attempt to milk that old tradition.)

Given these disciplines, Al Jolson then found his key inspiration in the impromptu jazz rhythms associated with New Orleans and introduced into his performance a forceful element of the 'soul' implicit in jazz. He thereby created the singular and much-imitated *persona* of the cheerful but heart-aching troubadour of syncopated songs, full of yearning for parent (for instance, *Mammy*) girlfriend (*Rosie, you are my posie*) child (*Sonny Boy*) place (*Swanee*) or mood (*When April Showers*). In his choice of songs, he was helped by his life-long association with the song writer, Harry Akst. For many seasons he dominated New York's Broadway in theatrical showcases for his talent, while he was also an eager tourist, insistent that all should have a chance to witness his gifts.

It was an electrifying performance, with the warm, throbbing voice, as smooth and lubricious as golden syrup, the exact match for the amazing range of facial expression and extravagant gesture, occasionally tricked out with *virtuoso* whistling. The whole was fuelled by an almost demonic and certainly hugely egotistical drive that has led many critics to judge as correct Al Jolson's billing as 'the World's Greatest Entertainer', as he left in the shade talented rivals like Eddie Cantor and George Jessel. British audiences had to rely on his records to enjoy some of this explosive delight; he first made a disc in 1911, reputably strapped to restrain his exorbitant gesticulation, and was one of the first to sell a million copies. Then, in 1927, he was chosen to star in the first commercial sound film, the aptly-named, *The Jazz Singer*, which gave him a world stage. He also appeared in other films, such as *The Singing Fool* (1928) and *Mammy* (1930). Primitive film never quite captured the vivid magnetism of his live performance and his career actually stalled somewhat in the 1930s. However, late in his career and after he had renewed his reputation with a heavy programme of war-time troops entertaining, he was accorded the accolade of not one but two heavily sanitised bio-pics, *The Jolson Story* (1946) and *Jolson Sings Again* (1949) in both of which Larry Parks mimed strenuously to the beguiling tones of Al Jolson himself. They were very popular films on both sides of the Atlantic with a massive spin-off by way of records.

On the night of his death, and unprecedentedly, the lights were dimmed on Broadway and the traffic halted in Times Square. No one has ever hit a stage with such furious gusto and there was much truth in his enduring catch-phrase, 'you ain't seen nuthin' yet'.

 **GRETA GARBO** (Greta Gustafson, 1905-1990, born Sweden)

Taken to Hollywood from Sweden by her director, Mauritz Stiller, Greta Garbo deployed her extraordinary screen presence to considerable effect. The remoteness of her aloof beauty fuelled the stereotype of the gorgeously fair Nordic ice-maiden, as, according to one critic, she became 'the dream princess of eternity'. Another spoke of 'her alluring mouth and volcanic, slumbrous eyes' and her wintry, inscrutable loveliness created one of the most powerful cinematic legends there has been. In a relatively short career that ended in sudden and typically mystifying retirement, her leading films were *Flesh and the Devil* (1927); *Anna Christie* (1930), *Grand Hotel* (1932); *Queen Christina* (1933); *Anna Karenina* (1935); *Camille* (1936) and *Ninotchka* (1939), all testifying to her overall role as the tragic, dignified heroine.

She memorably uttered 'I want to be alone' in *Grand Hotel* and that huskily murmured wish has forever been identified with her as a kind of signature. Mae West never did say 'come up and see me sometime' on film, but that phrase, too, was to be her personifying line — and it was the exact opposite of Greta Garbo's wish. For all the modern talk of spin and hype, those early Hollywood experts knew a thing or two about publicity, especially when it came to the so-called 'screen goddesses'. Thus they introduced to a worldwide public differing styles of sexual appeal.

Mae West (1882-1980) was mockingly raunchy where Greta Garbo was broodingly reserved. Such were Mae West's hourglass proportions, with high, bulging bust, corseted waist and flamboyant hips, that the pneumatic air force life-jacket was named after her in the second world war. She made films like *She Done him Wrong* and *I'm no Angel*; again the titles are redolent of the species, for she was invariably the confident broad treating men as, one of her favourite epithets, 'suckers'. Like Greta Garbo, she is remembered as an image rather than for particular characterisations. A bright lady, she wrote much of her own scripts and has a thousand quips to her splendid name. Almost all of them demonstrate — 'it's not the men in my life, it's the life in my men that counts' — how she crumbled the edges of taboo and censorship in an often prurient era.

Another prototype rival was the 'the Platinum Blonde' of Jean Harlow (1911-1937, originally, Harlean Carpenter) who created *furore* both public and private with her sharp-tongued, sophisticated, crackling performances. '. . . the spirit of her era all but shines from her eyes', said one admirer, as, in films like *Hell's Angels!*; *The Public Enemy* and *Dinner at Eight*, as well as in her scandalous antics off-screen, she fully earned the 'sensational' label hung upon her by the studio system.

At another remove there was Mary Pickford (1893-1979, the Canadian actress, Gladys Smith) who, via silent films, had become 'the world's sweetheart' and an extremely rich woman. Demure, with a sometimes prissy innocence, this pretty, sweet-hearted 'Glad Girl' captivated millions in films like *Her First Biscuits* (her first movie in 1909) *Tess of the Storm Country* and *Coquette*. In contradistinction to Greta Garbo, Mary Pickford concentrated on waif-like, Cinderella-ish parts.

Like Greta Garbo, if not with the same intensity and endurance, they all became legends — and also innovators. Think, for instance, how Bette Davis, Jayne Mansfield, Marilyn Monroe, and Aubrey Hepburn were to step into the appropriate four pairs of shoes.

ERROL FLYNN (1909-1959, born Tasmania)

A house called Cirrhosis-by-the-sea, shared with drinking pals like David Niven, is something of a give-away, for Errol Flynn, fleeing from his Australian creditors to find fame and fortune in Hollywood, lived life to the over-full and paid the penalty of premature death. For some twenty or more years he demonstrated that the film industry could produce male as well as female stars, although it is perhaps fair to remark that there was more variety on the distaff side. Tall, dark and handsome was the cliché descriptor for the men, preferably with a large dash of impudence, and that was Errol Flynn, sleek-haired and of imposing build, to a 't'. *My Wicked Wicked Ways* was the not inapposite title of his autobiography, published in the year of his death.

He was the good-looking, always-got-the-girl hero of costume drama, western and war film. He was as ebullient thwarting the Sheriff of Nottingham in *The Adventures of Robin Hood* in 1938 as he was foiling the Japanese, not without some English sarcasm by way of critique, in *Objective Burma* in 1945. He starred in popular action-packed movies such as *Captain Blood*; *They Died with their Boots on*; *The Charge of the Light Brigade*; *The Dawn Patrol; Dodge City; Elizabeth and Essex; The Sea-Hawk; Gentleman Jim* and dozens more.

Douglas Fairbanks Jnr (1909-2000) was another debonair and dashing performer in period pieces like *The Prisoner of Zenda, The Corsican Brothers* and *Sinbad the Sailor*; his name became synonymous with cavalier, chandelier-swinging stunts.

Then there was Clark Gable (1901-1960), known as 'the King of Hollywood', and, despite being described by Howard Hughes as having ears that 'made him look like a taxi-cab with both doors left open', an actor of implacable masculinity. His wife, Carole Lombard, was apparently less moved by his appeal; 'listen', she commented, 'he's no Clark Gable at home'. For all that, he sustained his massive screen repute for over a quarter century, in films such as *Red Dust, It Happened One Night; Mutiny on the Bounty* and his final movie, *The Misfits*. Many will recall his famous closing remark to the Scarlett O'Hara of Vivien Leigh in *Gone with the Wind* when, as Rhett Butler, he drawled, 'frankly, my dear, I don't give a damn'. It might have been his epitaph.

Britain's Ronald Colman (1891-1958) was another elegant and virile romantic lead of the day, bringing suavity as well as manliness to a string of films such as *Her Night of Romance; Bulldog Drummond; Condemned; Raffles; Clive of India; A Tale of Two Cities; Talk of the Town* and *Random Harvest*. Honest, pensive and slow-moving, Gary Cooper (1901-1961) brought the backwoodsman's appeal where Ronald Colman was ever the English toff. Cooper's long series of films included *Lives of a Bengal Lancer, Sergeant York, Beau Geste, Mr Deeds Goes to Town* and *High Noon.*

As with the female stars, everyone will have their own favourites to recall and add to this brief roster of Errol Flynn and his enviably handsome fellow-stars. As with the female stars, one has only to open the entertainment guide for the local cinema listings and find the names of their latter-day descendants.

SHIRLEY TEMPLE
(Shirley Temple, 1928 - , born Santa Monica, California, USA)

Mr Vincent Crummles, the theatre manager in *Nicholas Nickleby*, could have coined the billing, 'the Infant Phenomenon', for Shirley Temple. In actuality, the theatre had generally used children only in bit parts, often with stage families 'blooding' their offspring, or in juvenile groups, while there are few major child roles in mainstream drama. The less arduous schedule of film-making, at least in so far as it was possible to construct movies scene by scene, as opposed to the more comprehensive necessities of the stage, released a torrent of 'child stars' in every generation. Older movie-goers may recall Freddy Bartholemew (*David Copperfield*) or Jackie Coogan (*The Kid*, with Charlie Chaplin) while the likes of Mickey Rooney, Elizabeth Taylor and Donald O'Connor began their film careers at a comparatively early age.

Shirley Temple is, however, the abiding and *nonpareil* child star. Making her first film at three, she was a big star at six, winning a special Oscar in 1934, and the top Hollywood earner at ten, with a yearly income of $300,000. In all, she made about fifty films, a few as a teen-ager. She made nine films just in 1934. They were simple, sentimental, occasionally rather scrappily constructed vehicles for her rousing singing and dancing talents. Titles like *Bright Eyes; Curly Top; The Littlest Rebel; Poor Little Rich Girl; Dimples; Baby Take a Bow; The Little Colonel; Little Miss Broadway* and *The Little Princess* say it all. The songs she popularised are even more redolent of her charisma:

On the Good Ship Lollipop; Animal Crackers in My Soup; But Definitely and *That's what I want for Christmas* echo cocksurely down the years.

Blessed with sturdy limbs, golden locks, chubby features and, providentially, something of a photographic memory for scripts, Shirley Temple could tap-dance energetically and knock out a song like an old trouper. There was all but an evangelical ring as she convinced us that 'You gotta S-M-I-L-E to be H-A-double-P-Y'. It was schmaltzy but it managed to stay this side of sugary, and, whilst her undoubted assurance smacked of precocity, her likeable countenance drew affection, not the stomach-churning disapproval that attends the antics of some so-called gifted children. Looking back, one recollects those intelligent, beaming eyes and wonders whether, even then, she had the measure of what now would be called the hype and was able to preserve some sense of proportion. After all, here is a little girl who has wryly recounted how she stopped believing in Santa Claus at an early age because, when taken to see Santa Claus, he asked for her autograph.

Her professional after-life adds to the conviction. After a brief marriage, 1945-49, with the actor John Agar, she married a businessman, Charles A Black, in 1950 and has since been known as Shirley Temple Black. Apart from this ongoing and stable family setting, she became involved in Republican politics and, in an uncomplicated fashion, has undertaken several public duties, as, for instance, US ambassador to Ghana, to the United Nations and what was Czechoslovakia.

It has been said that she was that rarest of humans, 'a genuine prodigy'. It is as simple and as mysterious as that. Seek no further explanations.

FRED ASTAIRE AND GINGER ROGERS
(Frederick Austerlitz, 1899-1987, born Omaha, Nebraska; and Virginia Katherine McMath, 1911-1995, born Independence, Missouri)

Gene Kelly is Fred Astaire's only male rival in the annals of cinematic dance, his more rugged muscularity as distinguished as the latter's easy grace. Both had several partners. Fred Astaire, who was in vaudeville at the tender age of seven, first came to prominence with his sister, Adele Astaire (1898-1981). They had Broadway and West End successes in shows like *Lady Be Good; Funny Face; The Band Wagon* and *The Gay Divorcee*. Adele then married Lord Charles Cavendish, younger son of the Duke of Devonshire, a show-girl/stage door Johnny wedding where nature seemed to be imitating art, for it could have been the plot of one of their shows.

At first denied as a possible film performer, Fred Astaire was presciently teamed with Ginger Rogers in the 1933 movie *Flying down to Rio*, in which their dance duet, *Carioca*, atop gleaming white pianos, proved sensational. Fred Astaire was, during his lengthy and glittering career, to have other partners, such as Paulette Goddard, Rita Hayworth, Judy Garland, Vera-Ellen, Cyd Charisse, Jane Powell, Leslie Caron and

Audrey Hepburn. He also starred with Bing Crosby in *Holiday Inn* and *Blue Skies*.

Nonetheless, in the mind's eye of the watching public, it was the Astaire/Rogers combine that was to be memorable, more so than with any other duo of its kind. Ginger Rogers, too, had a vaudeville and stage start — in *Top Speed* and *Girl Crazy*, for instance — before she made a couple of films, most notably as Anytime Annie in *42nd Street*. After the white pianos *en route* for Rio, they were coupled together in, among others, *The Gay Divorcee; Top Hat; Follow the Fleet; Shall We Dance?*, all pre-war films, and then, in 1949, *The Barkleys of Broadway*. They made ten films together and, when they went their separate ways, success pursued them — Ginger Rogers won an Oscar in 1940 for her part in *Kitty Foyle*, for example. While Fred Astaire led a quiet life off the set — he was married happily twice; his first wife died prematurely and his second survived him — Ginger Rogers acted out the Hollywood stereotype and married five times.

Their private relationship is said to have been uneasy. Much of this arose from Fred Astaire's emphasis on extensive practise and on his detailed perfectionism. He was an adequate actor and an uncomplicated, perhaps under-rated singer, but he was a superlative dancer. Ginger Rogers was a splendid all-rounder, probably a better actor, but by no means as good a dancer, and, in the complex weaving of their choreography (a good deal of the credit for which should go to Fred Astaire's friend and collaborator, Hermes Pan) there was much to be learned. Fred Astaire, the stickler for faultlessness, and not too tactful in his instruction, occasionally found Ginger Rogers lacking in dedication.

She, on the other hand, spoke of times when she danced with bleeding feet. With his elegant, floating, debonair style, at his most characteristic in top hat and tails, he created a wholly original approach to screen dance — but it is unlikely that, without Ginger Rogers, his success would have become the stuff of legend. Not bad for a man a film auditioner had earlier assessed as 'Can't act. Can't sing. Balding. Can dance a little'.

 CHARLES LAUGHTON (1899-1962, born in Scarborough)

Overweight old king dribbling his food and chucking chicken legs over his shoulder; naval captain bawling threats — 'I'll hang you from the highest yard-arm in the British NAVEE' — at Fletcher Christian; hideous grotesque shrieking 'Sanctuary, sanctuary' among the bell-ropes of Notre Dame cathedral: every time anybody attempts an imitation of an angry, stout Henry VIII, or apes sadistic Captain Bligh aboard the mutinous 'Bounty' or sticks a cushion in the shoulder of his jacket and pretends to be the Hunchback of Notre Dame, they are, in essence, mimicking Charles Laughton. His heavily jowled features, lugubrious countenance and plump body provided the instrumentality whereby he became him one of the cinema's outstanding character actors in a long career from *Wolves* in 1927 to *Spartacus* in 1960.

His was a superlative series of characterisations. It is not given to many actors to so encompass a role that, even today, the public image of the character in question is as they created it. It really is very impressive. One might think of Laurence Olivier's Richard III, with maimed gait and crafty, gleeful phrasing of 'now is the winter of our discontent'; or Robert Newton's 'ahhh, Jim lad' portrayal of Long John Silver; or Sean Connery's urbane Bond, but to create three such luminaries is unsurpassed. Nor did it end there. Charles Laughton's Nero in *The Sign of the Cross*; his Rembrandt, his irascible Mr Hobson in *Hobson's Choice*, and his Edward Moulton-Barrett in *The Barretts of Wimpole Street* all have something of the same ineradicable stamp.

Orson Welles (1915-1985) was an actor in rather the same magnificent proportion, although perhaps now remembered more as a director and *bravura* personality. He himself admitted that 'I started at the top and worked my way down', but many will recollect with special pleasure his appearances in *The Magnificent Ambersons; Citizen Kane*, a film on many a critic's short-list as the best movie of all time, and as Harry Lime in the evocative *The Third Man*. What is perhaps different is that Orson Welles is remembered as Orson Welles in formidable person, whereas Charles Laughton is seen in the mental eye as Charles Laughton in the guises of Henry VIII, ridding himself of infertile and unfaithful wives, or of a scornful Captain Bligh, imposing savage punishments, or of Quasimodo, hands clamped over his deafened ears, hoarsely crying 'the bells, the bells, I cannot hear the bells'. In post-war England the infinitely gifted Alec Guinness was to manage this   extraordinary feat of losing himself in characters such as Fagin in *Oliver Twist* or as eight D'Ascoynes in the stylish black comedy, *Kind Hearts and Coronets*. Indeed, Alec Guinness subtly lost himself

entirely, while Charles Laughton contrived always to keep his own personage in the acting equation. His were theatrical performances brought to full fruit upon the screen and he should be forgiven his slight tendency toward bombast.

Charles Laughton is difficult to forget, and, because of him, some characters, fictional and factual, are equally difficult to disassociate from his vivid reconstruction of them. That is a truly great cultural legacy.

 ## RITA HAYWORTH
(Margarita Carmen Cansino, 1918-1987, born Brooklyn, New York)

A mixed blessing of modern technology is that a past sex icon like Rita Hayworth, tagged 'the Love Goddess', may be recalled, not just in the memory, but on larger-than-life film. The contrast between such glamorous screenings on present-day television, and an awareness of her decline during the 1970s, initially attributed, if unfairly, to alcohol abuse, into severe dementia is an agonising one. The last years of her life were spent under the legal care of her daughter, Princess Yasmin. The wealthy playboy, Aly Kahn, was the third of Rita Hayworth's five husbands, the others being the Texan business-man, Edward C.Judson; the grand Hollywood star, Orson Welles; the singer, Dick Haymes and the producer, James Hill. Understandably, her busy domestic affairs added to the mystique, in that she seemed to double up the ardent nature of her private life and her professional portrayals.

Rita Hayworth learned to dance and perform from the age of six. She first danced professionally in Mexico with her father, Eduardo Cansino, a Spanish dancer, and this Latinate flair remained the root of her exciting dancing appeal. Her voice was not strong and was often dubbed for film purposes, but her sheer allure gave her a very special screen presence. She started making movies at sixteen, among them *Music in My Heart* and *The Strawberry Blonde*, with James Cagney, but it was the 1941 when Rita Hayworth made a decided breakthrough in *You'll Never get Rich* with Fred Astaire, with whom she next made *You were Never Lovelier* in 1942. There followed, in quick succession, *My Gal Sal*, with Victor Mature, *Pal Joey*, with Frank Sinatra and Kim Novak, *Cover Girl*, with Gene Kelly, *Tonight and Every Night*, and, in all, some 60 movies, the last as late as 1972.

Apart from the several musicals in which she starred, she also indulged in tempestuous dramatic roles, sometimes with musical additions, such as *Put the Blame on Mame* in *Gilda* (1946) and *The Heat is on* in *Miss Sadie Thompson* (1953). These exotic creations were clearly to be the bench-mark of her cinematic life and those two pictures are usually regarded as her best. For a film industry under the cautious watch of prim censorship, her directors manage to convey, through Rita Hayworth, an unusually erotic heat, a tribute, in turn, to her personable seductiveness.

Rita Hayworth displayed, in performance, all the clichés associated with her Hispanic-Irish lineage. Fiery, sultry, unruly, her lissom dancer's frame, slender legs and excitingly sculpted body were surmounted by beautiful features and, most famous of all, that rich crown of lustrous auburn hair. Hers was a sensuousness that was the converse of the more earthy, playful appeal of, say, Betty Grable. The Rita Hayworth pin-up was, after Betty Grable's, the second most popular of World War II. It was taken from the cover of *Life* magazine and revealed her lying across a bed in diaphanous garb. It was to be drooled over by millions of allied servicemen. In its most macabre deployment, it was pasted to the side of the atom bomb that was detonated over Hiroshima.

 THE MARX BROTHERS (Leonard Marx, 1886-1961, CHICO; Adolph Marx, 1888-1964, HARPO; and Julius Marx, 1890-1977, GROUCHO; all born in New York)

'One morning I shot an elephant in my pyjamas. How he got into my pyjamas I'll never know'. . . such is one of the non-stop wisecracks of the Marx Brothers as they spread their reign of unholy terror across the stages and screens of the USA and elsewhere. Silent film, witness Charlie Chaplin and Buster Keaton, had thrived on mimed comedy, but then came the need to balance visual and audio comicalness. There were other comedy teams, like the Three Stooges, Larry, Moe and Jerry, or Olsen and Johnson, most noted for their crazy farce, *Hellzapoppin*; or duos among whom many will doubtless recall Bud Abbott and Lou 'I'm a ba-a-a-d boy' Costello. The Marx Brothers, however, attained cult status and are still much admired for their bringing of shrewd intelligence to familiar vaudeville settings. There was always a satirical note about even their wildest ventures.

Although the two other brothers, Milton (Gummo, 1893-1977) and Herbert (Zeppo, 1901-1979), were peripherally involved, it is the threesome that is best-remembered. They were an unlikely trio to share such congruence and create such chemistry. There they were: Groucho, with the moustache, the loping gait, the cigar and the vibrant one-liners; Harpo, with the angelic countenance, the flowing coat, the long fair locks, the harp, the horn and the pregnant silence; and Chico, with the Italianate argot ('there ain't no sanity clause'), the eccentric piano-playing and the plant-pot hat. These three, steeped in vaudeville from childhood, developed that spiked humour, characteristic of a Jewish New Yorker background, to an extraordinary degree. Using clever writers, like S J Perelman and George S Kaufmann, they worked unceasingly to hone their material, and some of their films were originally Broadway and toured farces, with lots of gags already well-tested before they reached the screen.

Some speak of them as zany, but it was more knowing, more subversive, than that. What they had in common was a healthy desire to cock a snook at those in authority, political, financial or social, in the American establishment. Few will forget, for example, Groucho's deployment of the stately Margaret Dumont, a personification of all these traits, as his constant butt. Like the other Marxism, it was revolutionary, but it was genial as well as disruptive: it was Marxism with a grin.

They made ten major films. These were *Animal Crackers* (1930); *Monkey Business* (1931); *Horse Feathers* (1932); *Duck Soup* (1933); *A Night at the Opera* (1935); *A Day at the Races* (1937); *At the Circus* (1939); *Go West* (1940); *The Big Store* (1941) and *A Night in Casablanca* (1946). Each paid tribute to their declaration of war on the orthodox and the authoritarian; they were displays of licensed anarchy.

Space for one other piece of Marxist dialectic:

Margaret Dumont (in *Duck Soup*): *my husband is dead.*

Groucho, as President of Fredonia: *he's just using that as an excuse.*

MD: *I was with him till the end.*

G: *no wonder he passed away.*

MD: *I held him in my arms and kissed him.*

G: *so it was murder.*

 JUDY GARLAND (Frances Gumm, 1922-1969, born in Grand Rapids, Minnesota, USA)

Had her tragic life been portrayed on screen, the critics would have scoffed at it as unbelievable. Born into an argumentative stage family and performing from the age of two as 'Baby Frances', her singing with her two sisters led to film and fortune. Married, usually unhappily, five times (most famously to Vincente Minnelli, father of her daughter, Liza, born in 1946) and committed to an extraordinary regimen of drugs from teen-age, much of her domestic life was characterised by turmoil. To the pills irresponsibly supplied for practically every disorder from not sleeping to not being wide enough awake, she added alcohol, and her sad existence was littered with an abortion, nervous collapses, suicide attempts and, in general, the sort of disturbances that made her an occasional professional liability. She died in 1969 apparently from an accidental overdose of sleeping pills.

Yet in the best traditions of theatre and literature, indeed, according to some observers, with her gifts informed by these sad events, Judy Garland grew to be a show-business legend of cult status. By Hollywood standards she was no 'glamour puss', to employ an Americanism of her day. Homely, if pleasing, of feature and inclined to a certain dumpiness (hence one set of the varied pills she swallowed) of figure, she still conveyed substantial *charisma* on stage and concert platform, as well as on screen. It was her resonant voice, from an early age suffused with emotional power, that did the trick. Its depths were genuinely tear-jerking and she succeeded in reinforcing over and again the devotion of her myriad fans.

As a young star, she made her mark singing *Dear Mr Gable*, followed by *You Made me Love you* in *Broadway Melody of 1938*, before partnering Mickey Rooney in the 'Andy Hardy' series. Then came her sensational and glittering success in the 1939 classic *The Wizard of Oz*, with the charming refrain of *Somewhere Over the Rainbow* acknowledged as her abiding theme-song. Throughout the 1940s she starred in a string of successful musicals. These included *For Me and My Girl; Thousands Cheer; Girl Crazy; Meet Me in St Louis* (which some

believe to be her best film); *Ziegfeld Follies; Till the Clouds Roll by; Easter Parade* and *In the Good Old Summer-time*. Later on she turned to more dramatic roles, as in *A Star is Born* (1954) a somewhat ironic picture of real-life Hollywood, and *Judgement at Nuremberg* (1961).

In 1969, the year of her last marriage and her death, she was pelted with food at some performances at London's 'Talk of the Town' night-club, an undignified tribute to her unpunctuality — in London, where, years earlier, she had known a glittering triumph at the Palladium. 'If I'm such a legend', she once pitifully asked, 'why am I so lonely?' Somehow it was this compound of popular acclaim and private grief that inspired so much affectionate admiration for Judy Garland. Never has so great a star found herself so completely overwhelmed by success. She was, so to speak, run over by her own roller-coaster.

HUMPHREY BOGART
(1899-1957, born in USA)

Just as Mae West never invited anyone to 'Come up and see me some time', so Humphrey Bogart never actually uttered the literal instruction, 'Play it again, Sam', but legends ignore facts, just as love laughs at locksmiths. And Humphrey Bogart was a similar kind of imperishable personage; the tough guy, whereas Mae West was the tough cookie. Moreover, his *persona* was heightened by a tendency to remain in character off the set. It was said of him that he 'was a helluva nice guy until 11.30 pm . . . after that he thinks he's Bogart.' His fourth wife was Lauren Bacall (born Betty Jean Perske in

1924) who made her debut as his co-star in *To Have and to Have Not* in 1944, and famously told him, 'if you want anything, just whistle'. She also played opposite him in films like *The Big Sleep* and *Key Largo*.

With its *genres* of Westerns and gangster plots, Hollywood was noted for its bad guys. Either they were smiling in sinister fashion, like George Raft, or unsmiling, like Alan Ladd. They were a far cry from, for instance, Charles Boyer, the suave Frenchman, billed as the screen's 'great lover'.

James Cagney (1899-1986) was another (and he never precisely cried, 'you dirty rat', as all his imitators did). Cagney strutted his unhesitating way through a whole series of hard-nosed roles, as in *The Public Enemy*, *Angels with Dirty Faces* or *White Heat*, but he could also turn his ebullient hand to vaude-villian dance of consummate ease and energy, as he did as George M.Cohan in *Yankee Doodle Dandy*.

Humphrey Bogart did not quite go that far, but he extended his repertoire to include not only gangsters but the cynical creatures of *films noirs*. Craggy, watchful, gravelly-toned, his chief mannerism a facial tic that pulled at his lips when he was thoughtful or aroused, he was ideally suited to the sombre mood of post-1940 scepticism, where Jimmy Cagney's was a personality more redolent of the 1920s and 1930s. Humphrey Bogart was not a large man, but his sturdy frame and his seemingly unemotional countenance could certainly dominate a screen, and this he continued to do from 1930 to 1956.

Space allows but a selection from his many films for his admirers to enjoy in the memory. These included *The Petrified Forest*, in which he played the gangster, Duke Mantee; *Marked Woman; The Roaring Twenties; High Sierra; Across the Pacific; Passage to Marseilles; Dead Reckoning; The Treasure of the Sierra Madre; Beat the Devil* and *The Barefoot Contessa*. Beyond these well-known films, he participated in the making of a handful of certain classics. There was, immortally, *Casablanca*, facing Ingrid Bergman's Ilse Lund, as Rick Blaine; and there was *The African Queen*, opposite Katherine Hepburn's Rose Sayer, as Charlie Allnutt, while others would place at the head of this particular list his role as the Bligh-like Captain Queeg in *The Caine Mutiny*. Others again would point to his archetypal characterisations of the Dashiell Hammett private eye, Sam Spade, in *The Maltese Falcon* and of the Raymond Chandler private eye, Philip Marlowe, in *The Big Sleep*.

What a laconic, sullen but loveable talent — and to think they initially pencilled in Ronald Reagan for Rick's part in *Casablanca*.

Celia Johnson in *Brief Encounter* in 1945

Laurel and Hardy were together from 1928 to 1956

Alastair Sim in *Laughter in Paradise*, 1951

Vivien Leigh in *Caesar and Cleopatra*, 1945

Charlie Chaplin first dressed like this in 1915

Robert Donat with Greer Garson as Mrs Chips in *Goodbye Mr Chips* in 1939

George Formby in 1938

Will Hay in 1936

James Mason as *The Man in Grey*, 1943

Margaret Lockwood as *The Wicked Lady* in 1945

Going To The Flicks ~ British Cinema
Ten British Film Stars

During this period, from about the late 1920s to just after the second world war, Britain boasted 5000 cinemas. In regions such as Lancashire and Scotland there was one cinema seat for every nine people in the population. The knowledgeable film critic, Leslie Halliwell, luxuriated in a Bolton childhood during which there were no less than 47 cinemas within five miles of the town centre. Over four out of every ten persons in the population went to the cinema once a week and nearly three out of ten twice a week.

The commissionaire's familiar cry to the queue of 'one and nines on the right; half a crown round the corner' gives some idea of the cost — 1s 9d would be 8p and 2s 6d would be 12.5p nowadays. Of course, many paid much less, either at low-grade venues that rejoiced in sobriquets like 'the twopenny crush' or 'the bug-hut', or at children's Saturday afternoon matinees. These later shifted to Saturday mornings, but for the bulk of our period it was a matter of finding three-pence or fourpence for a Saturday afternoon outing. There would be a cartoon or two and a 'big picture', but the chief interest often lay in the serial, wherein the heroine was frequently hissed as much as the villain. So it might be Buck Jones or Deadwood Dick of Western vintage, whilst what would now be called sci-fi was provided by Flash Gordon. These followed in the silent Pearl White, tied-to-the-railway-line convention, with a cliffhanger (a phrase coined from the cinema serial) at the end of the reel to bring us back for more next week.

The standard cinema routine was a short 'feature' film of documentary or informative kind — *The March of Time* series, discussing current issues, is one long-running example. Then there would be a cartoon, à la Walt Disney, with the spinach-stimulated Popeye or the irascible Donald Duck causing amusement. Another regular element was the news bulletin, with the booming, confident voice of some newscaster, such as Leslie

Mitchell, explaining matters somewhat patronisingly to the audience. Rather like television news, these would include light-hearted as well as serious items. Newsreels were of some import. Before the rise of television, the efforts of Gaumont British News or Pathe Gazette provided the public with its first moving pictorial record of events. Newspapers had photographs, of course, but here was 'live' action, like Neville Chamberlain returning from Munich, with his notorious scrap of paper, in 1938, or exhilarating sports occasions, like the FA Cup Final. For the first time in history, those, obviously the huge majority, unable to be present at the fringes of power and influence, could actually witness the comings and goings of Gandhi or Adolf Hitler or President Roosevelt. One was able, for instance, to follow the progress, suitably censored for security and morale purposes, of the second world war in moving pictures.

Finally, after the 'trailer' for next week's 'forthcoming attraction' and an interval for ice cream and a visit to the often dingy loos, there was the main film. Most cinemas ran through the programme twice, if not three times, beginning in the afternoon, so that patrons could join the performance at whatever time they wished, or, if there were a long queue, whenever — 'room for three in the balcony' went up the shout — vacancies occurred. It was not uncommon to risk separation from one's friends or loved ones, until other seats became empty and one could re-group. Then one 'sat round' until one caught up with the programme, or, of course, 'sat through' for added measure. The modern coinage of 'this is where I came in' stems from this habit.

Imagine, therefore, an ordinary market town of, say, 35,000 people. There would probably be four cinemas, as well as others to reasonable hand in neighbouring towns or perhaps an adjacent city. One or two would offer a week's programme, while the less luxuriant would change midweek, while, certainly by the middle of the war, all would have been likely to provide a separate Sunday schedule. Thus the perspicacious, if not too discerning, film fan might have watched a different film every single day without travelling more than a mile from home. These four cinemas, ranging from the quite plush to the downright dog-eared, might accommodate *in toto* some 2500 customers. On a Saturday, and apart from perhaps two that might offer a children's matinee, there could be the equivalent of ten showings, almost all of them jam-packed full. This meant that, in effect, practically the entire populace might attend the cinema on a Saturday, although it was not uncommon for some to visit two cinemas in the same day. They were the social venues for family outings, trysts for putative sweethearts as well as groups of friends. Although young people were the most persistent attendees, the cinema was cross-generational in appeal.

By the end of the 1950s most of these people were watching the television on a Saturday evening in the comfort of their own homes. It is fair to say that the cinema chains rather took their captive audience for granted: many will remember, for example, queuing in the rain or in draughty alleys, under the beady and wrathful eye of harsh commissionaires. Soon cinemas began to close rapidly, to be replaced by supermarkets, bingo halls and garages. A town of 35,000 souls would have been unlikely to have had a cinema at all by 1970. The multiplex cinema, with its several screens, caused a bit of a revival thereafter, but it was small beer compared with the 1930s and 1940s. Since that time cinema-going has plunged to only about 10% of the population attending a cinema at least once in the last month.

Films were categorised by the film censor as 'U' for universal distribution; 'A' where a child could only watch if accompanying an adult; and 'X' which ruled out children altogether. Many will recall an intermediate stage, round about the early teens, where youths were trying to get the best of both worlds — attempting still to cadge a half-fare on the bus journeying to the cinema, but then masquerading as an adult in order to enjoy an 'A' film. The alternative was to hang about the foyer of the cinema in the hope that some liberal-minded member of the public would accept your halfprice ninepence and, temporarily assuming guardianship, would buy your ticket for you. The standard plea was 'please take us in, mister'. The young lady in the box office, not wishing to lose custom, would turn a blind eye to this relatively innocent deception.

For some 30 years, not a long while in the historical record, this cinematic cult provided the present older generation with probably its most significant leisure outlet.

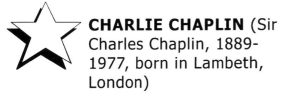 **CHARLIE CHAPLIN** (Sir Charles Chaplin, 1889-1977, born in Lambeth, London)

Very occasionally there are icons that are associated as intimately with the origins of an art-form as a god-head with a religion. Such a one was Charlie Chaplin. In the popular culture of the modern world there are maybe only two or three names that might appear alongside his in that limited pantheon: Elvis Presley in the field of rock'n'roll music and its successors, or Walt Disney, as the creative genius of animated film, or, from the world of global sport, W G Grace or Pele. Charlie Chaplin is to cinema what William Caxton is to printing or James Watt to steam-engines. To be frank, his chief contribution dates from the silent era, before the onset of the period actually under review. His 'talkie' work, like *The Great Dictator* (1940); *Monsieur Verdoux* (1947) or *Limelight* (1952) errs on the theatrical, and something of his earlier appeal is lost.

Nonetheless, 'the tramp' was a characterisation that has kept its black and white imprint throughout this period and beyond. The three o'clock waddle, the twirling cane, the lustrous eyes, the natty bowler and the expressive moustache — they formed an immemorial portrait. Initially with the Keystone Company and, after working for others, becoming his own producer, he starred in a lengthy series of silent two-reelers from 1914 to 1922, among them *The Tramp; The Pawnshop* and *The Immigrant*, the very titles revealing much of the approach. Of the feature films made in this vein few will forget *The Kid* (1920); *The Gold Rush* (1924); *City Lights* (1931) and *Modern Times* (1936).

Born in the denigrating poverty of South London, Charlie Chaplin certainly knew at vivid first hand the character he gave the world of 'the little man', struggling against the suffocating forces of industrial society. It is true that his grinding early days left him suspicious, mercenary and self-important in his professional life, while his private life, given his *penchant* for the nubile nymphet, was quite notorious. However, his transfer of the essential clown to the world screen was to strike a simple but emphatic chord internationally. It was, of course, sentimental, with the emotions tugged by grief as well as comicality, but, then, as Charlie Chaplin knew, that is the lot of the common man. Crucially, his creation passed the test both of popular appeal and critical acclaim.

Basically, he was a pantomimist who learned his exacting trade with Fred Karno, he whose famed 'army' of mime artists delighted music hall audiences with their adept sketches. It is no coincidence that both Stan Laurel and Charlie Chaplin, possibly the two salient lodestones of film comedy, were Karno apprentices who transferred their skills to the silver screen. 'The son of a bitch is a ballet dancer', gasped that other but very different film comedian, W C Fields, when he watched Charlie Chaplin and, not without some irascible despair, acknowledged his acrobatic prowess. Those light-footed, circus-oriented gymnastics gave Charlie Chaplin an extra dimension, and, plainly, some of his routines — with the blind flower-girl, for instance, or reduced to eating his boots — almost touch on classical dance for their inspiration and styling.

'I am a citizen of the world', he cried. The combine of cinematic technology and his extraordinary technique made Charlie Chaplin so.

GEORGE FORMBY
George Hoy Booth OBE
1904-1961, born Wigan)

The nascent British cinema, slow to recognise the true horizons of film, turned chiefly to music hall stars, like George Formby or Gracie Fields. Such was the success of George Formby that, eventually, he was just about the highest-paid film star, with earnings of some £85,000 a year, and was reputed to be, after Stalin, the best-known man in Soviet Russia. He was also justly remembered, and awarded the OBE, for his magnificent efforts in entertaining the troops in the second world war. There was a time when, on variety stage, typically a Blackpool summer show, on record, on radio, as well as on screen, it was difficult to avoid (not that one wished to) the insistent jingle of his insouciant ukulele strumming and the saucy vulgarity of his cheeky lyrics.

With his Donald Duck gait, toothy grin, jutting neck and uncomprehending fluster, his films continued from *Boots* in 1934 to *George in Civvy Street* in 1946, with such titles as *It's in the Air; Trouble Brewing; Let George Do It* and *Spare a Copper* along the way. Each saw the simple-minded, gangling George winning the battle over some nefarious foe and claiming the comely heroin; each was an acceptable excuse for him to regale cinema, as he did variety, audiences, with *double-entendre* numbers, like *With My Little Ukulele in my Hand; Auntie Maggie's Remedy; Chinese Laundry Blues* (Oh, Mr Wu), and his archetypal song, redolent of the prurience and *voyeurism* of the 1930s, *When I'm Cleaning Windows*. Aside from those, his nicely-judged singing of *Leaning on a Lamppost* was to make it one of the most heartfelt love-songs.

His father, George Formby Senior, had been a celebrated star of the Edwardian music hall, a northerner prominent in a largely London-oriented profession. His subtle portraiture of a fundamentally diffident and melancholy man, presenting as a frolicsome and extrovert one, was a classic. After being an apprentice jockey, his son vainly tried to adopt his father's mantle on the older man's death in 1921, after his long struggle with bronchitis — the phrases 'I'll have to get a bottle' and 'coughing better tonight' stem from the incorporation of his illness into his act. George Formby never saw his father perform, for he had been anxious to steer his son away from stage-life. It was only when he taught himself to play the ukulele, with that amazingly intricate dexterity of the right hand, and take on his goofy image, that fame came his way.

That and his marriage to the formidable Beryl Ingham . . . in his basic variety 'honeymoon' sketch, she played forward bride to his backward groom — and that somehow foreshadowed their relationship. Tales are legion of how completely she dominated his life and career, right down to the prudent watch on his leading ladies, only one of whom (Googie Withers) he ever kissed passionately on screen, and his tiny allotment of pocket money. Fact and lore grew closer, until, on Christmas Day 1960, the militant atheist Beryl died of cancer, leaving the roman catholic George without his dominatrice. Two months later, he announced his engagement to a Fylde schoolteacher, Pat Howson, but then died in the March of 1961, leaving a long trail of family litigation over his will and odd stories of suitcases stuffed with notes spirited from his Blackpool home, *Beryldene*. For

once his ebullient catch-phrase, 'it's turned out nice again', was scarcely apt.

 LAUREL AND HARDY
(Arthur Stanley Jefferson, 1890-1965, born Ulverston, England; Oliver 'Babe' Hardy, 1892-1957, born Georgia, USA)

Never was the Anglo-American alliance more fruitfully represented than in the coming together of the slight, nervous Laurel with the courtly, amply proportioned Hardy. It is possibly fair to include them in this British listing, for Stan Laurel undertook the third significant role of gag devisor and frequent director. He was, in fact, the motivating and creative force behind the duo. Obsessively dedicated to his craft, and with, perhaps consequentially, a string of failed marriages to show for his disorganised private life, he was the converse of the golf-loving, easy-going Oliver Hardy, as affable domestically as he was irefully pompous professionally. Stan Laurel, a practised scholar of the Fred Karno school, teamed up with the actor, often, until then, the 'baddie', Olly Hardy under the aegis of Hal Roach in 1926. From then until after the second world war, they produced a marvellous stream of films, short and long, among them, *You're darned Tootin'*; *Big Business*; *Towed in a Hole*; *Way out West*; *Blockheads*; *The Flying Deuces* and *A Chump at Oxford*.

The complements of character were beautifully maintained: weedily thin and complacently fat; fearful neuroticism and pained resignation; the twirled hair of unease and the twiddled tie of embarrassment, with the essential visual effects underpinned with a minimal dialogue of familiar types of phrases. From Punch and Judy onwards, the mark of the double act has been the straight man or woman outwitted by the clown. Not so with Laurel and Hardy: what makes them the premier double act ever is the manner in which they so cultivated their respective characters that it is impossible to assess them according to that time-honoured standard. They are both 'the comic'. Only Morecambe and Wise, whose vintage performance had echoes of their illustrious predecessors, have come close to emulating those two genuinely three-dimensional creations.

They came to be instantly recognisable in their lower middle class suits and pot hats and from the moment the jerky, rather juvenile notes of their opening music began. Sometimes they would exchange their normal wear for the uniforms of pilots or foreign legionaries, but their basic nature was never disguised. Cinematic techniques allowed them, of course, a wider range of disaster than the stage, and they courted disaster with the exuberance of the lovesick swain. Disaster, when it inevitably arrived, usually brought Oliver Hardy low and left Stan Laurel comparatively unscathed. Disaster looming; disaster, and the aftermath of disaster; these were alike the stages for their physical and verbal exchanges, the whole construct a veritable poem of praise to their strangely close and imperishable friendship.

Oliver Hardy's final judgement — 'here's another nice mess you've gotten me into' — belongs to the world anthology of quotations, whilst their very outlines continue to be exceedingly strong in the public mind. Any twosome adopting their dress and manner-isms, as, for instance, Harry Secombe and Roy Castle did a few years ago on television, is rewarded with instantaneous acknowledgement. Very few stars, whose chief output was over fifty years ago, are able to make that claim.

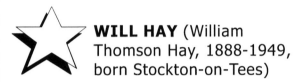 **WILL HAY** (William Thomson Hay, 1888-1949, born Stockton-on-Tees)

It is a tribute to the power of schoolboy literature, especially the *Magnet* and *Gem* comics, with their enthralling adventures of the 'famous five' of Greyfriars and the plump anti-hero, Billy Bunter, that theatre and radio audiences so swiftly identified with Will Hay, 'the Schoolmaster Comedian'. Having considered a career in engineering, he turned to the stage, and, like so many of his contemporaries, he gained some experience with Fred Karno. Then he created his legendary schoolmaster - and everybody understood what and who he was. Playing the floundering but stealthy incompetent of a teacher, with mortar board and *pince-nez*, in school-room sketches set in some minor boarding school, often the Narkover of J B Morton (Beachcomber of the *Daily Express*), everyone readily understood the argot of prep and dorms and beaks, even although the huge majority of people had left school about the same time public schoolboys entered their lofty establishments.

It was a wonderfully observed caricature, more dramatic, at times more pathetic, than comic in concept. The seedy garb, the devious face, the shifty look, the deprecating cough, the split-second timing: it was a masterpiece of theatrical construction that still stands service when one seeks an illustration of the bungling teacher. The battle for control with the smart-alec pupils in his dithering charge was as perceptive a performance as any produced by the variety theatre. From the hesitant, guarded 'good morning, boys', it was a masterly enterprise. This was a deeply-thought through character, sustained by a clever man and a noted astronomer in private life, although, it must be said, a trifle mean-spirited in some of his domestic and professional dealings.

Probably because of this fully polished and rounded configuration, Will Hay was to transfer his characterisation more successfully to the cinema than any other British comedian, and his series of some 18 films between 1934 and 1944 comprise a *genre* unmatched in UK film-making. Although several, such as *Boys will be Boys; Good Morning, Boys* and *The Ghost of St Michael's*, were school-based, what Will Hay also adroitly did was to transpose his study of failing authority to other institutions. Famously allied with Moore Marriott, as the old man, Harbottle, and Graham Moffatt, as the fat boy, Albert, he was prison governor, station master, fire chief and police sergeant in, respectively, *Convict 99; Oh, Mr Porter; Where's that Fire* and *Ask a Policeman*. Other well-known films were *The Black Sheep of Whitehall; The Goose Steps Out* and *My Learned Friend*.

Will Hay excelled in *ensemble* playing, surrounding himself with good players, with the humour bouncing around among them very fluently. Some critics have gone so far as to say that in *Oh, Mr Porter*, usually assessed as his greatest film, the trio of inadequate controller, knowing youth and witless ancient

came close to emulating, in a distinctly English idiom, the quality of the Marx Brothers at their sovereign best. It is a bold boast, but a close scrutiny of Will Hay's work persuades one that it is not unreasonable. His ability to evoke sympathy for his basically worthless and incapable character is positively Falstaffian in its merit.

 ROBERT DONAT
(Friederich Robert Donat, 1905-1958, born Manchester)

Gradually, the luminaries of the British theatre sloughed aside their disdain for the cinema and gave it their closer attention. One element in this metamorphosis was the beginning of a long and handsome line of quietly-spoken, understated heroes, normally described as 'typically English'. It was a cult that has lasted to the present day, although, in the hands of Sean Connery's James Bond or Michael Caine's Alfie, it has lost some of its gentler and more sporting virtues. The Americans had been swift to seize on the prototype, either moulding Douglas Fairbanks Jr to the Anglicised shape or recruiting the likes of Ronald Colman (1891-1958). The latter's romantic courtesies were to the fore as he adopted the identities, *inter alia*, of Bulldog Drummond, Sydney Carton in *A Tale of Two Cities* or Rudolf Rassendyll in *The Prisoner of Zenda*.

Robert Donat, although always struggling against the scourge of asthma, switched from a distinguished stage career to an equally distinguished cinema career. A good-looking, at times almost ethereal face, a trim physique and, most particularly, a voice of exquisite melodiousness were the honourable tools of his trade. For over 20 years he made films in which he always caught and descried the essence of some hero for whom all felt instant sympathy. He was much-wronged as *The Count of Monte Cristo*, in 1934; he was the much-chased Richard Hannay in John Buchan's *The 39 Steps*, in 1935, with Madeline Carroll co-starring; he was the much-tempted young doctor, Andrew Manson, in the film version of A J Cronin's *The Citadel*, in 1938; he was the much-stressed statesman in *The Young Mr Pitt*, in 1942. Possibly he will be mainly recollected for his gradually ageing role, shifting from uptight young teacher to wise old preceptor in *Good-bye, Mr Chips* (1939), after the James Hilton novel. As he matured, he was cast astutely in older parts, as in *The Winslow Boy*, in 1948, and *The Inn of the Sixth Happiness*, with Ingrid Bergman, in 1958.

Many followed in his courtly footsteps. He was near contemporary with Leslie Howard, born in 1893 and prematurely killed in a still controversial air-plane attack in 1943. Just as Robert Donat came from a Polish background, Leslie Howard was of Hungarian origins, but both were idolised as the unadulterated cream of English manhood. As Sir Percy Blakeney in *The Scarlet Pimpernel* (1935) or later as the unassuming archaeologist, in the updated *Pimpernel Smith* (1941) or as Mitchell, the Spitfire's inventor, in *The First of the Few*, he was ever the unaffected hero. David Niven carried on the good work. No one could have found more Englishry than he in such films as *Raffles* (1940), *Carrington VC* (1955) or as Jules Verne's Phileas Fogg in the 1956 favourite *Round the World in Eighty Days*. John Mills, too, could readily muster the necessary stiff lip and unflagging but never boasted courage. In war films he always seemed to be silently valiant on the bridge while Richard Attenborough was having hysterics in the engine room but that may be a figment of confused imagination. Certainly in films like *In which We Serve* (1942); *This Happy Breed (1944); The Way to the Stars* (1945) or *Ice Cold in Alex* (1958) he 'did his bit', as the pithy wartime phrase had it, and then, of course, treated us to a long life of sturdy character roles. Admired by the chaps and loved by the ladies, such actors as he and Robert Donat brought inestimable pleasure to cinema-goers.

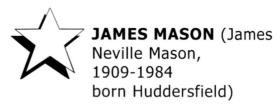 **JAMES MASON** (James Neville Mason, 1909-1984 born Huddersfield)

British cinema might find a Robert Donat as the English reflection of an American hero in the Cary Grant mould, but could it uncover the English equivalent of the more dashing champion, on the lines of an Anglo-Saxon Errol Flynn? Until the late 1930s it seemed unlikely that a true-blue swashbuckler would ever be in the offing, but along came Stewart Granger (1913-1993) who could buckle a swash with the pick of them, even if his real-life name — James Lablanche Stewart — was not exactly in keeping with that piratical convention. With gleaming black hair, strikingly aquiline features and a brawny torso in the Hollywood muscular tradition, he thrust and parried his cavalier way through a series of heroic roles, some of them co-starring with

James Mason, in chiefly period tales like *The Man in Grey* (1943); *Fanny by Gaslight* (1943); *Madonna of the Seven Moons* (1944); *Captain Boycott* (1947); *Saraband for Dead Lovers* (1948); *King Solomon's Mines* (1950), as Alan Quartermaine, and *Beau Brummell* (1954). Stewart Granger is quoted as saying he was not proud of any of his films, but, while it is true none of them are ever cited as classics, they gave a lot of straightforward, no-nonsense amusement.

The appeal of James Mason was more subtle and complex. The simplest explanation is that he was often cast as the leading man that women might love to distraction but never like. He could be broodingly cruel and mysteriously forbidding. His crumpled good looks and tousled dark hair, coupled with his moody eyes and decisive, gravelly tones, were utilised in some of the strongest and roundest acting in British and, later, American films. He was in over a hundred films from 1935 to 1984, rarely deviating to stage, radio or television. He was very much the professional and highly intelligent cinema actor. The long list of his credits include *I Met a Murderer* (1939, along with his wife, Pamela Kellino (actress, columnist, screen-writer, novelist, TV personality and 'progressive' mother of Portland), *Hatter's Castle* (1942), *The Night has Eyes* (1942), *The Man in Grey'* (1943), as the dastardly Lord Rohan, and, of course, with Judy Garland in the 1954 drama, *A Star is Born*. We watched him smash poor Ann Todd's fingers on the piano in the psychobabbling *The Seventh Veil* in 1945, whilst a year later he was roistering with Margaret Lockwood as the devil-may-care highwayman in *The Wicked Lady*. That same year saw him chalk up probably his best performance,

hunted, mentally as well as physically, as the lone Irish terrorist in *Odd Man Out*. He was Rommel in *The Desert Fox* (1951), Captain Nemo in *20,000 Leagues under the Sea* (1954) and Humbert in *Lolita* (1964).

An interesting aspect is that the sepia hues of black and white film admirably suited his rather bleak acting personality, whereas others, the bronzed magnificence of Stewart Granger being a case in point, looked pretty good in Technicolor. *Odd Man Out* is a downbeat illustration of this point. James Mason's painful flight through the wet back-streets of 1940s Belfast is well-crafted, the detail watchfully itemised, with the grainy, subdued tints ideal for the low-key story-line. There were not many laughs in a James Mason film, but few actors, even judging on an international criterion, have sustained so potent a screen image for so long.

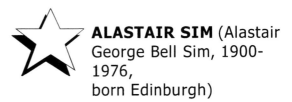

ALASTAIR SIM (Alastair George Bell Sim, 1900-1976, born Edinburgh)

Once British films came of age a consistent feature in their success became a treasury of delightful character actors. These drolls were especially notable in the famously quirky post-war Ealing comedies, like *Passport to Pimlico; The Lavender Hill Mob* or *The Man in the White Suit*. The last two starred Alec Guinness, born in 1914, and just beginning on his spectacular career — from Fagin in *Oliver Twist* in 1948 and his incredible eight roles in *Kind Hearts and Coronets* in 1949 to epics like *The Bridge over the River Kwai* in 1957 and *Star Wars* in 1977. His amazing portrayals lie more outside than inside our relevant period, and something of the same applies to Richard Attenborough, born in 1923, who moved decorously from youth roles, as in *Brighton Rock* (1947) or even as a 13-year old in *The Guinea Pig* to searching characterisations like that of the murderer, Christie, in *10 Rillington Place* (1971). But there were also less well-known actors offering shrewdly observed support. Some of them were enlisted in the 'I know him but I can't think of his name' brigade. For example, the bespectacled Richard Wattis (1912-1975), icily stern or frigidly angry, appeared to be in practically every British film.

The doyen of British character acting was Alastair Sim, for whom the adjective 'lugubrious' might have been specifically coined. He somehow managed to combine the music hall skills (there was something of Will Hay in his timing and facial expression) with high legitimate arts, creating a fascinating once-off study impossible to imitate. His angular, almost vulture like posture; his long-drawn countenance, itself a screen for the less pleasing human emotions, such as avarice, fear, crocodile tears or unwonted glee; his careful dominie-like diction; his scale of gestures, his arms waving like a gale-blown windmill — these were the instruments in the Sim one-man band. The resultant compositions were to be enjoyed in such films as *Let the People Sing* (1942); *Waterloo Road* (1944); *Green for Danger* (1946); *Hue and Cry* (1947); *Laughter in Paradise* (1951) and *The Green Man* (1956). His *Scrooge*, in 1951, is by far the finest celluloid representation of that Dickensian conversion, for, moving from grasping miser to generous host, he retained — and it is a difficult feat — the core of the same personality, chiefly through its abiding force of energy. Memorably, he played the beleaguered headmaster in a number of films, including *The Happiest Days of your Life* (1950) and a comical set of St Trinian's films. These also demonstrated, in the differing approaches of the bashful Joyce Grenfell and the exuberant Margaret Rutherford, that the females could hold their own in the character acting stakes. Needless to say, he was also a consummate stage actor, as witness his definitive Captain Hook in several productions of *Peter Pan*.

His *protégé* was George Cole, and aptly so, for George Cole, on stage (in *The Brass Butterfly*), radio (*Life of Bliss*) and television (as the dubious trader, Arthur Daley, with his *Minder*, to say nothing of ''er indoors'), has revealed some of the same breadth of inventiveness as his mentor for a later generation. Born in 1925, he has had, from a young age, a noted film career, not least in many Alastair Sim vehicles, ranging from fumbling innocent to devious confidence trickster and always impressing with his well-humoured proficiency. The work of Alastair Sim reflects great credit on British cinema and its capacity to make plentiful room for so eccentric a character actor.

 MARGARET LOCKWOOD
(Margaret Mary Lockwood,
1916-1990, born Karachi)

But what about the ladies? Seven down and only three to go, and not a female in sight. To be candid, early British cinema did not offer actresses much scope. They were the insipid *ingenues*, gazing fondly into the eyes of posh actors or perhaps into the startled face of George Formby, with maybe an honest-to-goodness charlady, usually cockney, thrown in for low-brow measure. Gracie Fields, of course, made one or two stout efforts, but very much in her music hall mode, while attempts to employ the charm of the London musical stage, even with a talent like Jessie Matthews, were not too convincing. There were some powerful older roles, like those Dame Flora Robson played in *Fire over England*, in 1936, or *Frieda* in 1947 — 'would you take Frieda into your home?' was its much-quoted billing. Plainly, there were no reasonable opportunities for young aspiring women. Curiously, it was the Methodist tenets of J Arthur Rank, financial saviour of British films which were introduced by gong-striking Bombardier Billy Wells, that prevailed. The Rank starlets did begin to bring some glamour to the British screen.

Many will remember the rosebud prettiness of Patricia Roc (Felicia Riese for real, born in 1915). She was cast in the 1940s as the chaste, comely heroine, and she excelled in such roles in films like *Millions Like Us*, the 1943 story of girls directed to wartime munitions factories, or *The Brothers*, the melodramatic 1947 yarn about Skye fisherfolk. Later there would be the more lusty invocation of one Miss Diana Fluck, happily re-tagged with the stage-name of Diana Dors (1931-1984). The physical and emotional converse of Patricia Roc, 'the blonde bombshell' was Britain's tart with the heart from 1946 on, as much photographed off as on the screen, her buxom figure, pouting lips and long yellow tresses proving to be a sex symbol for the 1950s.

Where, however, was the UK approximation to the USA's golden mean between the nice and the naughty, the attractive but tough-minded 'doll', as the then current argot had it, of the Bette Davis, Joan Crawford, Kathleen Hepburn school? Margaret Lockwood was the nearest to an answer. It was a long-term response, too. That invincible lady was in *Lorna Doone* in 1935 and in *The Slipper and the Rose* in 1976. Nonetheless, it was as the arch-villainess or, if not that, the militant female of the middle years that brought her enduring fame. A stunning brunette, with shapely curves, luminously glowing eyes and imposing manner, she graduated from juvenile leads to become, in 1946, the most popular star of the year. Her films included *The Lady Vanishes* (1938); *The Stars Look Down* (1939) and *Quiet Wedding* (1941). Most typically, there was *The Wicked Lady* (1946), where she played the thrill-seeking, aristocratic highway-woman, Lady Skelton, the beauty spot high on her left cheek bone a tiny emblem of her sinfulness. We felt quite grown up to learn that her low-cut bodice was causing concern to the American film censor.

Popular English literature and theatre had tended to concentrate on innocent young girls and wicked old ladies. With an echo of *Vanity Fair's* Becky Sharp, Margaret Lockwood very seductively concocted a blend of allure and depravity that, paradoxically, seemed somewhat wholesome in a rather prurient age.

CELIA JOHNSON (Dame Celia Johnson, 1908-1982 born Richmond)

Celia Johnson made her stage debut in 1928 and within three years was a star. Retaining a very sane and un-starstruck view of the theatre, she balanced professional and domestic life with delightful skill. She retired from the stage during the war and was an auxiliary policewoman; she appeared in all manner of productions from ancient classics to modern pot-boilers, and she was amazed at her well-merited DBE. She has been described as having 'outstanding charm, wide eyes, a *retroussé* nose, and a remarkable voice'. She was certainly an adornment to the West End stage both before and until well after the war, with everything from *Major Barbara* (her first play) to *The Reluctant Debutante* effortlessly within the scope of her fine gifts .

Indeed, many may view her more as a stage than a screen star and it is true she appeared in many more plays than films. As in the theatre, the film roles tended to be rather genteel in character. Her cinema debut was in 1942, as the wife to Noel Coward's naval captain in *In Which we Serve*. This was followed by parts in *Dear Octopus* (1942), *This Happy Breed* (1944); *The Astonished Heart* (1949); *I Believe in You* (1952); *The Captain's Paradise* (1953); *The Holly and the Ivy* (1954) and *A Kid for Two Farthings* (1956). Then she was a prim but determined Miss Trant in the 1957 version of J B Priestley's concert party story, *The Good Companions*, and a sceptical headmistress in the 1969 filming of Muriel Spark's *The Prime of Miss Jean Brodie*.

However, Celia Johnson's real claim for inclusion in the cinematic gallery arises from her beautifully controlled role in *Brief Encounter*. Made in 1945, set in Carnforth railway station, grimy and smoke-blown, it is still a riveting film and one that, deservedly, appears high on both popular and critical lists of all-time great films. Few will need reminding that it tells the bleak little fable of the suburban housewife and general practitioner who, beginning with a trivial bit of first aid when he removes a speck from her eye, fall in intense but intensely inhibited love.

Written by Noel Coward and others, from the Coward play *Still Life*, and directed by David Lean, it is a middle-class tear-jerker of uncommon quality. Trevor Howard (1916-1988) was to be the tough-minded Englishman in scores of films, but here he was the understanding but frustrated leading man, who takes a post abroad to preserve the sanctity of comfortable if unexciting marriage. As counterpart to the cut-glass tones and Anglican values of the leads, there is the brazen flirtatious banter of the working class couple, Stanley Holloway's railwayman and Joyce Carey's refreshment room attendant.

Brief Encounter has grounds for being assessed the best of British films. The film critic, Richard Winnington, has spoken of 'the tight realism of its detail', for it was an immaculately crafted piece of work. Moreover, it was a parable of the period. There are no physical flings flung; the passion is emotionally cooped up, with mundane duty victorious over romantic bliss. In her touching encapsulation of mid-century, middle class ethics, Celia Johnson etched a genuine portrait that well may stand the test of centuries of time. Unlike the average film, this was real-life: they did not all live happily ever after.

VIVIEN LEIGH (Vivian Mary Hartley, 1913-1967 born Darjeeling)

Born in India, Vivien Leigh's girlhood was spent in travel and acquiring aesthetic knowledge, a marinating in 'good taste' that was to be of much value to her. It informed the gracious style of her personality, while she was blessed with a lovely, flawless complexion, expressive greeny-blue eyes, glossy chestnut hair and a decorous ease of movement. All was set for a magnificent career on stage and screen.

Her stage-life was dominated by her impassioned and intimate partnership with Laurence Olivier. She was Ophelia, for instance, to his Hamlet at Elsinore in 1937, and this was but one of many times they appeared together, frequently in Shakespearean dramas, such as *Anthony and Cleopatra*. They first met in the world of films. They played together in the 1937 *Fire over England*, that pageant-like re-creation of the defeat of the Spanish Armada, and this led to another dual engagement, as Lord Nelson and Emma in *Lady Hamilton* in 1941. She made several other likeable films. These included the spy romance, *Dark Journey* (1937); the Anglo-American hit, *A Yank at Oxford* (1938), co-starring handsome Robert Taylor; *Waterloo Bridge* (1940), again with Robert Taylor, he the army officer to her impulsive ballerina; *Caesar and Cleopatra* (1945), after the George Bernard Shaw play; *Anna Karenina* (1948), from the searching Tolstoy novel; *The Deep Blue Sea* (1955), the screen adaptation of Terence Rattigan's sorrowful drama, and *The Roman Spring of Mrs Stone* (1961), a study in widowed decadence. She also re-created her successful stage role as Blanche in the strong Tennessee Williams piece, *A Streetcar named Desire*.

One cannot but be conscious of the way so many of those characterisations saw art mimicking nature and *vice versa*. Vivien Leigh's health was delicate and, increasingly, she became subject to nervous collapse and manic phases. Driving herself incessantly, she died of tuberculosis in her early 50s. The lights of the West End theatres were dimmed for an hour on the day of her death.

What film-goers will, needless to say, remember is her portrayal of Scarlett O'Hara in *Gone with the Wind* in 1939. Its arrival in England at the beginning of the war was timely, for it provided luscious escapism at that dreary time, but, by any standards, it remains, if not a classic piece of film-making, a glorious example of truly popular art. Although Vivien Leigh is said not to have liked the character as such, she was delighted to shed the 'English rose' image that had attached to her in her few early films, and she proceeded to invade the screen and our collective cinematic memory with an unforgettable *tour de force*. Spunky, egotistical, vain, manipulative, the scheming Scarlett flaunts her charms and her valour, so much so that, in film terms, Olivia de Havilland and Leslie Howard are left looking slightly two-dimensional and weak-kneed and even Clark Gable's Rhett Butler has to battle arduously to find some sort of foothold in the story.

No English actress has made so forceful an impact in a single film, and Vivien Leigh's lustrous name will forever be associated with that of the uppity Miss O'Hara.

Alvar Lidell in 1939

Al Read

Arthur Askey in *Bandwaggon* in 1940

Professor Jimmy Edwards in *Whack-O*

Sandy Macpherson

Uncle Mac, Derek McCulloch in 1940

Wilfred Pickles

Tommy Handley in 1940 in *ITMA*

Jack Warner as PC George Dixon
in *The Blue Lamp* in 1949

Professor C E M Joad
on *The Brains Trust* 1942

Those Radio Times ~ Listening To The Wireless
Ten Radio Stars

Guglielmo Marconi . . . how indebted we must be to him for realising the potential of wireless broadcasting. He was the intrepid entrepreneur who spotted the functional possibility implicit in laboratory theory and experiment and, in 1895, produced the first 'wireless' signals. By 1901 he had increased the transmission distance to 200 miles, and there was soon much military and naval usage. Indeed, it was only after the 1914-1918 war that private civilians were really allowed their chance and, in 1920, *The Daily Mail* sponsored an historic broadcast of songs by Dame Nellie Melba. The chief impetus came, on the one hand, from the equipment manufacturers, anxious to sell receivers, and, on the other hand, from the listeners, many of them in 'wireless societies', who wanted something to receive. The Post Office, under an act of 1904, was the licensing authority for wireless stations, but arguments about which manufacturers should have leave to build stations and where rumbled on, while

foreign broadcasting ominously took shape. In 1922 the British Broadcasting <u>Company</u>, funded by a group of manufacturers, was granted an exclusive license by the Post Office, and, rather casually, public service broadcasting was born. It might have been invidious to pick and choose among several contenders — and a single body was easier to control. It has been said that the Conservative politicians liked such staunch authority and the Labour politicians disliked private enterprise. Either way, it was still the actual sale of wireless sets that dominated the thinking, from which curio arises the oddity of financing the BBC from individual wireless licenses.

A puritanical Scot, John Reith, became General Manager of this new network of several regional stations, with London's 2LO at the centre. In 1923 the headquarters moved from the Strand to Savoy Hill, the first issue of *Radio Times* was on 28 September in that year, and, in 1924, the first Greenwich Mean Time 'pips' were heard. In 1927, by royal charter, the BBC became a Corporation, with John Reith as director general, in part a reward for the BBC's good behaviour during the General Strike of 1926. He imposed an austere regime, keen to deploy 'the brute force of monopoly' (his words) to give the public what they ought to like, the whole stamped with his Calvinistic morality. Hence the Sabbath was held dear and free from the taint of popular music and, in total, censorship was ferocious and overbearing. Drama and light entertainment were at a discount, while the true winners were serious music (popular music was only allowed about 30% of the time) and 'talks'. It was not surprising that the early commercial stations to penetrate Britain, like Radio Normandy in 1931 and Radio Luxembourg in 1933, proved acceptable to many listeners.

John Reith's strict rule ended in 1938, providentially, perhaps, because wartime needs were to blow asunder so rigid an attitude, while transatlantic influences were beginning to tell. Nevertheless, Reith, later Sir John, then Lord Reith, had laid the important foundations of broadcasting as a public service, with the civic responsibilities that entailed. This was illustrated by, for instance, the monarchical Christmas and other royal broadcasts and by the growing political use of the medium. Where Lloyd George and Ramsay MacDonald had been magical 'live' orators, the composed Stanley Baldwin took readily to the microphone, whilst, needless to say, Winston Churchill was to make radio his own personal weapon in the coming fight for democratic freedom.

By the outbreak of war there were some 10m wireless licenses, so that, in effect, the BBC could and did communicate with the entire nation. Not only that, it contrived to communicate with many other nations — as opposed to eight in 1939, it broadcast in 47 languages by 1943. In fact, the BBC grew enormously during the war period, increasing its staff from 4000 to nearly 12,000, its transmitters from 23 to 138, and its hours of broadcasting from 50 to 150 hours a day, with its Home Service and Forces Programme the central dishes. To be fair to John Reith, there were other reasons why the popular culture had not been too prominent in the BBC's early days. Theatre magnates were suspicious of the competition, while some artists either could not translate easily to radio or were scared of seeing a years-old, lovingly nursed act vanish in just one broadcast. Whatever the case, and when due regard is paid the pioneers of the 1930s, in shows like John Watts' *Songs from the Shows*, Ernest Longstaffe's *Music Hall* and Harry S Pepper's *The Kentucky Minstrels*, it was the decade of the 1940s and the early years of the 1950s which were to witness the glory days of BBC light entertainment.

By accident and by design, the BBC produced a consensual diet for a consensus audience. Although John Reith had insisted on a narrow menu, he was not altogether out of touch with the prurient suburban thought of the 1930s, but the loosening effects of the second world war shook up those values both at Broadcasting House and among the BBC's clientele. What emerged was a mixed bag of light and heavy material for a people that apparently were prepared to enjoy both. Thus a schedule of dance and classical music, of educative and light-hearted 'talks' and discussion programmes, and of serious dramatic and hilarious comedy shows, was not only acceptable but became a norm rarely thought of as lopsided. For all the talk of national cultures, it is, historically speaking, rare for a country to appreciate instantaneously a single such experience. It requires an uncommon degree of technical and social collusion for a vast population to enjoy some such presentation together. In shows like *ITMA* or Wilfred Pickles' *Have a Go*, as well as in the daily news bulletins or the uplift of prime ministerial speeches, there was a period of some 20 years when the broadcasters achieved that pinnacle. Like the family novels of Charles Dickens or the cross-class urban folk-operas of Gilbert and Sullivan before them, they served the nation as a whole. They were the genuine 'voice of Britain'.

By the mid-1950s the might and allure of television would begin to hack away at this integrated culture — although, for a while, especially with one or two of the 'soap' operas or, most definitively, with the Morecambe and Wise shows, TV would itself emulate that sense of national togetherness. At the same time as it began to lose ground, radio responded nobly with creations like *The Goon Show*, with its alternative nightmare universe, *Hancock's Half Hour*, with Tony Hancock's superb three-dimensional personification of the ambiguities of the era, and even, with its record-breaking runs between 1958 and 1972, to say nothing of its 10m listeners, *The Clitheroe Kid*. For those of what prudent writers used to call a certain age, the 'wireless' will always be fondly remembered for its good cheer and for its good will.

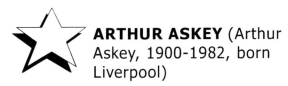 **ARTHUR ASKEY** (Arthur Askey, 1900-1982, born Liverpool)

The first light entertainment programme to find real fame was *Band Waggon*, which ran for 52 editions (1938-1939). The BBC was under increasing pressure from commercial radio and transatlantic influences, especially on the comedy front. Thus it set British radio comedy on a new, pacy and inventive path, with the *Band Waggon* driven by 'Big-hearted' Arthur Askey, with Richard 'Stinker' Murdoch, so to speak, riding shotgun. The lively, diminutive comic had the gusto — 'hello, playmates' — of the concert party, rather than the more abrasive edge of the music hall, and it was this sunny disposition that won the fans. He featured his nonsense songs about tiny creatures, like the moth, the worm, the sea-gull and, most memorably, the busy bee. His agile bounce, gleaming beam and large spectacles were well-known, for he had a coveted place among the strip cartoons of the comic *Radio Fun*. Richard Bernard Murdoch (1907-1990), tall and charming, of Charterhouse and Cambridge, was his admirable antithesis. He was to find later glory with Kenneth Horne in *Much-Binding-in-the-Marsh*, perhaps the most renowned of all fictional military installations, and a mock-RAF station from which broadcasts were seemingly made from 1947 to 1953.

The core of *Band Waggon* was the splendid notion that Arthur Askey and Richard Murdoch had a flat above Broadcasting House. Arthur Askey was to prove skilled at adapting to new media in this way — on television, for example, there was to be his diver-like descent from camera view, 'before your very eyes'. They had a cleaner, Mrs

Bagwash, whose daughter, Nausea, was Arthur's sweetheart; two pigeons, Basil and Lucy, and a goat called Lewis. With lots of sound effects, some music and some spots like *New Voices* or *Chestnut Corner*, the show was one of the first to be granted a regular weekly timing, something the BBC had hitherto been reluctant to permit.

That magazine construct was very popular in those days. *In Town Tonight* was an example. Eric Coates' *Knightsbridge* march introduced a string of surprise and topical items, prefaced by the ringing declaration, 'once again we stop the roar of London's traffic to bring to you some of the famous people who are — IN TOWN TONIGHT'. There was also *Monday Night at Seven* (later 'at Eight'), a title that firmly located it on the calendar. The cameos called for listener participation. There was *Inspector Hornleigh Investigates*, (*Meet Dr Morrell* was his successor) with the solution to the mystery later in the programme; there was *Puzzle Corner*, with Ronnie Waldman ('Get your pencil and your paper out; you're the winner if you know about . . .'), again with the answers later, including — its original coinage — a 'Deliberate Mistake'; there was, transferred from *Band Waggon*, Syd 'What would you do, chums?' Walker, the rag-and-bone-man, raising a problem and later in the programme, offering his homespun remedy.

In terms of comedy, it was Arthur Askey who created the first true 'radio' material, as opposed to transposed stage matter, and from that would spring *The Goon Show, Round the Horne* and many other successes. All those who want to show their appreciation may now cry in concert, quoting the tiny master's citing of a bus conductor, 'Aythangyow'.

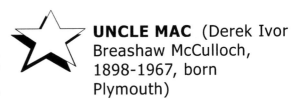

UNCLE MAC (Derek Ivor Breashaw McCulloch, 1898-1967, born Plymouth)

Those now, as the 21st century opens, aged between 65 and 80 formed the first generation of children to benefit from the blessings of radio. In *Children's Hour* the BBC established a unique presentation. It tacitly recognised that the Victorian stand-by of family-based entertainment, like the Dickens-type family story or the pantomime aimed alike at children and adults, was no longer sufficient. In the wake of the post- 'Alice in Wonderland' development of children's literature, there was a growing appreciation — witness the clothes, games and comics, for instance — that children were not little adults, but had a distinguishable childlike quality. This BBC decision was of compelling significance. It was made at a time when even educationists had barely begun to recognise that childhood had an essential character that should be nurtured; indeed, unfortunately, it is a lesson still to be learned by all too many of them. In its alertness to this truth, the BBC, often derided for being old-fashioned, was years ahead of its time.

The rather progressive psychology of 'Children's Hour' endured for many years; then it became a 40 minutes programme, beginning at 5.20 instead of 5 o'clock. With the advent of TV, which, in turn, soon engrossed itself in children's programmes, it was discovered that many of its listeners were now quite ancient adults, yearning still for the cultural nourishment of their childhood. It was quite a compliment, but the unsentimental BBC axed it forthwith, in 1965, to the horror of Uncle Mac.

Uncle Mac was the personification of *Children's Hour*. The doyen of children's presenters down the ages, his soothing, deliberate, empathetic tones were assuredly avuncular. In a modern culture awash with the over-familiar usage of matey forenames, the idea that all presenters then were uncles and aunties may seem preposterous, but it suited the times. The BBC was to become a corporate 'aunty', so its maternal embrace of children was widely accepted. A BBC announcer from 1926, and *Children's Hour* Organiser from 1933, then Director from 1938, Uncle Mac presided with some aplomb over a daily dosage of child-oriented magazine-style items, although he diversified slightly, we were amazed to find, by playing Larry the Lamb, bleating and timid, in *Toytown*. He accomplished this despite dreadful wounds on the Somme in WWI and a later crippling road accident. He introduced playlets, often historical in mode, many of them, such as *Castles of England*, written by L du Garde Peach, and what would now be termed short documentaries. Perhaps conscious of its listeners' urban-bound majority, *Children's Hour* made a supreme effort to provide nature study. Each week we would follow Romany and his faithful dog ('down, Rack') in search of nature's secrets, and, after Romany, there was a weekly opportunity to go *Wandering with Nomad*. Ever present were the ubiquitous uncles and aunties, compering, describing, storytelling, playing music, joining Romany on his rural jaunts, ready with bright question and pleased reaction.

Among them, unhurried, composed, possibly close to a great-uncle, ruled Uncle Mac. There was, for thousands of children, many of them the unlucky victims of a depressed economy or evacuation, something infinitely calming about his final words: 'Good night, children, **everywhere**'.

TOMMY HANDLEY
(Thomas Handley, 1894-1949, born Liverpool)

Tommy Handley was the finest reader of a radio script there has ever been. That simple but emphatic encomium leaves room for nothing much but exegesis and examples. A melodious baritone, with concert party experience, his variety sketch was Eric Blore's *The Disorderly Room*, a post Great War *pastiche* of balladic parodies, what was then known as a 'song-chainer'. Especially on radio, he also partnered the slightly *risqué* Ronald Frankau as Murgatroyd and Winterbottom in a flowing stream of wordplay and patter-song. These rhythmic skills were to stand him in enormously good stead as he proceeded to host *ITMA*, the most successful radio comedy show in history. From 1939 to 1949 there were 310 episodes over twelve series, 170 of them in wartime. With 20 million home listeners, boosted to over 30 million worldwide, *ITMA* had inestimable quality as a morale-booster, and its appeal was cross-class and age-neutral. On his untimely death, with *ITMA* still on the air, the nation mourned as if an elder statesman or senior royal had perished. There were memorial services in Liverpool Cathedral and, unprecedentedly for a comedian, St Paul's Cathedral, with 4000 crammed in the church and 2000 listening outside to the broadcast service. There were 10,000 mourners packed around the crematorium and the streets for his funeral procession were lined six deep.

Tommy Handley's invaluable compatriots were the script-writer, Ted Kavanagh, and the producer, Francis Worsley, as they made their weekly assault on the nation's, to deploy Ken Dodd's physiology, 'chuckle-muscle'. With a couple of musical items and announcements, this left some 18 minutes, into which they endeavoured to pack a hundred laughs, one every 11 seconds. The same round of fantastical characters, with their Dickensian names and tasty catch-phrases, were trooped out each time, the whole an exercise in doting familiarity as well as bang-up-to-the-mark topicality. The familiarity is such that, if one listens to an *ITMA* recording, one can sense the studio audience arriving at the punch-lines in front of the artists.

Tommy Handley was the ringmaster of this circus of babbling clowns, his quick-fire delivery always racy but, and herein lay the secret ingredient, never for a second less than articulate. He was the animated Maypole around which they wove and re-wove the coloured ribbons of their highly-charged lines. The abiding sound effect was the opening and closing door, as his colleagues visited him with the latest gloss on their usual tale. A generous leader, and, strangely, offstage a man of considerable nerves, the normal time of 8.30 on a Thursday evening was avowedly anticipated with rarely disappointed relish. In an excellent psychological development, rather more sophisticated than in World War I, the humour was mildly skittish, with jovial mickey-taking, at the expense of the wartime bureaucracy, deflecting the citizen's grumble and complaint with a grin.

Stern space limits mean that mention may only be made of Dorothy Summers' charlady, Mrs Mopp ('Can I do you now, sir?' and 'TTFN') and Jack Train's bibulous Colonel Chinstrap ('I don't mind if I do'), each catch-phrase now part of the language. There was also his German spy, Funf. Curiously, 'It's That Man Again' was taken from a *Daily Express* headline about Hitler, but the show was our secret weapon against the Führer.

 PROFESSOR JOAD (Cyril Edwin Mitchinson Joad, 1891-1953, born Durham)

The BBC struggled hard to cultivate a cross-sectional middlebrow audience, beseeching the highbrows to enjoy *ITMA* or the fast-moving *Hi Gang*, and pleading with the lowbrows to lift their values and enjoy *Music for You*, with Dobson and Young. Although a little patronising, it was a worthy cause, much helped by a strange aspect of war, whereby, as counterpoint to a hedonistic fatalism, there was a genuine concern for serious pursuits. From the remarkable concerts of Dame Myra Hess in the National Gallery to the fact that, at one point, the army's Southern Command had no less than 30 chamber groups in rehearsal, there was cultural *gravitas*. As a consequence, the BBC produced pundits as a conjuror draws rabbits from a top hat, many of them with a common-or-garden tang. If it were not Mr C H Middleton earnestly solicitous about the manure at the bottom of your garden, it was the Radio Doctor gruffly asking after your bowels. (What a surprise it was to find the latter in his other incarnation, as Charles Hill,

Secretary of the BMA, tempestuously fighting Nye Bevan over the creation of the National Health Service; he was later a Conservative cabinet minister.)

With this increasing avidity for knowledge on both the home and military fronts, the BBC producer, Howard Thomas, borrowing the title from the sobriquet for President Roosevelt's advisory team, invented *The Brains Trust*. From its inauguration on 1 January 1941, it was an unparalleled triumph, only the news and mainline variety rivalling its pull. By 1943 it had 12 million listeners, that is close to four out of ten of the potential audience. The first 'Question Master' (a Howard Thomas branding, now universal in application) was the courteous Donald McCullough who presided over a panel of three regulars and a couple of guests. The questions, normally with a light-hearted one for relief, were sent in by listeners. The original trio were that eminent populariser of scientific topics and member of a humanely intellectual family, the lucid Julian Huxley; Commander A B Campbell, the plain-spoken one, yet with his exotic tales of 'when I was in Patagonia', and Cyril Joad.

Professor — although this was rumoured to be a self-styling — Joad was a working philosopher, and his qualifying clause, 'it all depends what you mean by . . .' is still much in vogue today among those wishing to clarify a question. Glistening of eye and bushy of beard, his high pitched, insistent voice was everyman's idea of the tweedy scholar. He had a rare ability to discourse on practically any subject with breathtakingly pithy assurance, and, in a programme purportedly unprompted and certainly live, his two-minute dissertation on, say, the nature of happiness was a puissant *tour de force*. Toward the end of his life he happily twinned farming with philosophising.

The Brains Trust, with C E M Joad as its salient personality, is a proper example of how the BBC sought to balance its information remit with dexterous production, at a time when the citizenry, both armed and civil, was in want of sound adult education. *The Brains Trust* was a staging-post on the arduous road toward the as yet unreached destination of lifelong learning.

 JACK WARNER (Horace John Waters, 1894-1981, born Bromley, London)

Jack Warner initially made his name as the truculent private soldier in *Garrison Theatre* (1939-1941) devised by Charles Shadwell, following his Great War experience of such entertainment. He was the balding conductor of the BBC Variety Orchestra, the composer of *the Spice of Life*, the signature-tune of BBC's *Music Hall*, and known as 'the comedian's friend' because of his high-pitched, infectious laugh. His daughter, Joan Winters, was Jack Warner's prim usherette — 'programmes, chocolates, cigarettes' — 'littel gel'. 'Mind my bike' was his still extant catch-phrase, as he intruded on a straightforward variety schedule with his censored letter, with its 'not blue-pencil likely' interpolations from 'my bruvver Sid'; monologues gently poking fun at reserved occupations, such as 'a bunger-up of rat-'oles' or 'a caster-up of alabaster plaster'; and edifying chats on 'ills for rill mills' (eels for real meals. . .'de-da-de-da-de-da . . .)

Jack Warner powered on to be the *pater familias* of the Huggett family on radio and film, to be a more than useful cinema actor, and to find undying renown as Dixon of Dock Green. Here he might stand surety for several comics and comedy shows on radio during this time. Out of the three services the programme *Merry-go-Round*, for example, spun three shows. These were the RAF's *Much-Binding-in-the-Marsh*, in which the stalwart Maurice Denham played 60 — 'Dudley Davenport at your service, sir' - roles; Charlie Chester's army-style *Stand Easy* (1945-1949), with Whippet Quick and Ray Ling, the Chinese fence; and the naval *Waterlogged Spa* (1944-1948) starring Eric 'heart-throb' Barker, Pearl Hackney and Jon Pertwee.

Shows ran the cultural gamut from *Hi Gang!* (1940-1949) to *Happidrome* (1941-1947). The former, gaining propaganda value by 'coming to you from the heart of London' was a fast-talking vehicle for the American couple, Ben Lyons and Bebe Daniels, who gave *The White Cliffs of Dover* its first airing, and the Austrian-born, violin-playing comedian, Vic Oliver. The latter show came from Llandudno and, like *Garrison Theatre*, was a simple music hall formula hosted by a regular team, to wit, the Mr Lovejoy — 'ee, if ever a man suffered' — of Harry Korris, the Ramsbottom of Cecil Fredricks and the Enoch — 'let me tell you' — of Robbie Vincent. Their theme-tune was a parody of the Inkspots' *We Three*. From the mid-1940s there was also *Variety Band-box* (1944-1953), which was almost entitled 'Band-box Variety', with resident comedians like Derek Roy and, most engagingly, the gossipy Frankie Howerd, while stars like Tony Hancock and

Harry Secombe were both 'discovered' on the show. Then there was the nonsensical quiz show *Ignorance is Bliss* (1946-1953), with Stewart MacPherson attempting to manage the inanities of Michael Moore, Gladys Hay and Harold Berens, with crazy musical interludes form Sid Millward and his Nitwits; or Jewell and Wariss, with Claude Dampier, in *Up the Pole* (1946-1953). Toward the end of our period, Ted Ray, spiritual inheritor of the Tommy Handley mantle, began his long-running success in *Ray's a Laugh* (1949-1961), with Kitty Bluett, Patricia Hayes, Bob and Alf Pearson and the young debutante, Peter Sellers, as, among others, Crystal Jollibottom.

Time to end this piece; so, as P C Dixon might have said, 'Evenin' all'.

ALVAR LIDELL (Tord Alvar Quan Lidell, 1908-1981, born Wimbledon Park)

The seminal revue, *Beyond the Fringe* had a 'war' parody that included the line, 'here is the nine o'clock news and this is Alvar Liddell bringing you news of fresh disasters'. It did seem a bit like that at times, but the sacred tone of the nine o'clock news was probably due for a little debunking. Hitherto, the newsreaders, while compelled by Lord Reith to wear dinner jackets, had been anonymous as well as invisible. Less the wavelengths fell into enemy control, the wartime newsreaders revealed their identities, so that an alert citizen might sense had security been breached. We learned to link the intonations with the names: Bruce Belfrage; Joseph McLeod, Stuart Hibberd, Frank Phillips, Frederick Allen, and so on. For a short time even Wilfred Pickles took on the job, his flat vowels and regional 'good neet' being very distinctive by BBC yardsticks. Partly because of the unusual forename and partly because the second syllable of the surname was stressed, Alvar Lidell, was the most memorable. Tall, of Swedish origins, with impeccably modulated enunciation, he could do *The Times'* crossword in six minutes, and, were that not enough fame for one man, he announced the abdication of Edward VIII and introduced Neville Chamberlain's declaration of war on 3 September 1939.

He serves to represent a small host of BBC informants over the period. There were prestigious commentators, like Stephen King-Hall, Raymond Gram Swing, J B Priestley, although his leftish hymning of the rights of the common man caused some *frissons*, and Quentin Reynolds, who taught us to imagine Hitler as Herr Schickelgruber, while Alistair Cooke would soon begin his effortlessly impeccable *Letter from America*, and Freddie Grisewood, counselling housewives on the *Kitchen Front*, was a martial forerunner of the glut of cookery programmes today. There were also radio war correspondents, men like Richard Dimbleby, who once described a bombing raid over enemy-occupied Europe. Kate Adie and Martin Bell are their descendants

Both before and after World War II, sports broadcasting had developed quite a momentum. Commentators became identified with particular sports. There was John Snagge for the Boat Race; Howard Marshall for the cricket; Stewart MacPherson for the boxing, always with blandly impartial inter-round summaries from J Barrington-Dalby; and handlebar moustachioed Raymond

Glendenning for the football. Older listeners will recall how, for instance, rugby matches utilised a squared grid system to make listeners aware of where the play was located, so that a secondary announcer would, every now and then, call, 'square three' or 'square five'. Is this where the phrase 'we're back to square one' originated? After the war the greatest of sports commentators, John Arlott, made his unhurried and urbane debut: when N B F Mann of South Africa bowled to F G Mann of England, he described it as 'Mann's inhumanity to Mann'.

Eventually, though, it was the calm, reassuring, extremely famous newsreaders who, in the darkest days, kept the nation informed, and, although we knew there were security and morale considerations, we trusted them implicitly. They won the propaganda battle, despite the calculating efforts of Joseph Goebbels and that other notorious wartime broadcaster, Lord Haw-Haw — 'Jairmany calling, Jairmany calling'.

 SANDY MACPHERSON (Roderick Hale MacPherson, 1897-1975, born Paris, Ontario)

During the fearful early months of the 1939-45 war, Sandy MacPherson apologised to listeners for being on the air so often. 'You must be getting fed up of me', he said ruefully, or words to that effect. My patriotic grandmother, with whom I was listening, would have none of it, and, speaking directly to the radio, as people then did in the most conversational tones, she told him that we were only too appreciative of his tuneful company and that we were fully aware of what a fine job he was doing.

It is strange how the organ, on electrification, was transmogrified from the theological to the theatrical. For long years, and since, the organ had been the ordained instrument of the church. There had been many experiments with electronic music, but it was only after the Great War that they reached functionality. The 1931 Rangertone was one of the first electric organs and this coincided with the rise of cinema and of radio. The colourful organ, all jazzy flashing lights, became the customary stand-by of the more exclusive cinemas. Typically, the organ, plus the smiling, head-turning organist, would ascend majestically to stage level, and a bobbing white spotlight would pick out the screened words so we could join in the choruses. The organ was equally a great broadcasting asset, for its grandiose booming range meant that, for the price of the organist, one could obtain something like the full gamut of an orchestra's power and versatility. Entire programmes were monopolised by organists, with selections that comprehended the light classical, the traditional, the dance tune and the march. Reginald Foort was the first BBC resident organist, a tribute in itself to the power of the instrument. There seemed to be a glut of Reginalds, for, apart from Reginald Porter-Brown, there was Reginald Dixon. Often broadcasting from his natural habitat in the Tower Ballroom, Blackpool, he was probably the most famous of the organists. With his jocund and apposite signature-tune, *Oh, We Do Like to be Beside the Seaside*, he was a year-on-year attraction for thousands of Blackpool holidaymakers as well as thousands of listeners.

Sandy MacPherson has been termed 'one of the heroes of wartime broadcasting'. The Canadian-born musician had served with the Canadian forces in the Great War and then worked as a musician in Hollywood studios thereafter. He came to England in 1928 and was appointed organist at the Empire Cinema in London's Leicester Square. Having enjoyed being organist at one of the nation's most prestigious cinemas, he replaced Reginald Foort at the seat of the BBC Theatre Organ in 1938. Twelve months on came war, and the London BBC personnel began its exodus, with, for example, the Variety Department evacuating first to Bristol and then to Bangor in North Wales. The BBC Home Service, as its one lone, non-regional schedule was called, emanated from near-empty studios, with news on the hour, official advice practically by the minute, record recitals with Christopher Stone, the grandfather of disc-jockeys (he had been active in the role since 1927) — and Sandy MacPherson. Hour after hour, his marathon endeavour at the organ continued, calming nerves with soothing melody and quietly spoken introductions. A meticulous as well as an indefatigable musician, Sandy MacPherson was truly the war hero of the Wurlitzers.

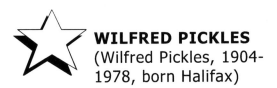

WILFRED PICKLES
(Wilfred Pickles, 1904-1978, born Halifax)

The stage-struck young Wilfred Pickles tried hard in amateur dramatics in his native Halifax and in Southport, where he met and married his supportive wife, Mabel Myerscough, who encouraged him in his tentative efforts to obtain radio work. Gradually, he gained a foothold, with programmes like *Kingpins of Comedy* and *Billy Welcome,* the latter a preliminary exercise in Wilfred Pickles' special skill in 'meeting the people'. There was also some variety and theatre work, a foretaste of his brusque northern roles in films like *Billy Liar* and *The Family Way* at the back-end of his career.

Radio's 'North Star', as he was billed, was asked by BBC producer, John Salt, to host a show called *Quiz Bang*, which Wilfred Pickles hurriedly altered to *Have a Go, Joe*, the forename being chopped very quickly. John Reith had frowned on the American vogue for quiz shows, but this was but a mild dosage, with simple questions and small prizes. It was mainly an excuse to visit some township or other location each week, the more obscure the better, and, in unscripted interviews, demonstrate that 'ordinary people' were the salt of the earth, hard-working, honest, cheerful and idiosyncratic. The whole formula was saved from mushiness by Wilfred Pickles' own genuine belief in the supremacy of ordinariness and in his naturally humorous sympathy both for the radio medium and for the workaday participants. Moreover, it was timely. There was a defined need for a hero in those austere years whose virtue was that he reflected, in values and in style, the very virtues of commonality.

Have a Go soon out-did anything the BBC had so far managed. Basically, given its consistently uniform pattern of over 20 million weekly listeners, it was and remains the most successful programme in British radio history. For some years it touched a national pulse and found a moment in the country's saga when listeners from all social classes were engaged. 'Lords and labourers, knights and knocker-uppers', was how Wilfred Pickles described it, as, week by week, town by town, the cries of 'give 'im the money, Barney' or queries such as 'are yer courtin?' or 'what was yer most embarrassin' moment?' kept all and sundry preoccupied. Old age was particularly idolised by Wilfred Pickles, and not without justification, for when an ancient contestant confided that his preferred drink was 'tea, wi' Senna pods in it', it attracted the longest recorded laugh in broadcasting history.

Wilfred Pickles was the categorical radio phenomenon. The radio historian, George Nobbs, has suggested that 'there was a brief period when Pickles was more powerful than anybody else in Britain, when had he chosen, or perhaps had someone chosen for him, he could have moved into politics as Ronald Reagan did later in America. His appeal was enormous and his sentiments and opinions found an echo in the hearts of the vast majority'. It is a forceful, in some sense, a frightening thought, but Wilfred Pickles, although a man of deep social conviction, never hinted at that constitutional possibility. Instead, rather then imagine him in Number Ten, let us relax in the fond remembrance of his homely introduction, after the jolly *Have a Go* signing-on tune, 'ladies and gentlemen of Gateshead (or Plymouth or Rochester . . .) 'ow do and 'ow are yer?'

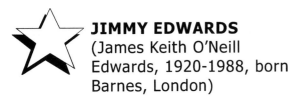

JIMMY EDWARDS
(James Keith O'Neill
Edwards, 1920-1988, born
Barnes, London)

Radio generations, like some of its wave-lengths, are short. Its critical comedy programmes form an hereditary chain of precious but tightly meshed links. Between *ITMA* which ended in 1948, and *The Goon Show*, which started in 1951, came *Take It From Here*, which ran from 1948 to 1960. There was nothing condescending about the sophisticated writing of Frank Muir and Dennis Norden; it made a wholesome post-war literate appeal to the intelligence of the radio audience. They were brilliantly served by two Australians, Dick Bentley and Joy Nichols, the latter's place later taken by June Whitfield, with Alma Cogan singing.

The underpinning force was provided by 'Professor' Jimmy Edwards. He dominated the proceedings with his ebullient authority and — 'Black mark, Bentley'; 'Gently, Bentley'; 'Clumsy clot'; 'Wake up at the back there' — employed the choicest catch-phrases. The show was a *pastiche* of wordplay, a constant scrutiny of the oddities of the language. The tree-surgeon is told that 'this hickory's a bit dickory, doc', while, in reply to Caesar's cry of 'where's me army?', came the response 'just off the coast of Florida.' Much of this delicious punning, extensively cited in work-place and school-yard next morning, was crammed into the final sketch, a lampoon of a cinematic *genre* — the western, the Roman epic, with the legionaries using Roman numerals on parade, the American newspaper drama ('Ace Bentley; he's got a big nose for a scoop' — 'he looks more like he's got a big scoop for a nose') the court scene (the judge to the weeping accused, 'you miserable pleader'). Later the Glum family emerged and, in fact, took on an existence of its own, satirising the cosy cliché families of much radio and cinema. Dick Bentley's naive Ron and June Whitfield's excruciating Eth were constantly under the satyr-like gaze of the florid Mr Glum of Jimmy Edwards, in this close-to-life study of a not too bright couple seeking romance in squalid circumstances. Mr Glum thoroughly understood the limitations of his 'baby boy'; 'he starts every day from scratch; it'll be eleven o'clock before he remembers there was a yesterday'. Not until the Royle family on television in the 1990s was there to be so fiercesome a denouncement of slovenly, inhibited and unintelligent domestic life.

Jimmy Edwards proceeded via the Cambridge Footlights and, in that postwar flush of comic talent, the Windmill Theatre, developing a strong variety act. He replaced Will Hay as the schoolmaster comedian, although his teaching methods at Chiselbury were more bucolic, more hearty, than his predecessor's. The audience was the class and he roared loaded questions at them, like 'why did the Australian go in the bush?'. Additional material included beery and salacious incarnations as a judge, Jimmunist electoral candidate, and ancient lighthouse keeper. With trombone, imposing plumpness and flowing RAF moustache, he made a vigorous impact. Privately, this Master of Arts, this valiant winner of the DFC for bravery at Arnhem, this squire-like figure with a taste for huntin' and shootin', was also, it transpired, a prey to uneasy sexual identity. Thankfully, radio listeners will mainly think of him in juicy form as the lynch-pin of *TIFH*.

AL READ (Alfred Read, 1909-1987, born Salford)

'You'll be lucky; I say, you'll be lucky' and 'Right, monkey' were the quintessential catch-phrases of the quintessential radio man, Al Read. Of all performers, he was most wholly a voice, managing his own *ensemble* of characters with immense virtuosity, so much so that, on stage or television, something of his capacity to bewitch listeners was, frankly, lost. It was a game played in the mind, with his audience envisioning his plain-spoken northern repertory to its heart's content. The observation was superb, presaging the critical eye and ear of artists like Alan Bennett or Victoria Wood today. The fact that the 'you'll be lucky' line was first heard by Al Read at a turnstile at Old Trafford football ground immediately gives the *locus classicus* to his creations.

His grandfather had been one of the first successfully to pack meat into tins, and Al Read inherited a flourishing sausage and meat pie business, so that, rather like the businessman, Kenneth Horne, he at first soldered together the entertainment and commercial elements of his busy existence, using what he called his 'pictures from life' mainly for private and professional purposes. Later his vans would bear the insignia 'Right, monkey', so that he also then cleverly used showbiz to support the trading. After these somewhat desultory beginnings, he made his radio debut in 1950 in *Variety Fanfare* and was an immediate success. From 1951, for seventeen years, if sometimes sporadically, 'the Al Read' programme wooed the beguiled listener with its gallery of northern voices. There was the football supporter, the teacher, the know-all, the bus passenger ('watch this dog ring this bus off'), the dentist, the gasman, the decorator, the patient, and scores more — his 'teaching his wife to drive' sketch was, for example, the inspiration for Bob Newhart's Americanised cameo on the same theme. All were day-to-day situations. All were easily recognised as situations one might find oneself in or overhear. All were very, very funny. Remember the bus conductor when the passenger, having arrived at the wrong destination, complained that the bus had had Moston on the front: 'it's got Harpic on the back, but we're not going there'.

Many were family-oriented. There was the inquisitive child, with his insistent 'dad, dad, dad, dad, dad . . .'; there was the nervous husband, with his 'ju-ju-ju-ju-ju-ju-ju-just a minute'; and there was the disgruntled and sardonic spouse — 'that's the wife in the kitchen'. Her scoldings included such beauties as, 'well, are you going to cut that lawn, or are we putting some sheep on it?', or 'when are you going to fix that garden gate — all tied up with rope?; I'm fed up of those dustmen with their 'we're dustbin men not mountaineers''.

Al Read, arriving just in time, before radio became overshadowed by the ubiquitous television, was the ultimate radio figure. His catchy theme tune was *Such is Life*. Such is life indeed. Could there be anything more Delphic and mystifying, yet somehow replete with tangible meaning, than the darkly uttered mantra of the wife embroiled in some familial feud: 'there was enough said at our Billy's wedding'.

JOE LOSS   BILLY COTTON   TED HEATH

CARROLL GIBBONS   GERALDO   HENRY HALL

GLEN MILLER   JACK PAYNE   VICTOR SILVESTER

AMBROSE

Dancing Cheek To Cheek ~ The Dance Band Era
Ten Famous Band Leaders

'Dare I ask her?'; 'will he ask me?'. . . in a social clime where the male of the species was supposed to take the lead — literally, when it came to ballroom dancing — those were the kinds of questions that were spinning through the minds of the thousands who thronged the dance halls of the era. These ranged from the mighty citadels, like the Hammersmith Palais or the Lyceum Ballroom in London, via the resplendent Meccas, Ritzes and Locarnos of the large towns and cities, to the smaller dance halls which every self-respecting town boasted. Beyond that, church and village halls, sports clubs, work places and, during the war, a vast array of civil defence groups and military units, ran dances or 'socials' that were largely dance-based.

These dance halls and ballrooms have been defined as 'a release of tension in wartime, a social centre in peacetime, and an informal marriage bureau at all times'. It would be interesting to calculate how many of the cur-

rent older generation did their 'courting', as such premarital negotiations were widely known, slowly revolving to the dreamy sound of a sedate waltz, on a dimly-lit dance floor, with light angling off the moving reflectors. The convention of 'the last waltz', with its implicit promise of the young man escorting the young woman home, with maybe the reward of a good night kiss, was very much part of this ritual. Although men were supposed to take the lead, in courting as in dancing, there were a variety of signals and boosts available on the distaff side.

What might approximately be termed 'ballroom' or 'modern' dance music filled the gap in the popular canon between ragtime, much enjoyed but rarely used for dancing, and rock and roll. The music was, in effect, a regularised and scored version of jazz, from a brand introduced into Britain by Nick La Rocca and the Original Dixieland Jazz Band in 1919, with its renditions of tunes such as *The*

Darktown Strutters Ball. With Paul Whiteman, the American band-leader, born in 1890, a major source, British musicians soon began to copy and present these new sounds. The largely string assemblages of the 'old-time' combines were superseded by the trombones and banjos of the jazz dispensation, but, in the fullness of time, possibly the most characteristic dance band tone would be rendered by the cooler sophistication of the saxophone.

Although the straightforward 'one, two, three' waltz survived, the other 'old-time' dances, such as the polka and the military two-step, faded. To fit the new music, they were replaced by the foxtrot, first brought to main public attention by the American dancing duo, Irene and Vernon Castle, in 1914, and, in London, by Elsie Janis and Basil Hallam. This came in two speeds, quick and slow, but by 1924 the 'quick' version became the better known quickstep, leaving the slow foxtrot as its tranquil complement, although, in popular usage, the 'trot' became a 'saunter'. This gave three simple basic patterns to the average or even mediocre dancer, and, although, from the hectic machinations of the Charleston to the heavier exotic typologies of Latin-American gyrations, there were more complex alternatives, these stand-bys were sustained.

During this period there was, of course, a sudden burgeoning of dance bands, with the Savoy Hotel giving a lead when it replaced its banjo-led quartet with a dance orchestra in 1921. For the ten profiled hereafter, many readers will be able to rattle off 20 or 30 more without pausing for breath. The smallest town had its dance band — Percy Pease is a localised personal recollection — but the famous bands were more likely to be playing at the swanky hotels, restaurants and clubs, where guests and diners were offered the chance to foxtrot to the best of British music. However, modern technology meant that their music could be disseminated very widely. Apart from colossal sales of sheet music, for use by local bands or, in popularised versions, for domestic pleasure, there were the millions of records, there was a chance to see some of the famous bands as, especially, in the 1930s, they toured the theatres and ballrooms of the nation, and, very importantly, there was the radio.

The BBC, despite some Reithian suspicions of the 'hotter' forms of transatlantic music, simply had to adopt dance music as the key popular music of the day. As the bands also deployed distinctive vocalists and as romantic lyrics were highly favoured by the public, this all leant itself naturally to the audible medium, in spite of an early BBC ban on what they thought of as song-plugging. The best-known bands had their regular weekly spot, while other bands were employed around them and record programmes were instituted — Christopher Stone was one of the first-ever disc-jockeys, although, needless to say, he would not have recognised the designation.

Dance bands and dance music, therefore, provided both a common and an intense cultural product in the era under review. Enjoyed by affluent socialites at classy night spots, no less than by those less fortunately placed, gallantly quick-stepping to a scratchy gramophone in their local church hall, it was very much a cross-class experience. Although by its nature it was mainly the province of younger people, both the music and its accompanying dance steps were also enjoyed by their elders. The dance as part of the wedding reception, for instance, with all generations waltzing and foxtrotting together, is one illustration of this.

It is difficult to exaggerate the concentrated character of dance music during this time. It appeared to be everywhere. Of course, few social phenomena start and stop abruptly: the waltz survived sturdily from the old regime; and some still enjoy ballroom dancing today. Nonetheless, one may point to a fairly tight period, from about 1920 to the mid-1950s, when the phrase 'all the rage' is not too strong an epithet for the prevalence of dance bands — and, inevitably, a group of extremely famous dance band leaders.

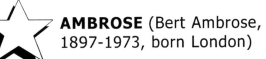 **AMBROSE** (Bert Ambrose, 1897-1973, born London)

Ambrose used to tell his bandsmen that, if they couldn't hear the swish of the ladies' dresses on the dance-floor, then they were playing too loud — a far cry from the louder sound of some of his younger contemporaries, let alone the high disco decibels of today. Trained as a violinist, he began his career playing piano in New York cinemas before three years directing the Palais Royal band there. Then, apart from another brief American visit, he led his own orchestra at London's Embassy Club until 1927, when he was signed on by the Mayfair Club at the, for those days, astronomical sum of £10,000 a year, probably worth some £500,000 at current prices. In 1933 he returned to the Embassy and also played at, among others, Ciro's and the Cafe de Paris, indeed at all London's 'society' loci. From the 1920s he was involved in much record-making, on, just one example, the Decca UK label, and broadcasting, while work on the variety stage and entertaining the forces in World War II brought his music ever closer to the ordinary public. In 1956 he disbanded his famous orchestra and went into artist management, notably as the agent for the talented singer, Kathy Kirby.

A strong disciplinarian, insisting on the highest orchestral standards, it has been said that, from the mid-1950s, his 'was the finest dance band in the UK over the next twenty years'. The darling of the aristocratic socialite set, the suave, almost silky tones of his elegant and harmonious rhythms were quite captivating. One needs but to list some of the musicians and singers with whom he was associated in his band-leading days: Ted Heath, Sidney Lipton, Stanley Black, George Melachrino, George Chisholm, Sam Browne, Elsie Carlisle, Vera Lynn, Anne Shelton, Sid Phillips, Alan Kane and the drummer-cum-comedian, Max Bacon . . . it reads like a veritable index to British popular music in the 1930s and 1940s. His chief arranger, and thus a most influential figure, was Lew Stone, born in London in 1898. He later, of course, started his own band in 1932, after further experience with the influential Roy Fox.

Lew Stone was to lead a hectic and hard-working existence, playing at clubs, hotels and restaurants, such as the Southampton Hotel and the Trianon restaurant, as well as at the Mecca ballrooms, and doing considerable stage work. He introduced the first female singer — Ella Logan — into British dance band performance and his regular Tuesday night broadcasts are especially memorable. A convinced socialist, he was always uncomfortable with the upper class focus and was greatly respected by every musician.

Ambrose, on the other hand, rather enjoyed the flamboyant high life: he is reputed to have lost £28,000 in a single night at Monte Carlo — just try calculating what that adds up to at today's valuation. A firm favourite of the then Prince of Wales (later Edward VIII) Ambrose secretly encouraged his poorish ability by starting slowly, then accelerating as the Prince caught the tempo. Ambrose will long be remembered for the serene euphony of his music, as in his well-known theme-tune, *When Day is Done*. No Saturday night then was complete without his mild melodies being wafted over the breezes of the 'wireless'. One dance band historian has judged that his was, in the pre-war years, 'the most listenable, and probably as a result the most danceable band in England, even in Europe'.

CARROLL GIBBONS
(Richard Carroll Gibbons, 1903-1954, born Clinton, Massachusetts, USA)

Dance band leaders varied from some who were not great musicians, but could manage a combine successfully, to those who were classically trained. American-born Carroll Gibbons fell into the latter camp, for he was taught as a classical musician in Boston, the cultural centre of his home state of Massachusetts. He soon turned to the more populist strain and he came to England in 1924, along with Rudy Vallee, hailed as the first chief singing star of the 1920s. Another character-

istic of band leaders was their youthfulness. The 23 year old Carroll Gibbons formed his first group — the Sylvians — in 1926, and they played at the Savoy Hotel as well as its companion hotel, the Berkeley.

The Savoy Hotel was fast becoming the fount for both high-living and for the popular dissemination of dance music. The American saxophonist, Bert Ralton, began the trend in 1922 with his Savoy Havana Band, and they broadcast first in the April of 1923. They soon became the first band to have a regular broadcast date, direct from the Savoy Hotel. By a curio, and contrary to how people recall their rightful fame, they were not the first British band to broadcast. That honour lies with a somewhat obscure band directed by one Marius B Winter, who broadcast from an attic in Marconi House, London, 26 March 1923. His also became the first dance band to play on commercial radio, courtesy of Radio Paris: he remains an apposite base for the difficult quiz question. After one or two fits and starts, the hugely famous Savoy Orpheans emerged as the top band. It was started by Debroy Somers who had been musical director at the Savoy Hotel (one wonders how many hotels employ a musical director these days) for several years. Debroy Somers, an ex-army bandsman with much of the martial presence about his imposing personality, ensured that the orchestra was very successful, not least in the matter of selling records. In fact, the various Savoy ensembles made over 300 records between 1922 and 1927. Carroll Gibbons was soon musical director in his stead, certainly as from 1927, and he was next appointed Director of Light Music for HMV, with artists like Paul Robeson and Gracie Fields on the books. He instituted the New Mayfair Orchestra and did film work for MGM. In 1931 'Gibby' returned to re-form the New Savoy Orpheans, with the help of the American saxophone player, Howard Jacobs. For 23 years until his untimely death in 1954, there was a Carroll Gibbons band charming dancers at the Savoy Hotel and beguiling listeners to the BBC. As a composer, he is fondly remembered for *Garden in the Rain* and his trademark theme-tune, the aptly-titled *On the Air*.

No one more benignly produced than he the soothing, emollient romantic dance music urgently sought in the 1930s, as counterpoint to the anxieties of depression at home and militarism abroad. Many will recall his hits in that temperate mood: *Room 504; These Foolish Things; A Nightingale Sang in Berkeley Square*, each of their lyrics indicative (the posh hotel, 'an airline ticket to romantic places', Mayfair) of the well-to-do lifestyle most listeners would have been glad to adopt. Affable, bespectacled, ever-courteous, many will also remember his distinctive and amiably drawled signing-off tag: 'good **night,** everybody'.

 **JACK PAYNE** (John Payne, 1899-1969, born Leamington Spa)

Jack Payne was a child pianist and a teenage pilot, serving with the Royal Flying Corps during World War I. He retained his musical interests, despite this sky-borne derring-do, and, from about 1925, he organised varied combinations, among them a sextet with which he rose to some prominence at the Hotel Cecil and on radio. In 1928 the BBC established its own resident band under Jack Payne's direction, although an earlier temporary house band, the London Radio Dance Band, conducted by Sidney Firman, had broadcast in 1926. Jack Payne's BBC Dance Orchestra broadcast for an hour every weekday late afternoon, leaving, as was the norm, the Sabbath free from such frivolity. They also did a substantial number of evening shows, so that Jack Payne, with the help of records and sheet music, soon became one of the nation's most famous names.

He was influenced by the work of Paul Whiteman and attracted to the showmanship of the American idiom. His approach had somewhat more vigour and sparkle than that of his more mellow successor, Henry Hall, and his orchestra, sixteen or more strong, was bigger. The purists wondered whether his orchestrations erred on the 'top-heavy' side, but he used his radio foundation cleverly. He was one of the first band leaders to scent the profitable possibilities of theatre and film, and he was very much aided by the deft arrangements of Brighton-born (in 1907) Ray Noble, most talented of musicians, who, apart from leading his own orchestra, composed such delightful standards as *Goodnight, Sweetheart* and *The Very Thought of You*.

A determined and bustling figure, Jack Payne offered a broader diet than some of his contemporaries, with comedy numbers (*You can't do that there 'ere*) and semi-classic concert numbers included. He first led his band on stage at the London Palladium in 1930, and, at this time, amazingly, made almost a hundred records a year. Among his associates were vocalist Billy Scott-Comber, saxophonist, Sid Millward, of 'the Nitwits' notoriety, and trumpeter, later band leader, Jack

Jackson, whose *Record-Round-Up* programmes from 1948 on both radio and television will be remembered by thousands. After 1937 his bands worked less regularly, as Jack Payne concentrated on his stud farm and his impresario affairs, but he returned to the BBC for much of the war. Dogged by ill-health and business problems, he died in Tunbridge Wells in 1969.

His only rival as a 'show-business' band leader was Jack Hylton, another man of vital personality and drive, born in Great Lever, Bolton, in 1892. His big show-band, over 20 in strength, with Billy Ternent on tenor sax, was formed in 1924 and undertook many European tours, as well as being well-known in Britain. It has been calculated that, in 1929 alone, the band travelled over 60,000 miles, had packed crowds at some 700 performances, and sold over 3m records, among them *Tiger Rag* and *Ain't that a Grand and Glorious Feeling*. However, from the late 1930s, he concentrated more on his theatrical business.

Returning to the equally versatile Jack Payne, his celebrated theme-tune, *Say it with Music* somehow sums up the entire *genre*.

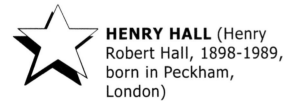 **HENRY HALL** (Henry Robert Hall, 1898-1989, born in Peckham, London)

The Salvation Army, ever eager not to let the devil have (as not its founder, General William Booth but, much earlier, Rev Rowland Hill, insisted) all the good tunes, had one called *The Sunshine March*. It was composed by Henry Hall, who worked as a young man in the 'Sally Ann' music department. Later it was transposed to being his legendary signature-tune, *Here's to the Next Time*. Henry Hall was one of the first band leaders to have both signing-on — to wit, *It's Just the Time for Dancing* — as well as -off tunes. Following that skirmish with evangelism, he became pianist with, then leader of, the orchestra at Manchester's opulent Midland Hotel, one of 30 belonging to the LMS (London Midland and Scottish) railway company. Indeed, he soon took charge of much of the musical output of these railway hotels and made his first broadcast from their Gleneagles Hotel in 1924, about the same time as he made his first Columbia records.

Dance band and broadcasting history was made in 1932 when he replaced Jack Payne as Director of the BBC Dance Orchestra. Almost at once he had an enormous success with the still popular *Teddy Bears' Picnic*, written by the American composer, J W Bratton, in 1908, the last full year of the American presidency of 'Teddy' Roosevelt, whose *persona* the toy celebrates. Another highlight for Henry Hall was his acting as conductor on the maiden voyage of the luxurious *Queen Mary*. There was no stopping him. Henry Hall, quiet and genial behind his glasses, was no vivid showman, nor did his music stir the stumps with what were then termed 'hot' arrangements. But he touched an essential broadcasting chord, seeming to buttonhole you in your own living-room. Others of his best-known songs were *One, two, Button my Shoe; Little Man* (you've had a busy day) and *Play to me, Gypsy*.

He possibly benefited from arriving at the BBC about the time it moved to its new and purpose-built premises, Broadcasting House in London's Langham Place. In any event, he stayed around for some 20 years, although in 1948 he 'disbanded' and established an entertainments agency dealing with such names as Norman Wisdom, Donald Peers, David Hughes and Reg Dixon. During the 1930s and into the 1940s, he usually broadcast eight times a week, an amazing record, whilst, at his peak, he received as many as 35,000 letters a year. He was also well-regarded in the USA. Nonetheless, he will always be remembered for *Henry Hall's Guest Night*, the radio programme that enjoyed approaching a thousand performances. It has some claim to being the first media chat-show in the United Kingdom, as Henry Hall introduced and talked disarmingly to the visiting performers. He was awarded the CBE in 1970 and died in Eastbourne aged over 90.

Many will recall, among his associates, the drummer-vocalist, George Elrick (*The music goes 'round and around and it comes out here*) and the glamorous singer, Phyllis Robbins. Another of his favourite vocalists, Betty Driver, still serves a mean hotpot, as Betty Williams, across the bar of *Coronation Street's* 'Rover's Return'. Everyone will recall his legendary hesitant introduction: 'this **is** Henry Hall speaking, and tonight **is** my guest night.'

GERALDO (Gerald Bright, 1904-1974, born London)

The flavour of the age was very much established by the opening line of Geraldo's cheerful signing-on number, *Hello again; we're on the Radio again*. Geraldo's

band so often was exactly that — on the radio again. His musicians — his were further bands to be associated with the Savoy Hotel — made some 2000 broadcasts from its formation in 1930 to the outbreak of the second world war, and he was on the BBC practically every day of the war. He supervised the dance bands controlled by ENSA during WWII and was later responsible for the dance bands entertaining on Cunard liner cruises. His orchestra also toured the variety theatres in the late 1940s. He retired from band-leading in the 1950s and died in Vevey, Switzerland.

Geraldo was classically trained in organ and piano at the Royal Academy of Music — his piano solos, alone on stage, were an essential aspect of his show-band presentation — and his brother, Sid Bright, was pianist with Al Starita's Piccadilly Players. But he soon turned his professional attention to dance music both at home and abroad. He conducted the Light Orchestra at the Majestic Hotel, St Annes-on-Sea, but he was attracted by Latin rhythms and it is said he spent time on the continent attempting to research the genuine South American model: hence the 'o' suffix to Gerald, in a less authentic essay in conveying that culture. In 1930 he formed his Gaucho Tango Orchestra and immediately found himself a radio and record star, with the accolade of a Royal Command Performance in 1933 and the label of 'the Tango King'. With guitars, accordions and strings, and clad in the loose scarves and baggy slacks that passed for South American garb, they were a colourful addition to the metropolitan social scene. The Latin-American tangos, rumbas and sambas were persuasive enough, but, for the broadstream of British everyday life, they were a trifle limiting, so that, in mid-1930s, the name and style were changed to Geraldo and His Sweet Music. It was under titles like this that he went on to command greater success, switching his signature tune from *Lady of Spain* to *I bring you Sweet Music*.

Geraldo set a high standard of scrupulous musicianship and he was noted for the tastefulness and virtuosity of his arrangements. Eschewing the louder vein, he concentrated on the sweetness he advertised, but it was never cloying nor unduly sentimental, with some jollier melodies as make-weight along the way, while, as the years progressed, he was not a little venturesome in altering mood. Future well-known band leaders, like Ted Heath and Nat Temple, competent solo instrumentalists, like the trumpeter, Eddie Calvert (*Oh, My Papa*) and much-loved singers, like Dorothy Squires, Rosemary Squires and Dick James, were among the personnel who helped him reach those heights. Such was his musical probity that, in his later years, he was very reluctant to allow the re-issue of his many scores of published records, among them fine hits like *Idaho* and *Soft-shoe Shuffle*.

Speaking of the 1940s and early 1950s, one commentator has gone so far as to suggest that 'Geraldo occupies much the same niche in Britain as does Glenn Miller in the United States.'

 VICTOR SILVESTER
(Victor Marlborough Silvester, 1900-1978, born in Wembley)

Imagine the son of a vicar, giving a false age and finding himself, a 14 year old, in the cruel midst of the 1914-1918 war, in which he is wounded then returned to the notorious Etaples holding camp where he is ordered to join five firing squads to execute deserters, a gruesome exercise that leaves him limp with hysterical nightmares, before going up to the Italian front and winning many battle honours. Now visualise the tall, stately figure of the impeccably clothed band leader, with his elegantly disciplined ballroom melodies and gracefully displayed dance routines. The child, in Victor Silvester's case, was hardly father to the man.

Free of that horror that haunted him his life long, he played and danced, and, in 1922, he won the World's Dancing Championship, partnering Phyllis Clarke. With his wife, the former beauty queen, Dorothy Newton, he set up a chain of dance studios, but he was frustrated by the lack of music rigorous enough for the exacting precision of dance instruction and competition. He persuaded EMI to record, in that fixed mode, *You're Dancing on my Heart*, which immediately sold 17,000 copies and which became his legendary signature tune when he formed his own 'strict tempo' orchestra in 1935. Many older people will automatically hum the opening bars of that song, but very few will know the words, for Victor Silvester, emphatic in his accent on dancing, rarely if ever employed vocalists.

In 1937 came the first of an astounding

number of over 6500 broadcasts, the majority of them under the heading *Dancing Club*. There would also be 17 years on television, latterly with his son, Victor Silvester Junior, in the maestro's dignified place. His band was comparatively small, but what gave it a special and tuneful effect was the use of two tinkling pianos, offering steady underpinning to the fragile employment of alto sax, violin, guitar, string bass and well-moderated drums. The programmes were dedicated, in part, to dance education, steps that could be practised at home on the lounge carpet or kitchen linoleum. Each week *Radio Times* included a diagram, a little patter of tiny black and white feet, as a help-meet. Practitioners would attend their local palais — and this was a curiously and peculiarly British institution — to put the lessons into dashing use. Victor Silvester's book, *Modern Ballroom Dancing* went through 50 editions and sold, worldwide, over a million copies. At the time of his death in the south of France in 1978, it was estimated that his record sales topped 75m. He was awarded the OBE in 1961. Oscar Rabin, who began his professional life with his Romany Five at the Derby Palais de dance in 1922, and Jack Harris are two of the best-known of the several band leaders who also catered for this unquestionable demand from dancers for unyielding meter.

Although non-dancing music buffs perhaps preferred the more versatile range of some other top bands, the dancing fraternity, of whom there were many thousands, rejoiced in the austere, but always melodic, regulo of the world's most effective dance teacher. Many will think of him gratefully whenever that seminal phrase is uttered: 'slow, slow, quick. quick, slow'.

 JOE LOSS (Joshua Alexander Loss, 1909-1990, born Spitalfields, London)

Joe Loss very much fits the band-leader blueprint. He was classically trained as a musician — there were high family hopes of his becoming a concert violinist — and he was extremely youthful — just 16 — when he led his first band. He was but 20, and the youngest band-leader in the West End, when he first became a well-known and tuneful adjunct to London's clubs and theatres. He was especially associated with the Astoria Ballroom, where, after an early spell, his was the resident band from 1934 to 1940. During this time he began a recording career that was to endure over 50 years. He had, for example, a big hit with *The Woodpecker's Ball*. The second world war found him undertaking a gruelling schedule entertaining the troops, before he settled in, from 1945 to 1970, at the famous Hammersmith Palais. For a number of summer seasons, holidaymakers sought him out at the Villa Marina at Douglas, Isle of Man and, of course, he was often to be heard on radio and, later, on television, notably with the *Come Dancing* programme.

Joe Loss also fits the mould in that his appeal was both popular and socialite. His band, now 18 strong, often cruised aboard the resplendent liner, *Queen Elizabeth II,* and the Royal Family was particularly fond of him and his effervescent music. He played at many royal wedding and birthday receptions, including Princess Margaret's wedding, the Queen's 50th and the Queen Mother's 80th birthday celebrations. Scarcely surprisingly, he was awarded the OBE in 1978 and a

Queen's Silver Jubilee Medal in 1978. He was made a Freeman of the City of London in 1979.

A smallish, stocky but neat figure, with brilliantined black hair, the careful sleekness of which did not always withstand the gyrations of his energetic conducting, and a generously broad grin, he kept going in bustling fashion for an astonishing 60 years in the band business, whilst his support of showbiz charities was enormous. Perhaps his nearest emulator, in style and approach, was Harry Roy (Harry Lipmann, 1900-1971) whose bouncy rhythms — witness his ebullient rendering of *Tiger Rag* — were much in appreciated evidence during some of the same period. Both bands managed to find a golden mean between swing and strict tempo that kept both avid listeners and keen dancers happy: both bands enjoyed a lengthy phase of popularity.

This much-loved conductor was shrewd in his choice of vocalists. Apart from playing for Vera Lynn's first broadcast (she sang *Red Sails in the Sunset*, signature tune of the comedienne, Suzette Tarri) the Joe Loss band was to be found backing such great voices as Adelaide Hall, Monte Rey (*The Donkey Serenade*) and Chick Henderson (*Begin the Beguine*) Poor Chick Henderson was killed by shrapnel in 1944, a war-victim like the even more famous singer, Al Bowlly.

In 1939 *Begin the Beguine* became, in fact, the first huge record success for Joe Loss. In 1940 came another. It was *In the Mood* and that jaunty, toe-tapping sound became his signature tune and the melody with which his name will be long associated.

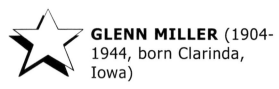 **GLENN MILLER** (1904-1944, born Clarinda, Iowa)

Although, from Paul Whiteman to Jimmy and Tommy Dorsey and Benny Goodman, records, radio and occasional film appearances brought American dance orchestras before the consideration of the British public, it is difficult to over-estimate the still enduring influence in the United Kingdom of Glenn Miller.

A trombonist, operating on the West Coast of America, he toiled doggedly away until, by the late 1930s, he had formed his own band to his own liking. His orchestra began recording in 1939 and in 1942 they took a prominent role in the Hollywood films, *Sun Valley Serenade,* with Sonja Henie, and *Orchestra Wives*, with Cesar Romero. It was in that same year, in the wake of the USA entry into World War II, that he joined the army and was commissioned first as captain and later as major. For the next two or three years he directed the large but intimately meshed AEF Band, eventually with a posting to England. Interestingly, Hollywood would repay him with his own biopic in 1954 — *The Glenn Miller Story*, starring James Stewart.

In 1939 Glenn Miller had recorded *Moonlight Serenade*, an urbane, attractive melody that was to become his theme-tune. The choice duality of clarinet and sax that was to be his mellow hallmark is stamped on that unforgettable arrangement, and the distinctive Miller sound echoes clearly down the years. In effect, one is surprised, given that singular melodic flavour, to recall how wide-ranging was his repertoire. His virtuosity covered the Tin Pan Alley sentiment of *April in Paris*; the jump blues of *St Louis Blues*; the pseudo-western rhythm of *Blueberry Hill*; the straightforward jazz beat of *Tuxedo Junction*; the modern notes of *Pennsylvania 6-5000* and the folk-song, written in 1869, *Little Brown Jug*. What a catholic and eclectic collection — and yet the Miller imprint is unmistakeable. With the effortless warmth of the melodious Dinah Shore, very smart in her army best uniform, in vocal tandem, he played and recorded such numbers as *Long Ago and Far Away; Stardust* (which became appropriately enough, the signature tune for the Carroll Levis *Discoveries* talent-spotting radio show) and *I've got a Heart full of Love*. *Chattanoga Choo Choo, I've got a Girl in Kalamazoo* and *American Patrol* must be definitely added to the list. It is a quite wondrous canon of magical music.

There were other 'military' bands, among them the RAF's own Squadronaires, with pianist Jimmy Miller perhaps their best-remembered leader, which included instrumentalists from the Ambrose and Lew Stone combines, or the Blue Tones, directed by Eric Tain, once a trombone-player with Ambrose, the dance band of the Royal Army Ordnance Corps. Many armed forces and civil defence orchestras broadcast and even the National Fire Service had a dance band, assisted by some of Billy Cotton's players — it is possibly superfluous to remark that its signature tune was *I don't want to set the World on Fire*.

Glenn Miller was a studiously bespectacled, undramatic personality. Just after the liberation of Paris, he slipped away in a single-engined plane from a Bedfordshire airbase to prepare for a concert in the French capital. With the same lack of fuss that surrounded his life, he simply disappeared.

 **TED HEATH** (Edward Heath, 1900-1969, born Wandsworth, London)

Ted Heath was another child prodigy who was coping with the tenor horn at the age of six. Musical folklore has it that he was heard busking on trombone outside the Queen's Hall, London by Jack Hylton, who promptly hired him for his Queen's Hall Roof Orchestra. After his time with Jack Hylton, Sydney Lipton and others, he played with Geraldo throughout the second world war, and then, literally on VJ (Victory over Japan, for younger readers) Day, 1945, he formed his own band. He did so on the proceeds of royalties from songs his wife, Moira, and he had composed, by far the finest, and most profitable, amongst them being *That Lovely Weekend*.

A meticulous director, he insisted on only the most highly-trained and hard-working musicians, all devoted to his firm intention to create a reputable swing orchestra. Ted Heath was determined to pick up the stronger traits of the American bands for this purpose and, by that token, his band is less a dance band in the Victor Silvester mien and more after the transatlantic fashion of Stan Kenton. It was a brasher, maybe noisier but no less musicianly a style and Ted Heath, as a consequence, was one of the few English bands to have an American following. He provided the music for *London Town*, the English film musical which, vainly, was supposed to challenge the Hollywood monopoly of that *genre*, but his main vein lay in the concert hall and the broadcasting or recording studio.

With Jack Parnell as his chief right-hand-man, he proffered hits like *Opus One, Dragnet, Hot Toddy* and *Skin Deep* to his adoring fans, the very labels indicative of a shift from the more languorous character of ballroom dance music. He was ably assisted into the early and mid 1950s by such high-ranking vocalists as Lita Rosa, Dickie Valentine and Dennis Lotis. Ted Heath, as a conductor, was laid-back and self-effacing in the Henry Hall/Glenn Miller tradition, rather than hyperactive à la Joe Loss. The dichotomy between his shyly hunched body and barely gesticulating finger, and the robust, rousing sounds that he manufactured was indeed curious.

The newer patterns of dance, of jitterbugging and then bop, were invading the dance floors, and Ted Heath's music was a little too complex for such lively antics. In one sense, his arrangements built a bridge across from the pacific calmness of the Ambrose idiom and accompanying dance routines to the rougher, heavier, if marvellously well-devised and performed, clamour of Bill Haley and the Comets. *Rock around the Clock* introduced the nation to Rock 'n' Roll in 1956, yet another convenient yardstick for the termination of the period we are reviewing.

For all that, and for ten and more years, Ted Heath was a highly successful band leader. His orchestra 'is accepted', judges one standard source, 'as the best swing band that Britain ever produced'. This is a fine epitaph for a band leader who brought much pleasure to keenly-cocked ears, anxious to catch his latest painstaking exercises in swing arrangements.

 BILLY COTTON (William Cotton, 1899-1969, born Westminster)

Tenth of our band-leaders is the redoubtable Billy Cotton, and, like most of the rest, he was born within a short phase of time around the turn of the century, and, like all but three, he was born in the London area. Chorister, soldier-boy bugler-drummer, survivor of the gory Gallipoli campaign of World War I, intrepid pilot with the Royal Flying Corps, bus driver, footballer, motor cycle and car racer, then drummer with the Laurie Johnson band . . . that was the variegated apprenticeship of this colourful man whose son, Billy Cotton Junior, went on to be head of BBC Light entertainment and who himself was meritoriously elected Show Business Personality of the Year for 1962.

Again like most of his peers, he was a relatively young man when he started his first band, the London Savannah Band, and he played at the Wembley Exhibition of 1924. The genuine beginnings fell in 1925 when he joined forces with Clem Bernard, who, for 40 years, was the quiet eminence behind the glittering Cotton throne, as initiator and arranger. They played at the fancy nightspots, but they soon found a significant *niche* in ciné-variety, that intriguing hybrid whereby short films and live 'turns' were interwoven, significant because it motivated Billy Cotton to develop a show-band, rather than an honest-to-goodness dance band or, after the style of Ted Heath, a serious concert band.

His popularity, and that of his band, grew during World War II, with radio worthy of particular mention. Sunday's roast beef and Yorkshire pudding was hardly possible of digestion for twenty years without the accompanying tumult of *Wakey Wakey!*, introduced by the raucous bellow by Billy Cotton of that same phrase, a borrowing from reveille in both military barracks and Butlin's holiday camps. From 1957 he added a regular TV date, with *The Billy Cotton Band-show*, complete with middlebrow guests of the Alma Cogan and Russ Conway ilk. He was also much in demand in variety theatres. Here his band-show usually occupied the whole programme, where others, such as Harry Roy's or Geraldo's, might only have taken up a half of the show. With his band at full-pelt, threatening the roof of several of Britain's old-established variety theatres, he was one of the last of the great stars to pack out such arenas, as they started their sad decline under televisual pressures.

His menu mixed the avowedly sentimental with the outrageously comic, the diet eked out by strong vocals from the likes of Dorothy Stevens, Kathy Kaye, the Highlights and the versatile Alan Breeze, practically an ever-present. The titles say it all: examples are the theme tune, an uproarious version of *Somebody Stole My Girl; New Tiger Rag; Oh,O,O,O, what a Referee!; Maybe it's because I'm a Londoner; Oh, Nicholas, don't be so Ridiculous; Fall in and Follow me; I'm just a Little Pecunia in an Onion Patch; Friends and Neighbours* and *I saw Mummy Kissing Santa Claus*.

His ample girth and his grinning chubby countenance formed the perfect conduit for his Cockney *bonhomie* and overwhelming gusto. In 1969 he was buried at St Margaret's Church, Westminster, where, unbelievably, he had begun his professional career as a cherubic choirboy.

Evelyn Laye

Ivor Novello

George Robey

Anna Neagle

Gertrude Lawrence

Binnie Hale

Laurence Olivier

Jack Buchanan

Jessie Matthews

Noel Coward

The Light Fantastic ~ Stars of Stage
Ten Famous Theatre Stars

English drama tends to have peaks, like the heady days of the Elizabethan theatre or the Regency days of Sheridan, with longish troughs in between. The somewhat impoverished theatre of the Victorian epoch had ended with the introduction to London of Ibsen and Chekhov, to say nothing of the Irish gifts of Oscar Wilde and G B Shaw but then there was another doldrums after the first world war. Such assessments are relative. Plays like R C Sheriff's *Journey's End* or Terence Rattigan's *Separate Tables* were well-crafted, but they did not quite carry the *gravitas* of their predecessors. This slightly downbeat phase lasted until the 1950s. The production of John Osborne's fiery play *Look back in Anger* in 1956 catapulted the theatre through the French window and confronted it with the kitchen sink. It provides our period with a book-end as conclusive, in theatrical terms, as the Coronation a year or so earlier.

This is to speak solely of the legitimate theatre and this did not, frankly, touch as nearly on the popular culture as did the variety theatre. The local variety theatre, together with its seasonal staples of pantomime and seaside concert party, was the more common stage experience of most people; such delights are considered in our comedy and singing sections. Although many towns had repertory companies or stages for touring troupes, they were much fewer in number than the music halls, and, for example, a large urbanised area might have boasted a dozen variety theatres and but one or two of the 'legit' type.

However, there was a third wave of theatre, overlapping both the serious and the variety stage. This might be termed the musical theatre. Even here there was something of a hiatus between the resplendent richness of the Gilbert and Sullivan *genre*, which, with some rivals in the musical comedies of George Edwardes, had dominated the musical stage before 1914. Again, it was to be the late 1940s before there was another major advance, with the folksy joys of *Oklahoma!* heralding the advent of the mature American-style musical play.

The Merry Widow is exactly the kind of Viennese operetta that appealed in the Edwardian era. With music by the melodious Franz Lehar, and English lyrics by Adrian Ross, it arrived in London, courtesy of George Edwardes, in 1907, a year and a half after its opening in Vienna. *Naughty Marietta* (*Ah, Sweet Mystery of Life*) launched in America in 1910, was another. Similar favourites soon after the war included the 1924 *Rose Marie* (*Indian Love-call*), the 1926 *Desert Song* (shades of the Red Shadow), and the 1928 *the New Moon* (*Stouthearted Men* and *Lover, Come back to me*).

The two most popular shows over the actual wartime period were *The Maid of the Mountains*, which opened in 1917, with Jose Collins, as the brigand's lady-love, Teresa, singing *Love will find a way*; and *Chu Chin Chow*, first staged in 1916 and loosely based on the legend of Ali Baba and the 40 thieves. The first ran for 1352 and the second for 2235 performances. The eastern promise of *Chu Chin Chow,* with its robber chief, Abu Hasan, played by Oscar Asche, the show's creator and director, was a ravishing achievement. Another show that brought some glitter to those grim days was *The Bing Boys are Here*, with George Robey and Violet Lorraine sharing the charming ballad, *If you were the only girl in the World*. It ran, with two sequels, from 1916 to 1920, introducing hits like *Another Little Drink* and *Let the Great Big World Keep Turning*.

The 'Bing Boys' format was revue, not in the later connotation of autonomous sketches and numbers, usually of a satirical bent, but where song and dance clung feebly to the thinnest strand of storyline. In the 1920s, 1930s and for most of the 1940s, the new fare was, after this pattern, frothier, with revue and light-hearted musical comedy offering rather two-dimensional entertainment, with little accent on plot and characterisation. Of course, the older pieces were revived and repeated, but the new mood — and one can see it underscored in the somewhat frenetic dances and intrepid fashions of the hour — was about seeking frolicsome relief after the bestial horrors of war.

Most of these were ephemeral pieces. A few endured to become part of the amateur operatic repertoire, but most were transient in form. This is not to belittle them. Metaphorically, they melted in the mouth, as do the choicest desserts. In chief, they provided the guise for dainty juvenile leads and good-looking matinee idols to chirrup and strut together. Sometimes the tunes have lived on: many who could hum *We'll Gather Lilacs in the Spring Again* may have forgotten its provenance. One reason for this is that, outside of the West End or the big cities with big theatres, these shows were not generally available to the ordinary public. People came by such airs on radio, on record and on sheet-music to play on the parlour piano — until the parlour piano began to yield place to the 'wireless'.

Eventually the more solid of these entertainments were filmed and, immediately, there was a mass audience. For every one who saw Jessie Matthews on the stage, there were thousands who enjoyed her at the cinema. It was estimated, astonishingly, that, when *King Lear* was televised, its not by any means record-breaking audience was larger than all those in Britain who had ever watched a professional performance of that tragedy in the four hundred years since it was written. That constitutes the power of the technological medium, and some of the same was true, in those intervening years, of film and radio.

Thus the ten stage artists who are paraded here could, in most cases, have found themselves in the roster of singers or of cinema stars, and, in some cases, radio celebrities. They are chosen because their talents were such that they forced their way on to the public consciousness and became household names. With the exception of Laurence Olivier, himself a film star of the highest rank, they are recruited, in the main, from the musical stage, for, again, in terms of the popular culture, that was where the major interest lay.

Whatever else, it was an era replete with harmonious strains, and it is certain that the very mention of these names will, in many cases, bring melody racing to the mind's ear.

 **GEORGE ROBEY** (Sir George Edward Wade, 1869-1954, born London)

George Robey was a bridge — one is tempted, given his comic front, to say, 'arch' — between ancient and modern. Round about the time of the first world war, the old-time music hall began its transformation into variety, and George Robey, 'the Prime Minister of Mirth', was one of the few to transmute with any *panache*. The change was substantive. Whereas variety was, well, varied, music hall was more uniform. Each

performer was a walking trinity, the three in one of the name, the character and the song or song-type. Thus Marie Lloyd was always the raunchy East End strumpet, identified by her boisterous songs, full of leering innuendo, like *My Old Man* or *Oh, Mr Porter*. Gus Elen and George Formby Senior were respectively the wry Cockney, full of social comment, and the Wigan melancholic, self-deluding and insecure, the one singing *If it wasn't for the 'ouses in between*, and the other *I'm Such a Hit with the Girls*. Incidentally, the only two performers Marie Lloyd would deign to watch were George Formby Senior and the much-loved Dan Leno, greatest of panto dames, and the nonpareil patter-songster, in numbers like *The Shop-walker*, *The Beefeater* and *The Bandit*.

George Robey set aside an engineering career to become the highest of low comedians, first singing his juicy ditties professionally at the Royal Westminster Aquarium, before making his full stage debut in 1891 at the Oxford Theatre. With those confidential eyebrows, the clerical garb and, as often as not, the shovel hat, he transfixed audiences with his knowing fruitiness and — 'desist; kindly temper your hilarity with a modicum of reserve' — outraged authority. His range of character studies, plus appropriate lyrics, included the Mayor of Mudcumdyke, the manager of the Splitz Hotel, the German musician and even the Prehistoric Man, but, at base, they were the same dubious sinner. Each song was a man-to-man admission of such failings, from his first hit, *The Simple Pimple*, through *Bang went the Chance of a Lifetime* and *Archibald, Certainly Not!*, to *I Stopped, I Looked and I Listened*. Sham erudition — ' a coarsening of the auricular appendage, in other words, a thick ear' — was his speciality.

Such was his priceless talent that he crossed from the pre-1914 to the post-1918 worlds by bringing his adept skills to the field of revue that flourished then. In 1916 he starred in the Alhambra revue *The Bing Boys are here*, which was followed, after 378 performances, by *The Bing Boys are there*, from which George Robey was absent, together with a further sequel, *The Bing Boys on Broadway*, in which he again starred. This ran for 562 performances and it included the massive hit, *First Love, Last Love, Best Love*. This non-stop series was specifically aimed at troops on leave — it was all but a badge of honour to have caught 'the Bing Boys' before returning to the front line — along with war-weary civilians. Such was the potency of the brew that it secured for a generation that style of slim plot, scenes like music hall sketches, pretty girls like the stunning Violet Lorraine, funny men (Wilkie Bard, Gillie Potter and Alfred Lester were also variously involved) and, above all else, singable airs. George Robey continued to foster his sterling career, in pantomime, on stage and on radio. As well as some silent filming, he contributed cameos to later movies, most memorably as the dying Falstaff in the 1944 *Henry V*. He was knighted not long before his death, just as, fittingly perhaps, our period ends.

BINNIE HALE (Beatrice Mary Hale-Monro, 1899-1984, born Liverpool)

Binnie Hale is a superb example of the kind of vivacious, shining light comedienne who adorned the London stage during its 1920s and 1930s phase of rather superficial musical comedy-cum-revue. Some critics have, indeed, judged her the brightest star amidst that galaxy of shimmering beauties. She was blonde and pert, the daughter of fellow-performer, Robert Hale, and, like so many of her ilk, she was a versatile all-rounder. Singing, dancing, imitating, acting — it all came glitteringly alike to the gifted Miss Hale. She first appeared on stage in 1916 in *Follow the Crowd*; she was in the chorus of *Hoop-la* for the opening of St Martin's Theatre; and then she did a stint in a gaggle of other shows like *The Kiss Call* and *Just Fancy*, titles forgotten today. *Hoop-la* was one of the scores of shows staged by C B Cochran, who had succeeded George Edwardes as the predominant theatre magnate.

More familiar fare followed. Binnie Hale was leading lady in *No, No, Nanette* of *I Want to be Happy* and *Tea for Two* fame, and then she co-starred with Jack Buchanan in *Sunny*, leaving everyone humming *Who Stole My Heart Away?* Bobby Howes (1895-1972) was her disarming partner in a number of shows, notably *Mr Cinders*, with the recently reprised *Spread a Little Happiness*. He enjoyed a lengthy career, and, in 1953, he appeared with his daughter, Sally Ann Howes (born 1930) in *Paint Your Wagon*. Binnie Hale's father joined her in *Bow Bells*, which included the haunting *Mona Lisa* number, whilst there were short runs of short-lived pieces, like *Rise and Shine*, *Yes, Madame* and the Cochran

Coronation special, *Home and Beauty*, which included the cheery *A Nice Cup of Tea*.

During and after the second world war, this string of transient successes was maintained in such shows as *Up and Doing* or *Flying Colours*. She occasionally appeared with her brother, Sonnie Hale (John Robert Monro-Hale, 1902-1958) in shows like *One, Two, Three!*. He was, like Bobbie Howes, a charming entertainer, who also wrote and directed in this same musical field. He will be remembered for having been married to both Jessie Matthews and Evelyn Laye, while, on the professional front, he was the first to sing the Noel Coward lyrics, *A Room with a View* and *Dance, Little Lady, Dance*. He was also in the Richard Rodgers and Lorenz Hart hit-show *Ever Green* when it came to the London stage. Binnie Hale underpinned her versatility by making a few films, by combining with her younger brother in a pleasant radio series called *All Hale*, and by her Christmas appearances as a most winsome principal boy in pantomime.

Especially during the inter-wars years, crowds of people living around London, or tourists holiday-making in the capital, would flock to enjoy the sight of Binnie Hale spinning and warbling the evening away against a canvas of colour and light. There was no pretence. C B Cochran and his cohorts never claimed that there was a message or a lesson. These shows were like a holiday romance, rapturous for the moment but leaving, not regrets, but merely a lingering whisper of delectation. Binnie Hale was the perfect partner for such delights.

JESSIE MATTHEWS
(Jessie Margaret Matthews, 1907-1981, born London)

Her early life could have been the plot for one of the many effervescent musical shows in which she, endearingly *gamin*, appeared. Jessie Matthews came from an impoverished background and was one of several children, but, by the age of ten, she was a professional dancer. She worked hard, first in the chorus, then with bit parts, some of them on film; suddenly she was a recognised star. Soon she was starring in productions such as *Andre Charlot's Revue of 1926; Earl Carroll's Vanities of 1926; Jordan; This Year of Grace; Wake up and Dream; Hold My Hand* and *Sally Who?*.

Critics argue that her effortless genius was never properly represented on screen, but, for the huge majority unlikely, for geographical or economic reasons, to witness it on stage, her several films gave them some measure of that talent. They included *Waltzes from Vienna; First a Girl; It's Love Again; Head Over Heels; Gangway* and *Sailing Along*, with most people believing that *Out of the Blue* and *The Good Companions* were her best two movies.

Jessie Matthews was the creature of that rather frantic hiatus between the two world wars. She worked much less after the outbreak of the second war and lived in Australia for some years. Late there were occasional one-woman shows and cameos on stage, screen and television, and, most famously of all, from 1963 to 1969 she undertook the role of Mrs Dale in the BBC's *Mrs Dale's Diary* saga. This was like a second career after a longish break, with the now stately, calm figure the antithesis of the former *ingenue*.

If one were only allowed one name to personify the light theatre of the 1920s and 1930s, it would ineluctably be that of Jessie Matthews. Less dashing and chipper than Binnie Hale, more principal girl than principal boy, Jessie Matthews, dark-haired and doe-eyed, was of dainty build and translucent loveliness; there was something positively avian about the sweetness of her voice and the delicacy of her movement. She captivated London and became a legend — and the chirruping refinement of her singing is still one of the sounds of that era which is instantly recognisable, but, above all, she was a dancer of exquisite fairy-like gentleness. It was all so right for the time of the nervy dances, the flat-chested, short-skirted fashions, the bobbed hair and the bright young things. Yet, rather like the epoch, she was ever insecure, beset by nervous breakdowns and other troubles: 'all my life I had been frightened', she confided in her autobiography.

But when, in 1930, she appeared in the Rodgers and Hart musical, *Ever Green*, the intangible, ghostly quality of its premier song, *Dancing on the Ceiling* suited Jessie Matthews ideally. In 1934 she appeared in the film version, with, for whatever reason, the title portmanteaued into *Evergreen*. In this movie she first sang her identity-song, *Over My Shoulder*. It will be for ever associated with her, not least because its theme was the text for the lifestyle she represented. It touched the self-consciously light-hearted mood and yet somehow anxious refusal to look ahead of the hour. Lark-like, she carolled, 'Over my shoulder goes one care; over my shoulder goes two cares'. Blithe and agreeable, it might well have served, at least for one age-group of one social class, as a national anthem.

 JACK BUCHANAN (John Buchanan, 1890-1957, born Strathclyde, Scotland)

While Jessie Matthews was stirring the male hearts, Jack Buchanan was breaking the female ones. A good example of the fallacy of national characteristics, it is difficult to envision anyone less like the so-called typical Scot. He was a British Fred Astaire, lanky-legged and casual, debonair in dress and appearance, floating disarmingly through 50 years of assorted show-business, very much the Metropolitan dandy. He came early to London, trained as a dancer and worked as a chorus boy, before his first breakthrough with a lead role in the touring version of *Tonight's the Night* in 1915. In 1917 he secured his first major London part in the Andre Charlot revue *Bubbly*. He took over from Jack Hulbert (1892-1978) who, particularly in tandem with his wife — they married in 1916 — Cicely Courtneidge (1893-1980) was the true-blue English, Wodehousian stage toff. The energetic Dame Cicely Courtneidge introduced more effusively popular songs than most, including *The Guards are on Parade; There's Something about a Soldier; All the King's Horses; We'll All Go Riding on a Rainbow* and her theme-song, the invigorating *Vitality*.

Jack Buchanan appeared in the 1921 *A to Z*, another Charlot show, in which he sang his own first identity-song, *And her Mother came too*. Then he took Broadway by storm, no easy errand for a British song-and-dance man in that land of strong musical comedy men, where the nonchalant West End style was considered a little effete. He conquered the critics in two Charlot showcases, before returning to the London stage to star in Jerome Kern's *Sunny*. Elsie Randolph, that piquant soubrette, was his spicy partner in a row of light musical shows, such as *That's a Good Girl; Mr Whittington; This'll Make You Whistle* and *It's Time to Dance*. He famously co-starred with Jessie Matthews in *Wake Up and Dream* and with Evelyn Laye in *Between the Devil*. Think of the songs he carried with his slightly nasal intonation, dancing the while in seemingly weightless fashion: *Goodnight Vienna; Weep no more, my Baby; I'm in a Dancing Mood* and — as much his theme-tune and a song for the times as Jessie Matthews' *Over My Shoulder* — *There's Always Tomorrow*.

He successfully branched into management, direction and choreography, while he made some 30 films. Some, such as *Brewster's Millions* and *The Gang's All Here* were light comedies, but there were also plenty of music-and-dance movies, like *Monte Carlo*, with Jeanette MacDonald, and screen editions of his stage successes, like *Goodnight Vienna* (its USA label was *Magic Night*) and *This'll Make You Whistle*. He touched the peaks in 1953 when he joined forces with Fred Astaire in a marvellous illustration of the USA/UK 'special relationship'. In MGM's *the Band Wagon* that sophisticated twosome crooned and twirled their unhurried way through *I Guess I'll have to Change my Plan*, and then turned, with Nanette Fabray, to the witty good fun of *Triplets*.

Behind the public Jack Buchanan, elegant in white tie and tails, was a private Jack Buchanan, cursed with ill-health and with sexual leanings alien to a narrow-thinking age. This he bore with a bravery that should commend him to those who do seek for 'Bravehearted' courage in the typical Scot.

 IVOR NOVELLO (David Ivor Davies, 1893-1951, born Cardiff)

Keep the Home Fires Burning was a poem by the American versifier, Lena Guilbert-Ford. It was set to music in 1915 and came to betoken the hopes of families wrenched apart by war. Ivor Novello, son of a Welsh singing teacher, was the composer, and it brought him instant fame. After war years spent with the Naval Air Service, he found multifaceted success. With his long, dark hair and Grecian profile, he was to be a stage and film actor who was idolised across the nation, whilst he pursued his young ambition to write for the musical theatre. Eventually he would play the romantic lead in his own productions, so that, one way and another, and without his homosexual orientation causing any hindrance, he built a huge, idolatrous train of female fans. The American actress, Mary Ellis, played opposite him in several of his concoctions.

He began with shows like *The Golden Moth* and *Our Nell*, but his contributions were a bit hit-and-miss until he found common interest with the lyricist, Christopher Hassall, with whom he wrote six of his most popular musical plays. Other lyricists he worked with included P G Wodehouse and Alan Melville.

Lush as dew-drenched grass and as romantically unctuous as the sweetest syrup, their compositions were devised precisely for audiences starved of lushness and romance. Crafted with loving attention to both words and music, and presented with lavish smartness, they were the consummation and acme of light operetta from the 1930s through to the beginning of the 1950s, when the American ear for earthier realism started to intrude. In later years there would be attempts to rediscover those, to coin a phrase, glamorous nights, especially with Sandy Wilson's light-hearted *The Boy Friend* — first staged in 1953, with tunes like *I Could be Happy with you*; Julie Andrews made her New York debut therein — and the pleasantly inconsequential Julian Slade/Dorothy Reynolds piece *Salad Days* — from 1954, with its Novello-ish refrain *We said we wouldn't look back*. Such shows proved popular, but, in essence, we **were** looking back and enjoying the sentiment retrospectively. Novello's glittering attainment was to compose for contemporary taste and sentiment.

For those in search of Novello nostalgia, little more need be done than to list the shows and the hits from the shows. The real success story began in 1935 with *Glamorous Night* (*Shine through my Dreams*) and continued with the 1936 *Careless Rapture* (*Why is there ever Good-bye?*); the 1937 *Crest of the Wave* (*Rose of England*); the 1939 *The Dancing Years* (*Waltz of my Heart; My Dearest Dear*); the 1943 *Arc de Triomphe* (*Man of my Heart*); the 1945 *Perchance to Dream* (*We'll Gather Lilacs*); the 1949 *King's Rhapsody* (*Someday my Heart will Awake*) and the 1951 *Gay's the Word* (*It's bound to be right on the night* and *Vitality*)

Faced with the question 'what links Lionel Monkton and Howard Talbot's *The Arcadians*' (1909) with the Lloyd Webber/ Tim Rice success, *Evita* (1978)?', the response must surely be Ivor Novello's *Perchance to Dream* — except one suspects his songs may live longer than *Pipes of Pan* or *Don't Cry for me, Argentina*.

 ANNA NEAGLE (Dame, Marjorie Robinson, 1904-1986, born Forest Gate, London)

While it might be argued that Jessie Matthews' gifts were never reflected as well on film as on stage, or, conversely, that Margaret Lockwood's talents found a better outlet on screen than in the theatre, Anna Neagle was proficient enough in both media to leave open such a dispute. Part of her comprehensive success lay in her durability, as, over, if one may borrow one of her film titles, 'Sixty glorious years', she commanded respect on both stage and screen. Anna Neagle started professional life as a dancer in 1925 in *Charlot's Revue* and was soon one of 'Mr Cochran's Young Ladies'. Then she developed as a singer-actress and co-starred with Jack Buchanan in *Stand up and Sing* sharing the duet *There's Always Tomorrow*. Next came the films, and immediately her husband-to-be, Herbert Wilcox (they married in 1943) was in the frame, directing the great majority of her pictures. The first was *Goodnight Vienna* in 1932, and there followed other movie musicals, including *Bitter Sweet; No, No, Nanette; Sunny* and *Irene*, in which she sang and danced that standard favourite, *Alice Blue Gown*.

Anna Neagle was thus associated with three great showmen, for, apart from her long collaboration with her husband, who died in 1977, her early career involved the rival *maestri* of the musical stage, whose names automatically occur in several of these Thespian profiles. One was the Frenchman, Andre Charlot (1882-1956) who brought some of the sparkle of Paris to the intimate revues of these years, and who discovered or gave initial openings to big names such as Jack Buchanan, Gertrude Lawrence, Noel Coward and, in particular, the acute-minded Beatrice Lillie (1894-1989), who, between the wars, earned the tag of being 'the funniest woman in the world'. Unluckily, her cabaret-style humour really required an audience for its most telling effect, and her film-work was sparse and, by her incomparable standards, tepid. The other, of course, was C B Cochran (1872-1951) 'the English Ziegfield', who, from 1914 to 1949, controlled the London non-classical stage, and much else, with substantial flair and authority

During the late 1940s Anna Neagle was partnered by the debonair Michael Wilding in a string of romantic comedies, like *Spring in Park Lane; The Courtneys of Curzon Street* and *Maytime in Mayfair*. She also made *Lilacs in the Spring; King's Rhapsody* and, with the buoyant Frankie Vaughan, *The Lady is a Square*. Her other *forte* lay in the filmic creation of chiefly patriotic heroines. These included Nurse Edith Cavell, Nell Gwynne, Queen Victoria, Amy Johnson, Florence Nightingale and the French resistance fighter, Odette. It is a most impressive rota of studies, all affectionately received by audiences who had a vested psychological interest in wishing that both the actress and the relevant brave woman would achieve their goals.

However, the theatre was not forgotten. She starred in *The Glorious Days* in 1953 and, from 1958, moving beyond our chronological remit, she concentrated on theatre-work, in shows like the highly acceptable *Charlie Girl*, a revisiting of *No, No, Nanette, Maggie*, and a touring version of *My Fair Lady*. Over the winter of 1985/86 she played the Fairy Godmother in *Cinderella* at the London Palladium; soon after she went into a Surrey nursing home where this most beloved of English artists died in the June of 1986.

 NOEL COWARD (Sir Noel Coward, 1899-1973, born Teddington, Middlesex)

'Destiny's tot', as Noel Coward was once wittily described, was a show-business polymath. He acted; he wrote; he sang; he directed; he did plays, films and cabaret; he managed tight-lipped sentiment and playful humour equally adeptly; such was his 'talent to amuse'. Sometimes fame is about being 'imitable' rather than inimitable. The glossy dressing-gown and cravat; the tilted, ascetic profile; the languidly held expensive cigarette; the precise modulation, fluted and slightly staccato — a thousand mimics have tried to master 'the Master'. A child actor on stage as early as 1911, he first came to prominence with his songs, like *Parisian Pierrot* in the 1923 revue, *London Calling!*, and his first play, *The Vortex* in 1924, its outspoken comment on drug-addiction causing something of a *furore*. Henceforward he spent a lifetime in the brilliant spotlight, crowding achievement after achievement into his glittering career.

Among his many stage triumphs might be mentioned *Hay Fever; Private Lives; Cavalcade; Tonight at Eight Thirty; Bitter Sweet; Present Laughter; This Happy Breed* and *Blithe Spirit*. There was a conversational crackle about many of his scripts which recalled the clever dialogue of Oscar Wilde, and yet, as well as the flippancy, there were moving moments — *Brief Encounter*, of course, was his composition — whilst Noel Coward, eschewing the fashionable disdain of such matters, upheld a very ordinary brand of patriotism. This is very noticeable in the fine war film, *In Which We Serve*, the naval epic he starred in and co-directed with David Lean. As well as the filmed versions of his own plays, like *This Happy Breed, Bitter Sweet* and *Blithe Spirit*, he contributed several calmly observed cinematic cameos in, for instance, *Our Man in Havana* or *Around the World in Eighty Days*.

His serious songs include *Mad about the Boy; Poor Little Rich Girl; London Pride* and the touching refrain, *I'll See You Again*. His cabaret-style funny songs, hailed in Las Vegas and New York as jubilantly as in the West End, are proverbial: *Don't put your Daughter on the Stage, Mrs Worthington; Mad Dogs and Englishmen go out in the Mid-day Sun; There is Bad News Just around the Corner; Don't Let's be Beastly to the Germans*. His impudent parody of the Cole Porter standard, *Let's Fall in Love,* is another favourite. Each ripped snappily along, with agile facility of rhyming pattern: 'Tho' the pipes that supply the bathroom burst/ And the lavat'ry makes you fear the worst/ It was used by Charles the First/ Quite informally/ And later by George the Fourth/ On a journey North' (from the 1938 song, *The Stately Homes of England*.) Noel Coward is a much-quoted playwright — solely from *Private Lives* we might cite 'Very flat, Norfolk'; 'Extraordinary how potent cheap music is'; and 'Some women should be struck regularly, like gongs.'

It is difficult to judge whether his own private life was as august and self-assured as his public demeanour, especially in an era when society and the law regarded homosexuality as aberrant. The distinguished theatre critic, Kenneth Tynan, perhaps came close to a sound and not unkindly *résumé* when he wrote, 'Coward invented the concept of cool, and may have had emotional reasons for doing so.'

GERTRUDE LAWRENCE
(Alexandra Dagmar Lawrence Klasen, 1898-1952, born London)

The George S Kaufman/Moss Hart play and 1941 film *The Man who Came to Dinner* included spoofs of both Noel Coward (the character, Beverley Carlton) and Gertrude Lawrence (the character, Lorraine Sheldon). Although the caricatures exhibited the more egotistical aspects of their natures, it was a sincere tribute to their quality that Broadway and Hollywood audiences already recognised the models for these two impersonations. In 1968, 16 years after her premature and abrupt death from a rare form of cancer, Gertrude Lawrence became one of the few English stage stars to be granted the accolade of a ciné-biography. To be frank, *Star!* did not move the critics to raptures, but it gave Julie Andrews the chance to demonstrate some of the reasons why Gertrude Lawrence had become so big a name. Noel Coward — the pair met as child actors — was played by his godson, Daniel Massey. Disappointment in *Star!* perhaps echoed earlier frustration that Gertrude Lawrence had never contrived quite to recapture her stage flair on film. Her very last film, *the Glass Menagerie* (1950) was probably the pick.

All the more reason, then, to marvel over a star who was able to build an immense reputation on both sides of the Atlantic almost entirely on the basis of her theatrical presence. Born into a show-business family, she was on stage at 12, learned dancing and elocution, hence the disappearance of her cockney twang, and busied herself in all manner of shows. Her West End debut was in 1916, inevitably in a Charlot production, *Some*. Soon she was partnering Jack Buchanan in the 1921 *A to Z* and singing *Limehouse Blues* on Broadway. In 1926 she became the first British actress to originate a part in New York before bringing the show to London. This was the George and Ira Gershwin musical, *Oh, Kay!*, in which she played the eponymous heroine and sang such standards as *Maybe* and *Someone to Watch over Me*. She sustained her close working relationship with Noel Coward by appearing with him in *Private Lives*, and enjoying a hit with the tenderhearted waltz, *Someday I'll Find You*. Gertrude Lawrence also appeared in straight plays, such as *Behold We Live* and *Skylark*, while, more memorably, she introduced Cole Porter's amusing *The Physician* ('He went through wild ecstatics when I

showed him my lymphatics, but he never said he loved me') in his 1933 show *Nymph Errant*. Back with Noel Coward, she shared with him the deft pleasures of *Tonight at Eight Thirty*, his set of one-act plays, including *Red Peppers*, the argumentative variety duo with their brash number, *Has Anybody seen our Ship?*. In 1941 she had a great Broadway success with *Lady in the Dark*, composed by Kurt Weill and Ira Gershwin, and, throughout the 1940s, she continued to entertain elegantly around the world.

In 1951 Gertrude Lawrence undertook what she regarded as the best role of her career, in a show she actually suggested to Rodgers and Hammerstein, when she played Anna against Yul Brynner's powerful monarch in *The King and I*. With Valerie Hobson as Anna in 1953, it made history in the West End as well as on Broadway, but, alas, Gertrude Lawrence died only 18 months into the long run. Vivacious to the very end, she was a polished ornament of the Transatlantic stage, one for whom her film-title, *Star!* was completely justified.

EVELYN LAYE (Elsie Evelyn Laye, 1900-1996, born London)

Evelyn Laye, daughter of the actor-composer, Gilbert Laye, almost comprehended the century, just as, between the ages of 15 and 92, she captivated theatre audiences. She enjoyed an early success in 1920 in *The Shop Girl*, with its hit song, *The Guards' Parade*, while C B Cochran, who raved about her as 'the fairest *prima donna* this side of heaven', first show-cased her in *Madame Pompadour*. An attractive, accomplished singer and capable actress, she sought the stronger roles of operetta and the more solid musical plays, such as *The Merry Widow* and the London *premiere* of *The New Moon*, in which she enchanted everyone with her rendition of *Lover, Come Back to me*. She was also leading lady in the New York opening of *Bitter Sweet*, and later appeared in the London version.

Film-work naturally followed, but, like several others of those gracious inter-wars stars, the cinema was not her *métier*. Perhaps the techniques were as yet too elemental and unsubtle to catch the alchemy of her appeal; perhaps celluloid dulled the essential starlight that shone so effulgently across the footlights. Nevertheless, Evelyn Laye made some passable musical films. These included *Luck of the Navy; Queen of Scandal; One Heavenly Night; Princess Charming; Waltz Time; I'll Turn to You* and *Evensong* — considered by most commentators to be her best movie. She also joined with Ramon Navarro in the 1934 film, *The Night is Young*, in which she sang the song most intimately connected with her, the Sigmund Romberg/Oscar Hammerstein composition, *When I Grow too Old to Dream*. Back in theatre-land she was the heroine of Troy in *Helen!*; she played opposite the juvenile John Mills, another enduring example of English stage and screen craft, in *Give Me a Ring*; she partnered the vibrant tenor, Richard Tauber, in *Paganini*; and she joined forces with Jack Buchanan and Adele Dixon (the soprano and trim principal boy whose clipped tones — *Bringing Television to You* — introduced British television in 1936) in the American production of *Between the Devil* in 1937. This show was booked for a special presentation to celebrate President Roosevelt's birthday, thought to be the first time there had been an American equivalent of our royal command performances.

Evelyn Laye served as Entertainments Director for the Royal Navy during the second world war and is remembered for topping the bill when the first-ever variety show penetrated to the Orkneys remoteness of the Scapa Flow fleet. Equally memorable was her feisty presence in the 1940 revue, *Lights Up*. In this she sang not one but three hits: *You've done Something to my Heart; Only a Glass of Champagne* and *Let the People Sing*. It was an extraordinary *tour de force*. With the musical theatre a trifle becalmed after the war, there was something of a lull in her career, filled by some rather desultory straight acting and trips around the variety circuit. 1954 then found her triumphant in the musical comedy *Wedding in Paris*, and her course was again fairly set, travelling far beyond the end of our period, for another 40 years. 'Boo', as she was familiarly known from infancy, was married first to Sonnie Hale and later, with rather more stability, to the English actor, Frank Lawson, who many will have seen in films like *Young Woodley; David Copperfield* (as David himself, no less); *The Four Just Men* and *Went the Day Well*. Evelyn Laye is affectionately remembered as a great lady of the theatre.

 LAURENCE OLIVIER
(Baron, Laurence Kerr Olivier, 1907-1989, born Dorking)

Alone among the ten stage stars chosen to represent the era from about 1922 to 1953, Laurence Olivier is the only one to have concentrated on the legitimate stage. By its nature, the field of music and dance throws up the more popular stars, while the serious theatre has a more limited, if more thoughtful, audience. There was a rival or two, such as that pre-eminent speaker of verse, John Gielgud, born in 1904 and surviving the Millennium, and Ralph Richardson, 1902-1983, a raffish and mettlesome actor. Laurence Olivier, however, by his potent contributions to screen as well as stage, and as director as well as artist, contrived to become a household name in a convincing fashion not usually found among the 'legit' component of the English stage.

The child of a clergyman, his ambitions were energetic and fiery from the onset. He was quickly the matinee idol in plays like the preview of *Journey's End*, as Beau Geste in a dramatisation of the P C Wren novel, and as Victor Prynne in *Private Lives*, by Noel Coward for whom Laurence Olivier had immense regard. Then, as swiftly, it was the none too certain glare of Hollywood, and then, as abruptly, back to England to be directed by John Gielgud in the 1934 production of *The Queen of Hearts*, the prelude to his attachment to the Old Vic and to the Shakespearean repertoire, with roles as varied as Toby Belch, Henry V, Hamlet, Iago and Coriolanus. His sheer animalism and gusto, with his astounding resource for audacious movement and speech, especially in marked contrast to the classical style of John Gielgud, had already secured his place in the pantheon of outstanding English actors. In 1939, as Heathcliff, in *Wuthering Heights*, he painfully learned from the pitiless director, William Wyler, that screen was not lower than stage, but a different art-form. He soon put the agonising lesson

to proper account with the spirited 1945 film of *Henry V*, thought by some critics to be the best as well as the first of his own films. His 1956 *Richard III* was another film in which, gleeful, sinister and capering, he created the model of how everyone now imagines that monarch to have been.

The postwar theatre saw him in mixed classical and modern plays, including new work from Terence Rattigan, Christopher Fry, Tennessee Williams and Thornton Wilder. By now he was at the pinnacle of his fame and power, but, bold as ever, he plunged, where many of his classical colleagues feared to tread, into new wave drama. In 1957 he created the swaggering, seedy stand-up comic, Archie Rice, in John Osborne's *The Entertainer*, a parable of England's ambiguous plight in the 1950s. It would remain one of Laurence Olivier's favourite parts. In 1963 he became first Director of the newly established National Theatre, and, despite the alarums and excursions that such a prominent appointment brought and despite the frightening amount of ill-health with which he grappled, his life and career just went soaring onwards and upwards. In 1970 he became the theatre's first life peer, and an obituarist said of him that 'he did more to advance the art of acting than anyone since Sir Henry Irving'. Laurence was married three times, to the actresses Jill Esmond, Vivien Leigh and Joan Plowright. He enriched the cultural life of the English-speaking world with a fascinating series of stage and cinematic characterisations and has some claim to be England's cultural giant of the 20th century.

The Andrews Sisters in a Chesterfield commercial in 1939

Gracie Fields

Flanagan and Allen

Bing Crosby

Betty Grable

Vera Lynn

Al Bowlly, killed in an air raid on London in 1941

Donald Peers

Anne Ziegler and Webster Booth

The Inkspots

Let The People Sing ~ Popular Singers ~ Ten Vocalists

It is song-time in the day centre or the residential care home. Someone benevolently punches out old-time music hall songs on the piano, numbers like *Down at the Old Bull and Bush* or *Hello, Hello, who's your Lady-friend?*. There is nothing wrong with music hall songs. They had — and have — forceful *panache* and many embraced pertinent social comment; when Marie Lloyd was perkily following her old man's van, for example, she was remarking on the frequent 'flit', invariably by moonlight, of a private rental, pre-owner occupied and publicly housed society. The curio is that these music hall songs have now served about three generations of old people as if they had been the staple diet of the youth of each. This runs the hazard of becoming yet another negative symbol of old age, like the 'elderly persons' crossing sign or the woolly cardigan. The current over-sixties enjoyed a much more mid-Atlantic musical menu and that obliging pianist should be tickling the ivories with Vera Lynn, Bing Crosby and Glenn Miller standards.

In the quarter century after the first world war, records, radio, the dance hall and film brought music to the people, although, certainly until the 1950s, the sales of sheet music, to be played at home on the parlour piano, remained quite high. The taste turned to dance band music, with many of the vocalists who became famous as single acts starting life as dance band singers performing as solo acts, with full orchestral accompaniment. It is true that there was a more serious aspect. The sacred song and the choral society were still in vogue. The records of Dame Nellie Melba, said to be the first human voice to be broadcast, Dame Clara Butt or the boy soprano, Ernest Lush, were in much demand, with songs like *O, for the Wings of a Dove* or *The Holy City* much favoured. A long line of tenors, from John McCormack (*The Rose of Tralee*) and Peter Dawson (*The Floral Dance*) to Joseph Locke (*Hear My Song; Good-bye*) were also in vogue, while brass bands also enjoyed a following. What has to be remembered is that purchasing power then lay with an older, staider and more suburban social group than in the post-1950 decades when the youth cults took hold.

Nonetheless, the shift towards the more romantic mood of the dance tune was very marked. The gramophone really started to have a thorough-going influence from 1926, when electrical replaced acoustic recording, and, in price and quality, the product improved substantially. 'His Master's Voice', with the dog's head cocked inquiringly by the huge gramophone horn, was set to be one of the most enduring of marketing slogans. Both the piano and the pianola, which had competed fiercely with the primitive record, slumped in popularity. Already by 1926 there were two million holders of 'wireless' licences, so that the everyday world had access to these popular songs. In the 1920s the remarkable total of 40,000 composers were to be found on the books of the Performing Rights Society. The profits from sheet music, band parts, records and radio transformed the enterprising composer's life and bank account.

The British tradition of communal singing was alive and well. Once it had been the Victorian choral societies, especially in South Wales and Yorkshire, with their *penchant* for the oratorio; or, rather more vulgarly, music hall audiences following the 'all together now' instruction. The amateur light operatic societies remained strong, tempering their wholesale reliance on the Savoyard comic operas with the frothier musical comedies of Edwardian times. Hymn-singing in church was another example, and the fact that the BBC now imprints the words of its 'Songs of Praise' on the TV screen for living-room participation is a tribute to the national affection for hymns.

But the communal singing after 1918 had a semi-formal dimension, possibly stimulated by the collective rendition of ditties by soldiers in the 1914-1918 war. 'Community singing' was a phrase much in use during these decades, never more so than in the 1939-1945 war when, once more, the armed forces took up the melodious cudgels. They were joined by practically everyone else. Factory workers, especially as the tuneful distaff side were now to be discovered at the lathes, were to the fore, and their concerted efforts were honoured during and for years after the war by the daily *Music While you Work* programme that blared out over loud speakers. Couples often crooned to one another on the dance floor; cinema organists led audiences through choruses, with words flashed on the screen; there were even halls booked just to provide community singing.

The accent on lyrics in a 'singing' culture was immense and, for all that they may seem either hollow or syrupy in cold print, these compositions were often eloquently devised. In turn, the popular singers of the age, the leading soloists, so to speak, at this communal concert, were invariably cleanly articulate in their enunciation and phrasing. Although there were several duos and trios, the 'band' kind of group, with instruments and voices combined, was a phenomenon of the future. The emotive rhythm and beat of such effusions were to mean that there was less emphasis on lyrical clarity — not a worse, but assuredly a different approach. Before the Rock 'n' Roll years, the words were as significant as the melodies.

The romantic *motif* was maintained. It had not been absent from the first world war — the yearning tones of *Roses of Picardy* or

There's a long long trail a-winding testify to that — but the typical songs were cheery marching songs. The second world war, too, had its martial airs, like the *Beer-barrel Polka* (Roll out the barrel) or *Bless 'em all*, but songs of sundered lovers took precedence, in pursuit of the mood that had evolved through the dance music of the post-1919 era. Thus, while *Tipperary* and *Pack up your Troubles* will always be remarked as the representative songs of the first war, the second war's prototypical songs would be *Yours, We'll Meet Again*, and, borrowed from the German *Werhmacht, Lili Marlene*. A normal 'Music while you work' edition might include cheerful but still often romance-oriented quicksteps, alongside the slow fox-trots, with their deeper message of fondness or craving.

It was J B Priestley who coined the war-time phrase 'let the people sing' and it became the title of ENSA's signature tune. It was, however, an invocation that had equally applied in the hard times of the 1920s and 1930s, and it was to be needed for quite a few years after the war. Community singing brought a humane gaiety and decent tenderness to what was too often an arduous existence. We profile now some of the famed voices who were among its proclaimed leaders.

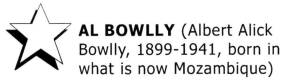 **AL BOWLLY** (Albert Alick Bowlly, 1899-1941, born in what is now Mozambique)

Between the dawn of modern record-making and the blitz, Al Bowlly was by far the most pre-eminent vocalist on the popular music scene. Born of Greek and Lebanese parentage and bred in Johannesburg, he played guitar and banjo with the Edgar Adeler and Jimmy Liquime bands, introducing vocals into his contribution almost immediately, and trekking around various parts of the world. His first record was made in 1927 in Berlin and he came to England a year later to sing with the Fred Elizalde orchestra at the Savoy Hotel. Soon, unusually for a dance band vocalist of that date, he went freelance. He sang and recorded with Ray Noble's New Mayfair combine, encompassing a trip to the USA, with Roy Fox at the Montseigneur restaurant, with Lew Stone, Geraldo, Maurice Winnick, Ken 'Snakehips' Johnson and a litany of other conductors. He also teamed up with Jimmy Messini as 'the Radio Stars with Two Guitars'. Incredibly, he recorded 700 songs in the short period of 1930 to 1933.

Excitable and extravagant off-stage, he was urbane, composed and lucid upon it, his delivery sophisticated and his phrasing impeccable. Although few tunes were outside his range and style, his chief achievement lay in the interpretation of ballads. Probably his most affectionately received standards were *Blue Moon; My Melancholy Baby; The Shadow waltz; Love is the Sweetest Thing; I'm Saving the Last Waltz for You; Louisiana Hayride; I'll String Along with You; Have You Ever Been Lonely?; Goodnight, Sweetheart* and *The Very Thought of You.*

The tingling sensation he generated was compared by one admirer to 'having fizzy lemonade poured down my spine'. Few could rival him, with Sam Browne perhaps coming nearest. Others may think of Leslie Hutchinson, familiarly known as 'Hutch'. Born in Grenada in 1900, Hutch turned from law studies to concentrate on accompanying his own singing at the piano. C B Cochran brought him from Paris to London in 1927 and, for many years, his velvety keyboard touch and smoky vocal style were to be heard on radio, stage and record, as well as in the swell London night-spots, in such numbers as *Out of Nowhere* and *Begin the Beguine*. He died in 1969. Another similar singer from that time was the American, Turner Layton (1894-1978). His enjoyable and lucrative partnership with Clarence Johnstone was ruined in 1935 when the latter was cited in a divorce case involving a white woman. The racist London society of the 1930s could not tolerate such conduct and he died in obscure poverty back home in the United States, Turner Layton prospered as a solo act. *Alabamy Bound*; *Bye bye, Blackbird* and *The Song is Ended* were the major Layton and Johnstone hits.

During one night of the London bombing, Al Bowlly left his girl-friend in bed to seek the makeshift shelter of the bedroom doorway. Unluckily, a bomb exploded outside his flat and the blast killed him, while his companion was fortunate to survive. Critics have labelled him 'the best popular singer of the 1930s', and few would quibble. An ambitious singer — he was the first dance band vocalist to risk touring as a variety act — the sad question hangs in the air as to whether he would have achieved his stated aspiration to become a solo international star. Competent judges think he would have done.

BING CROSBY (Harry Lillis Crosby, 1903-1977, born Tacoma, Washington, USA)

Whatever the disturbing notes of his private life that have emerged since his death, Bing Crosby's public image was overt, affable and direct. Across all the audio-visual media he conveyed an easy-going and amicable approach that belied, as is the case with many seemingly laid-back entertainers, among whom Perry Como was to be an example, a hard core of professional efficiency. His nickname around the recording studios — 'One-take' Crosby — exemplifies this, for his grasp of musical notation and phrasing was, by dint of considerable practice, almost instantaneous. While not, like Frank Sinatra (who, in many senses, was Bing Crosby's heir and whose celebrity fell chiefly beyond the period under review) he was not the most original of song interpreters. But he was extraordinarily adept, over many years, at presenting popular ballads to a world-wide audience. He had an acute ear for what audiences wanted to hear.

The explanation of this smooth and mellifluous performance lay, it is sometimes forgotten, in the new sophistication of amplifying equipment. Instead of the near-bellowing that a vast theatre had demanded of singers, sensitive microphones allowed the likes of the supremely gifted Bing Crosby to develop that intimate style which came to be called 'crooning'. Taking his forename from a cartoon character, he started singing with the Rhythm Boys, a vocal trio for the Paul Whiteman orchestra, and he also sang with the Jimmy Dorsey, Tommy Dorsey, Bix Beiderbecke and Louis Armstrong bands. His lazy, confidential intonation was well-suited to radio, while soon his record sales eclipsed all others, as, by the 1940s, he became the world's biggest singing star.

Like other American entertainers (his 'friendly rival', Bob Hope, is another example) he diversified his work, principally into film, where he had dramatic (for example, *The Bells of St Mary's*, in which he played a priest, or *The Country Girl*) as well as musical (*Blue Skies, High Society*, with Frank Sinatra and Grace Kelly) and light comedy roles, notably in the much-loved 'Road' (to Hong Kong, Singapore, Morocco, Rio. . .) films with Bob Hope and Dorothy Lamour of the ogled-over sarong. Bing Crosby was in demand to offer cameo stints, for instance, again with Frank Sinatra, in *Robin and the Seven Hoods*. During his long film presence, he remained, whatever the part or the plot, as amiable as was his melodic line.

Crosby's first wife was the actress and fellow Roman Catholic, Dixie Lee, and four of their sons tried their hand at show-business. It is mainly from that quarter that tales emerged of his strange, even cruel, moments behind the scenes. Whatever the truth — and there has been a fashion whereby the children of screen idols, among them Joan Crawford, have indicted their parents posthumously of dreadful deeds — the public *persona* of engaging ease remains untouchable. From the effortless charm of *Pennies from Heaven*, through the record-breaking constancy of *I'm Dreaming of a White Christmas*, to the emotion-kindling notes, complete with that tuneful whistle and crooner's 'boo-hoo-hoo', of his theme-song, *The Blue of the Night*, Bing Crosby was, for many, **the** singer of the 1940s.

 GRACIE FIELDS (Grace Stansfield, 1898-1979, born in Rochdale)

The biographers of American presidents were wont to hymn their subject's homely qualities with titles like 'from Log cabin to White House': Gracie Fields managed the British equivalent: from chip shop to Capri. From humble origins above a fried fish shop, her blazing trajectory carried her, via world stardom, to the idyllic surrounds of an island paradise, once the fit topic — *'Twas on the Isle of Capri* — for one of her songs. Yet, for all she was perhaps the most comprehensively talented British entertainer of all time, her personal life was marred by unhappiness. Touring as a child dancer, she suffered a nervous breakdown, possibly the result of sexual abuse; she had passages of ill-health; for a brief time at the beginning of the war she was unjustly accused of not 'doing her bit'. Her three marriages, to Archie Pitt, the father-figure producer, to Monty Banks, the Italian comic dancer, whose nationality gave rise to her war-time problem and who died in her arms aboard a speeding continental express train, and to the possessive Capri wireless mechanic, Boris Alperovic, were not free of grief.

Her public face betrayed none of this *angst*. From 1918, when she starred in the West End, as Sally Perkins in Basil Dean's *Mr Tower of London*, she was 'the most famous person next to royalty'. 'Our Gracie' began her recording career in 1928 and by 1933 had sold four million records. She made 12 simple but heart-warming films, beginning in 1931 with *Sally in our Alley*, whence came her beloved signature-tune, and with *Sing as we go* (which gave its title to another hit song) the best-liked. From 1933 she had a villa on Capri and in 1979 she was appointed a Dame of the British Empire, a year after her last London appearance which was, in fact, her tenth Royal Command Performance.

Like Fanny Brice of Brooklyn, Gracie Fields of Rochdale was ordinary in countenance and demeanour, but she had the command to hold audiences in thrall with her unspoilt confidence and the amazingly flexible instrument of her voice. It is difficult to think of another performer who has emulated her range. Gracie Fields could produce deathless hush with a deeply-felt *Ave Maria* or *Now is the Hour*. She could touch hearts with moving ballads like *Little old Lady Passing by* or, some years later, *Around the World*. She could lift the rafters with brisk chorus songs like *Sing, Soldier, as you March Along* or *Wish me Luck as you Wave me Good-bye*. She could tickle ribs with her laconic, resigned musical monologues like *Walter, Walter, Take me to the Altar*; *My Little Bottom Drawer*; *I Took my Harp to a Party*; *Following the Rochdale Hounds* and *With my Head Tucked underneath my Arm*.

At one moment the husky, broad-accented mill-girl droll, the next warbling and carolling high above the music and chorus, Gracie Fields was that *rara avis*, a class act. It was versatility on an uncommon and colossal scale, precisely because she could have been an international star, such was the jewel-like brightness of her talent, merely by concentrating on just one of those four disciplines. It only required the opening chord of 'Sally, Sally, don't ever wander away from the alley and me' and the audience was in the palm of her hand. There was considerable mourning when she died on the Isle of Capri in 1979.

 FLANAGAN AND ALLEN
(Reuben Weinthrop, then Robert Winthrop, 1896-1968, born in Whitechapel, London; and William Ernest Allen, 1896-1982, born London)

You may be surprised to find the 'Oi comedians' in the singing section, but, truth to tell, the fruits of their singing alliance has far outlasted their never more than homely humour. Bud Flanagan was the child of Polish refugees who was a call-boy at the age of ten and who took his name from his anti-Semitic sergeant-major in World War I. Chesney Allen, son of a master builder and intended for solicitors' articles, joined Florrie Forde in revue instead and then teamed up with Bud Flanagan. The differing origins showed in their costume: Bud in his voluminous, moth-eaten fur-coat and battered straw hat; Ches in his good suit and natty trilby. Again, Bud was the noisier comic and Chesney the steadier, more courteous 'feed'. They joined forces, memorably, as 'the Crazy Gang', with Naughton and Gold, Nervo and Knox and 'Monsewer' Eddie Gray, and, with umpteen London runs and royal command performances, they were the nearest those years had to court jesters. Ches Allen fell ill in 1946, but then outlived his colleagues. Bud Flanagan was appointed OBE in 1959.

There were other light-hearted male singing duets, usually with one playing the piano: the Two Leslies, Leslie Sarony and Leslie Holmes, with rather facetious songs like *I Lift up my Finger and I say 'Tweet Tweet'*; Flotsam and Jetsam ('We'll tell you our names in case anyone forgets 'em' ran their jolly opener) in real life the brisk tenor of

B C Hilliam and the profound bass of Malcolm McEachern, with sharp, up-to-the-minute novelty numbers like *Little Betty Bouncer loves an announcer down at the BBC*, or the Western Brothers, in reality cousins, Kenneth and George, languid and immaculately attired, drawling their topical commentary in public school 'play the game, you cads' argot. Michael Flanders and Donald Swann were to build on this stable platform for the next generation.

Flanagan and Allen, who, unlike most double acts, never showed a moment's Punch and Judy animosity, had a similar harmony, although they did not evince the same refinement.

Together their songs composed a hymn-book to ordinariness. Strolling across the stage, one hand on the other's shoulder, the affable, almost cantor-like notes of Bud holding the melodic line, the calm, all but spoken tones of Ches the perfect complement, they lauded the resilience of ordinary people coping with the vicissitudes of day-by-day life. The titles speak for themselves: *Ordinary People; Yesterday's Dreams; Home Town; Let's be Buddies; Down Forget-me-not Lane; Nice People.*

In 1926 Bud Flanagan scribbled a song while the couple were appearing in Derby. Next week they sang it at Southport. Not only did it become their immortal signature tune, it became the English 'depression' song, a whisper of hope among the debris of impoverished lives. It was the equivalent of the American *Buddy, can you Spare a Dime?*, although it did not convey the anguish of that mournful lyric. *Underneath the Arches* would live on triumphantly. Not many months before his death Bud Flanagan recorded the *pastiche* theme song for TV's *Dad's Army*, and, such was his magical imprint, many people thought it a 1940 original. As Ches often murmured, as they slowly sauntered front-stage, 'lovely melody, Bud'.

 ANNE ZIEGLER AND WEBSTER BOOTH
(Irene Frances Eastwood, 1910 -, born in Liverpool; Leslie Webster Booth, 1902-1984, born in Birmingham)

The orchestra strike up with the opening bars of *Only a Rose* and the audience, whether listening to the radio at home or sitting expectantly in the variety theatre, at once pick up the clue: the most famed male/female pairing of their generation are about to join their tenor and soprano voices in singing of exceptional quality. What, in fact, Anne Ziegler and Webster Booth did was to throw a bridge from the near-classical to the popular, bringing serious music to the populace. Webster Booth, dark and moustached, and Anne Ziegler, fair-haired and with strikingly handsome features, met in 1934, married in 1938, and formed their double act in 1940. The critical period of their popularity was from then until 1956. In that year they emigrated to South Africa, although in 1978 they returned and found a home in North Wales. Fame pursued them and their purported retirement was dotted with teaching and with all manner of singing engagements; they last sang together at Bridlington a few months before Webster Booth's death.

Webster Booth, a Lincoln Cathedral chorister and erstwhile accountant, found friendly refuge with the D'Oyly Carte Opera Company, before embarking on his own solo career, while his wife-to-be had first trained as a classical pianist before turning to singing. She met her husband when she was filming an early colour version of Gounod's *Faust*. Their essentially middle-brow appeal, during a period when many looked for a degree of serious but not solemn quality in their entertainment, was unrivalled. One might compare them with the Hollywood duet of Jeanette MacDonald (1901-1965) and Nelson Eddy (1901-1967). or even see the American pair as their forebears. Jeanette MacDonald had enjoyed considerable success partnered with the mercurial Maurice Chevalier and some feared that her animated mien might swamp that of the much more dour Nelson Eddy. However, from 1935 to 1942 they achieved enormous popularity in the filming of well-tried musical comedies like *Naughty Marietta, Rose Marie* and *New Moon*. Hits like *Indian Love-call* or *Lover Come Back to me* or *Stout-hearted Men* are still indelibly associated with them.

The strict purity of intonation of Webster Booth and Anne Ziegler was their hallmark. Faultlessly attired on the stage, rarely succumbing to any break in the general seriousness of atmosphere, their two voices blended excellently in their repertoire of mainly good quality show songs and old-time ballads. A concert by Anne Ziegler and Webster Booth might have contained some of the following: *If you Were the Only Girl in the World; A Paradise for Two; Ah, Sweet Mystery of Life; Deep in my Heart, Dear; You, Just you; Love's old Sweet Song; When we are Married; So Deep is the Night; Hear my Song; Violetta* and *Love's Last Word is Spoken.*

Nearly half a century on, and yet there will be many theatre-goers and radio-listeners who will respond, should you hum the first few chord of *Only a rose*, 'Ah yes, Anne Ziegler and Webster Booth.'

VERA LYNN (Vera Margaret Welch, 1917-, born East Ham, London)

A hit record — *Red Sails in the Sunset* — aged 20, the imperishable 'Forces' sweetheart' in the 1939-1945 war and dame of the British Empire is a reasonable career for a little girl banned from singing in school concerts because her voice was too low. Vera Lynn's voice, with its distinctive and much-imitated 'catch', was unusually low and band-parts had to be transposed several keys down on her behalf, while, outside her suitable range of slow-moving numbers, she was not quite as comfortable. Nor was she glamorous or sexy. Nevertheless, this dark-haired, good-looking, smiling young woman had the exceptional gift, not only of being heartfelt, but of conveying that virtuous earnestness in all she did. Her famous BBC programme was aptly named *Sincerely Yours*. It was this quality that appealed to serving men, and to their women-folk as well, for they rightly perceived no threat of the imagination, as might be posed by, say, the sensuality of Betty Grable or Rita Hayworth. Vera Lynn acted as a sisterly conduit for the proper emotion of spouses and sweethearts separated by war.

Having been a member of the Cracker Cabaret Kids troupe at seven and having sung with the Howard Barker band at 16, she joined the Ambrose orchestra at twenty years of age. She had enjoyed broadcasting, record and stage success before 1939, but it was, of course, during the war that she sprang to immense prominence. Critics wrote of her as 'the symbol of all the things we're fighting for' and she made the most strenuous efforts to meet the call. Apart from the *Sincerely Yours* broadcasts, with their formula of the introductory 'Wishing' song, messages, primarily about new-born babies, and more songs, she was an arduous tourer of military sites. Her work in Burma attracted the admiration and respect even of those who were not too keen on her type of singing. Of course, there were the compensations of hard cash: she made £50,000 in 1942 and invested most of it in war-bonds. She bought a house in Barking, married Aircraftsman Harry Lewis, a former clarinettist with Ambrose and genuinely played the role of the housewife-cum-celebrity. Such was the esteem in which she was held, to say nothing of the lovely way she handled the sentimental ballad, that her popularity was by no means short-lived. Her 1952 rendering of *Auf Wiedersehen, Sweetheart* unprecedentedly topped both American and British charts and, years later, she would have her own television series.

A blimpish coterie of politicians and brass-hats had abusively complained that her brand of song was morale-sapping — Anne Shelton, Vera Lynn's nearest to a rival, but who sang at a much brighter lilt as in *Lay Down your Arms and Surrender to Mine*, was not free from the same offensive assault. Both women better understood the more pensive mood of the citizen's army of World War II and, unlike their assailants, realised that the martial oom-pah-pah music they wanted would fall on deaf ears. Vera Lynn was also the victim of some pretty cruel impersonations, something she was sensitive about. At the end of the day, victory was hers and ours. *Yours; When the Lights go on Again; That Lovely Week-end; When they Sound the last 'All Clear'; I'll Pray for You; A Nightingale Sang in Berkeley Square; Goodnight, my Love,* not forgetting that old faithful, *We'll Meet Again*, will all be re-played and re-sung in her honour for years to come.

BETTY GRABLE (Ruth Elizabeth Grable, 1916-1973, born St Louis, Missouri, USA)

Little more really needs to be known about Betty Grable than that her pin-up picture was the most popular in World War II. In a stunning white bathing suit, she was portrayed peeping, with inquiring cheerfulness, over her shoulder. Her platinum blonde tresses framed her peaches and cream complexion and ruby-lipped grin, while her symmetrically-proportioned figure was resplendently set off by those sensational legs. In an era of legginess, her limbs, reputedly insured for $1m, reigned supreme and are perhaps the most famous legs the world has eyed. A lively, optimistic and wholesome young woman, she was, basically, one of the most competent song and dance leading ladies Hollywood ever produced.

She was a hoofer of energetic brio and sang in much the same vein. Hers was a clear, bold voice, the pleasant side of brassy, and, for slower, more thoughtful numbers, she could instil sufficient warmth to engage decent sympathy. Having had a chorus part in the film *Let's go places*, in 1939 she introduced the Cole Porter hit, *Well, did you evah?* (later revived in the film, *High Society*) in the stage show *Dubarry was a Lady*, starring the magnificent Ethel Merman. Immediately she sprang to prominence in a colourful host of films, thin on story but rich in exuberant song, many of them with old-time, backstage vaudeville settings. Her numerous films included *Tin Pan Alley; Sweet Rosie O'Grady; Mother wore Tights; Coney Island; Wabash Avenue* and *My Blue Heaven,* while her stream of leading men included Don Ameche, Victor Mature and Dan Dailey. In 1967 her fans welcomed the release of a compilation of no less than 48 of her songs, chiefly from the period 1940 to 1955.

After an earlier brief marriage to one-time child-star, Jackie Coogan, she married the trumpeter/bandleader Harry James in 1940, whereafter he had to suffer the indignity of being referred to as Mr Betty Grable. They were divorced in 1965, while Betty Grable died of cancer at the youngish age of 56. From Fanny Brice, more noted for her Broadway stardom, to Barbra Streisand, who played Fanny Brice in *Funny Girl*, the musical cinema has been a haven for songstresses; another such spectrum might be described by Canadian-born Deanna Durbin (*It's a Grand Night for Singing*) and Doris Day. Blonde and bouncing, Betty Hutton had some of the vitality, if not quite the curvaceousness, of Betty Grable about the same 1940s era.

It is an intriguing aspect of World War II that morale was boosted, not just by the exotic temptress, with which the first world war was quite familiar, but by a generous-spirited woman of guileless disposition. *Mens sana in corpore sano* might have been her sensible motto. Like, in a different way, Vera Lynn, Betty Grable was never the vamp. What you saw was what you got, and, the honest soldiery who watched over her picture in every tank and barrack-room might have added, very nice, if you can get it. Her war-winning exploits were a healthy counterpoint to the 'sultry sirens' of Hollywood, all mysterious allure, and she deservedly earned much credit for her never less than entirely committed and enthusiastic performances.

★ THE INKSPOTS
(Principally, 1939-1944)

Dance band vocalists, like Bing Crosby or Al Bowlly, emerged to become star solo performers. Another convention was that of the rhythm group, sometimes used to support well-known vocalists, but then establishing themselves in their own right. In 1934 Jack Hylton, so the legend runs, was in the USA, where he met a struggling quartet called the Riff Brothers, doubtless in an attempt to trade on the label of the already well-known Mills Brothers, who were to be their chief rivals in this field. Inspired by a messy desk blotter, he proposed the Inkspots as their name. These four American black men were given a chance by Jack Hylton on the British variety circuit and they also did moderately well back home at, for instance, the New York Paramount Theatre. In 1939 the lead singer, Jerry Daniels, fell ill, and his place was taken by the rangy tenor, Bill Kenny. At this point they abandoned their previous jazzy, even fevered approach, and, literally taking a deep breath, went to the other extreme. Their first record in this languorous style was *If I Didn't Care* and it was a smash-hit.

Apart from Bill Kenny (born in 1915), the quartet comprised the baritone and bass player, Orville 'Happy' Jones (1905-1944), Ivory 'Deek' Watson, the guitarist and occasional baritone and Charlie Fugua, on guitar and ukulele, with some tenor contribution. There were to be several changes of personnel. Kenny's brother, Herb, replaced Orville Jones while Billy Bowen replaced Ivory Watson; indeed, the lineage of the Inkspots, including two groups operating in the early 1950s, lingered on until the 1970s. Their main celebrity, however, coincided neatly with the war period. Their successors were to include groups like the Platters, but, all in all, the Inkspots could claim ascendancy in their chosen area.

The format was unfailingly familiar. A repeated guitar vamp — 'dum-dee-dee-dee; dum-dee-dee-dee; dum-dee-dee-dee-dum' — was followed by Bill Kenny's soulful melody line, his amazing range carrying into the falsetto register. Orville Jones would then pick out the lyric in a deep, half-spoken drawl, set off with typical mentions of 'honey chile' or 'honey lamb', and then it was back to a tenor reprise. The matching of featherweight and heavyweight would be disastrous in the boxing ring, but, in these close harmony routines, it was perfect. The pace was unhurried, almost drowsy; one still marvels at their audacity in singing and playing at so leisurely, even slothful, a tempo. They chose songs

exactly apposite for this consistent formula, songs that were invariably thoughtfully written, expressing poetic sentiment rather than mushy sentimentality. More often than not, the theme was one of thwarted or hopeful romantic love, with the medium ideal for the message, especially during a time when couples were split by the expediencies of war.

Maybe; Memories of you; My Prayer; I'll Never Smile Again; Address Unknown; Until the Real Thing Comes Along; Don't get Around much Anymore; Ring, Telephone, Ring; We Three (my echo, my shadow and me); *Someone's Rocking my Dream-boat; Do I Worry?* — the titles tell their own tale of romantic frustration and aspiration. Few will need reminding that their two best hits were *Whispering Grass* and *Bless you for Being an Angel.*

THE ANDREWS SISTERS (LaVerne, 1911-1967; Maxene, 1916-1995; Patti, born 1918, all born near Minneapolis, Minnesota, USA)

Apart from ethnic background, the Andrews Sisters were the converse of the Inkspots in every way. They were female and they were hectic in pace. Where the Inkspots were soporific, the Andrews Sisters were exhausting. Their vigorous delivery of swinging close harmony numbers at fairly high pitch was as satisfying as it was fatiguing, and they were simply the most successful female group ever, as their world record sales of over 60 million indicate. On this side of the Atlantic there were imitators, such as the

Cavendish Three, while, a little later and more sedately, the Beverley Sisters were to enjoy some fame, particularly with their song, *Sisters*. Even later, the Supremes, of Diana Ross association, might be seen as cultural descendants.

With the youngest sibling, Patti, acting as lead singer and soloist, the Andrews Sisters began their joint careers in the 1930s, fronting American bands like those of Larry Rich and Leon Belasco. A new manager, Lou Levy, who later married Maxene, directed them down the road of recording in their own right, with a terrific first hit in 1938, *Bei mir Bist du Schon*, from a 1933 Yiddish song. Then they recorded *Hold Tight, Hold Tight* and an Americanised version of an old Czech melody which, as *Roll out the Barrel* ('the Beer barrel polka') thus became one of World War II's most popular tunes. There followed a wide dissemination of their singing, with film playing a great part. They appeared with the Ritz Brothers and Abbott and Costello: it was whilst in the latter's *Buck Privates* that they launched their tremendous success, *Boogie Woogie Bugle Boy*. In the morale-boosting film, *Hollywood Canteen*, they offered another big hit, *Don't Fence me in*.

Riding on the first incursions of hotter swing rhythms into popular dance music, they mixed commercial boogie-woogie, often souping up old ballads, like *I'll be with you in Appleblossom Time*, with novelty numbers like *I, yi, yi, yi, yi, I like you very much*. Accompanied as a rule by the Vic Schoen orchestra, they had success after success, and they shrewdly partnered other artists along this affluent path — Burl Ives in *Blue Tail Fly*; Danny Kaye in *Woody Woodpecker*; Carmen Miranda in *Cuanto la Gusta* are examples.

They found a particularly rich vein in collaboration with Bing Crosby. *Pistol Packin' Mama; Is you is or is you ain't my Baby; Accentuate the Positive; Jingle Bells* and *Sparrow in the Tree Top* may be listed among these. They continued to bump near the top of the charts with recordings like *Says my Heart; Say si si; Beat me, Daddy, Eight to the Bar* and *Straighten up and fly right*.

In 1953, Patti's solo career led to the virtual disintegration of the trio's efforts, although there were to be occasional appearances both solo and together, and Patti visited England as late as 1990. War-time nostalgia and genuine talent combined to keep their names and work alive. For most of the generation that recalls their frenetic but impeccably expressed output, the abiding image must be from film, with the slim-built, smiling Andrews Sisters, clad in American service uniform, clustered about the microphone, heads pressed close and touching, intensely concentrating on the harmonies of *Boogie Woogie Bugle Boy* or *Don't Fence me in*.

 DONALD PEERS (Donald Peers, 1909-1973, born Ammanford, Dyfed, Wales)

Donald Peers didn't have much going for him paternally. Although he learned singing in his typically Welsh Sunday school, his father was a member of the Plymouth Brethren, so suspicious of showbiz sinfulness that he never watched his son perform; and he was also a brawny colliery worker who probably found his son's sentimental ballads a trifle effete. Little wonder that, marked down in the serious Welsh convention of the day to be a school-teacher, he ran away — not at first in any glamorous direction but, more mundanely, to be a house-painter and a steward on a tanker. There was little here to presage later stardom, but, in the mid-1920s Donald Peers found a more satisfying billet as singer in a concert party, *Tons of Fun* at Lowestoft. He made his first broadcast in 1927 with the comedy duo, Clapham and Dwyer, but his bookings were patchy. It was an appearance on the BBC *Music Hall* programme in 1933 that really established him as a capable performer in regular work, including a lengthy contract with the commercial station, Radio Normandie. After war service — he was invalided out of the army on D-Day — he quickly picked up the reins of his career with Blackpool shows and top-of-the-bill variety, with his first radio series, *Cavalier of Song* in 1947.

It was now that Donald Peers abruptly shot from minor to major stardom. He had a record 52 week radio series, broadcast live, during which the audience reaction was phenomenal. It led to bill-topping London Palladium dates, a one-man show, unknown for a variety artist to attempt, at the Royal Albert Hall in 1949, and, in general, almost unbelievable success. This was characterised, both during his broadcasts from the Kilburn Empire and elsewhere when he toured, by scrimmages of screaming, swooning girls exhibiting the most fervent homage. It was reminiscent of the bobby-soxer response the young Frank Sinatra had already invoked in the USA and, of course, for Johnnie Ray, the 'crying' singer and other later pop stars that treatment would become par for the show-business course. But, apart from the unusual nature of the reaction, Donald Peers was very much the

middle-brow trader in straightforward balladry without the obvious makings of a heart-throb. But heart-throb he became, so much so that the press ran articles like 'is Donald Peers a menace?' and sent psychiatrists to witness these Salem-like antics. By and large, the view was taken that, even if 'the stories of girls going into trances might easily be true', there was little unhealthy about his singing. Although this hectic furore did not last too many years, Donald Peers kept the attention and affection of the public for a very long time, his last hit being *Please don't go* in 1968.

In fact, perhaps the best way to recall Donald Peers is simply to jot down some of the standards he made famous. These include *I can't begin to tell You; Powder your Face with Sunshine; Lavender Blue; Clancy Lowered the Boom; Down in the Glen; I'll String Along with You; Music, Music, Music; If I'd have known you were coming I'd have baked a cake; Enjoy Yourself; Dearie; Dear Hearts and Gentle People*, and his Coronation special, *In a Golden Coach*. Donald Peers must occasionally have wondered whether some of his father's evangelical zeal had rubbed off on him, as, in his pleasingly modulated voice and unassuming manner, he yet again began his renowned signature tune, *In a Shady Nook* — and everyone joined in, 'by a babbling brook'.

Billy Bennett

Robb Wilton

Bob Hope

Jimmy James

Hylda Baker

Sandy Powell

Ken Dodd

Max Miller

Murray and Mooney

Norman Evans

Laugh And The World Laughs With You
Ten Comedy Favourites

Our period, that is, from the early beginnings of radio and 'talkies' to the breakthrough of television, roughly places the short history of 'variety' in a sort of chronological parenthesis. The child of the purer music hall, it was maimed by 'wireless' and cinema (although there was some reciprocal benefit as radio 'names' topped theatre bills and attracted listeners to see them) and then slaughtered by the telly. Variety was an apposite label. Although music hall had had its fair share of out-of-the-way acts, it had never been so varied as variety, where there were singers, comics, speciality turns, animal acts, magicians, ventriloquists, dancers, instrumentalists, old Uncle Tom Cobleigh and all. The music hall had been more uniform, with the performers adopting familiar characters and singing familiar songs, interspersed with patter. The variety bill was composed of a *mélange* of different turns. Moving around individually, they formed and re-formed bills at theatres all over the country, although,

latterly, 'road shows' became common, with a top-liner keeping the same supporting acts in regular assistance.

Generally speaking, it was the comedians who topped the bills and there were often two or three comics on each bill. This usage of 'comedian' dated from about the first world war. Hitherto 'comedian' had meant comic actor, the counterpart of 'tragedian' on the legitimate stage. Now it came to refer to the stand-up comic artist, who might use music, traditionally, ending 'with a song', but who depended almost wholly on jokes and monologues. They were not all single turns. There were double acts, like Flanagan and Allen, and there were 'sketch' comedians, like Will Hay, with two or more help-meets to help him. Idle sociological writing has sometimes argued that comedians are subversive, disruptive of established authority. One or two — the later American satirist, Lenny Bruce, for example — may have made this ideological essay, but it was far from being the norm, if only for the pragmatic reason that capitalist theatre managements would scarcely have submitted to paying good money to those who sought their downfall. Indeed, the general run of comedians has been rather conservative politically (the socialist Tony Hancock possibly being an unsurprising exception) for they have essentially been self-made men, re-selling their commercial product alone and twice-nightly.

Their social role has rather been that of community jesters, deflecting attention away from bothersome issues by making fun of them, not increasing awareness with a view to forceful remedy. During the depressed years before World War II and in the adverse circumstances of its aftermath, there was plenty of scope for comedians who could relieve the agony of the socio-economic condition with well-directed banter about it. In fact, many of the songs of the old-time music hall artists were more politically astringent than the jokes of the variety comedians: think of Gus Elen's complaint about rapid over-development in *If it wasn't for the 'ouses in between* or Albert Chevalier's bitter denunciation of the segregation of married couples in the workhouse in *My Old Dutch*.

Nine out of ten of these social lightning conductors profiled in the following pages are men, and that is arithmetically correct. Such a masculine preponderance raised the contemporary question as to whether women could be comic artists, a query which neglected the sublime reign of many queens of comedy in the music hall. What is more, they were often lovely women, the sex symbols of their day, artistes like Marie Lloyd, Lottie Collins, Ada Reeve, Vesta Tilley and Florrie Forde. Somehow this mix of comicality and sensuality vanished, and the few women comedians of the variety era followed in the bizarre footsteps of Nellie Wallace, 'the essence of eccentricity', and portrayed themselves in charlady or browbeaten drab fashion, after the manner of Suzette Tarri or Elsie and Doris Waters. In a succinct phrase, they tended to play dame in panto, whereas their predecessors had played principal boy, all buxom thighs and tights. But it was not that handsome comediennes had disappeared. They had become upwardly mobile, with performers like Beatrice Lillie moving into revue and cabaret, while it was Hollywood that inherited the concept of glamorous comedy in a fulsome descent from Mae West to Marilyn Monroe. Fortunately, the last decade or so has witnessed a return of the British comedienne who is quick-witted and not dowdy: Victoria Wood, for example, looks set to become one of the most inventive and perceptive of post-war comedians.

There were opportunities galore for comedians during variety's golden — variety's only — age. London alone had over 40 variety theatres and the most unprepossessing township might probably boast a weekly variety programme. It was not unknown for people to buy the local Monday paper in a moderately-sized urban area and plan their visitations to six nearby theatres over the week. In turn, this meant that comedians could hone one or two routines close to perfection, for it might be 18 months or two years before they returned to an individual theatre, so lengthy were the circuits. The great comedians were superb artists, understandably reluctant to deploy on radio and, more especially, on TV a life-time's professional accomplishment and see it swallowed up forever in their voracious maw — one night of television watchers might have been the equivalent of ten years of 'live' audiences. Bob Hope was not being disrespectful when he said that 'television is the box they buried entertainment in'.

In effect, TV has never been a happy hunting ground for the stand-up comic, usually reliant on the high-risk strategy of a response from a large audience to maintain their waggish attack. In the wake of Tony Hancock's superb adoption of the sit-com formula, television comedy has more resorted to actors, with talents like Arthur Lowe as Captain Mainwaring in *Dad's Army,* Ronnie Barker as 'Fletch' in *Porridge*, Warren Mitchell as Alf Garnett, David Jason as Del-boy Trotter and Leonard Rossiter as Rigsby in *Rising Damp* being exceptional illustrations. Morecambe and Wise were the rule-proving exceptions, who, after initial flops on TV, determined always to be, with brilliant success, the familiar 1930s/1940s double act, rather than to find a new format for television — hence their concentration on a stage setting, with their hilarious tomfoolery, for instance, with the theatre drapes, a constant reminder of their roots. Otherwise, one might say that, in the gifted hands of David Jason and company, 'comedian' has returned to its former definition of comic actor.

However, the ten comedians described hereafter represent a dedicated freemasonry of highly skilled craft-persons, each a genuine architect of comedy.

 BILLY BENNETT (William Bennett, 1887-1942, born Glasgow)

Billy Bennett built the perfect bridge from music hall to variety. The son of one half of a slapstick double act, Bennett and Martell, who, as a youngster made his first stage appearance as the back end of a panto cow, Billy Bennett was a 'canteen' comic and member of the Shellfire concert party. Just as the second world war produced its quota of bright new comedians, so did its grim predecessor, the Great War. But he also coupled the two disciplines by being a 'cod' monologist. In the old music hall, especially as it sought respectability, the serious narrative monologue, often a tale of valour with a flavour of Empire, had a regular place. The employment of a melodramatic reciter, pulling out all the oracular stops, was a cheap way of introducing a touch of *gravitas*, and the poems of Robert Service, George R Sims and Milton Hayes were much in demand — Rudyard Kipling, for instance, did very well out of the frequent use of his *The Absentminded Beggar*. Billy Bennett parodied these; indeed, in Billy Bennett's younger days an unfortunate actor might have declaimed the original earlier in the bill.

The titles of his lampoons, which he mainly wrote himself, included *It is Christmas day in the Cook-house; The Green Tie on the Little Yellow Dog* and *The Charge of the Tight Brigade*. He stuck quite closely to the original story-line but introduced a completely irrational, often impolite, version. It was nonsense of a Lewis Carroll kind, although, of course, much earthier, but, like Lewis Carroll's parodies, Billy Bennett's heavily relied upon the listener knowing the subject under attack. Attack is a good word for Billy Bennett's approach. His well-known bill-matter was 'Almost a Gentleman', and, in illustration of his shabby gentility, his garb was either too roomy — the baggy trousers — or too scanty — the curling shirt-front — while his bulging face and 'Old Bill' moustache added to this picture of clown-cum-hobo. In imitation of the old monologue actors, he roared out his own narratives with an air of accusatory defiance, with grotesque linguistics and rude *doubles entendres* liber-ally scattered throughout. Every verse ended with a thumping, rhyming punch, marked by a double 'boom boom' from the bass drum in the orchestra pit, a device which, many years later, younger souls innocently believed Basil Brush had invented. Sometimes it was songs that received the treatment, like his tat-tooed edition of *The Road to Mandalay*: 'On his back's he's got Calcutta; lower down he's got Bombay/And you'll see him sitting peace-fully on the Road to Mandalay'.

His guying was bellicose, absurd and laugh-able, and it carried him through a vigorous career bridging the two wars, from his first deployment of the 'cod' monologue in 1919 to his death, during a Blackpool booking, in 1942. Others have followed him: Ken Dodd's more surreal moments, especially in his own skits on *The Road to Mandalay* or *The Flo-ral Dance*; Ron Moody, that ebullient Fagin in the musical *Oliver!*, with his *The Face on the Bar-room Floor*; or Tommy Cooper, who, as well as being the greatest of the 'cod' con-jurors, also entertained with his many-hatted, pub-based monologue. Yet, for all this brag-gart nonsense, Billy Bennett was several times decorated for bravery in the 1914-1918 war. It is no bad epitaph to have fought valiantly for one's country and then to have amused it for over 20 years.

 **MAX MILLER** (Thomas Henry Sargent, 1894-1963, born Brighton)

The fact that 'the Cheeky Chappie' was born, lived and died in Brighton is somehow suitable. It was sea-side resort maligned in those times as the locus for 'a dirty week-end', with an unconvincing 'Smith' on the hotel register and a pair of co-respondent shoes at the bedroom door. Max Miller, the finest front-clothcomedian ever, for, on his own candid admission, 'there'll never be another', wholeheartedly embraced that dubious image. Where George Formby was nature's window-cleaner, pruri-ently sneaking a glance at underwear and bath-rooms, Max Miller has been called 'the eternal commercial traveller', a 'Popular Jack' figure, flirting and canoodling with the girls and offering a salubrious account of his spicy adventures to the covetous men.

His adopted cockney twang and cordial assault on the sensibilities gave him an admired reputation for blueness, although, in action, he was more the master of the sug-gestive and the unspoken than a crude blurter-out of crudity. Interestingly, his great hero was G H Elliott, 'The Chocolate Col-oured Coon'; bill-posting that would hardly be permitted in a more politically correct age. His black-face performance of songs like *The Silvery Moon* and *Lily of Laguna* was a tiny vignette of white-suited, dapper charm, and Max Miller, resplendent in his outrageous rig of plus-fours, multicoloured tie and dazzling white hat, never forgot G H Elliott's secret of being smartly-dressed and nimble-footed. Max Miller chirruped his *risqué* ditties and he tripped his jaunty dance-steps — 'give me a touch-up with the wire brushes' was his ambivalent request to the pit drummer, as he went into the splits, but only so far, then, 'half tonight; half tomorrow night' was the explanation. John Osborne said that when the orchestra struck up the opening bars of his lead-in music, *Mary from the Dairy*, it was 'an overture to danger'.

Peacock-strutting, blue-eyed and impudently smiling, he made a special appeal to the women-folk — 'what if I am, lidy, what if I am?' is his introductory and plaintive query as they welcome his gaudy entrance. Then he is off — ''ere a minute, lidy, 'ere a minute' on his insistent, confidential tap-room *reverie*. He records how, alone with a girl in the woods, he inquires whether she believes in the hereafter, which he raunchily defines as 'if you're not hereafter what I'm hereafter, you'll be hereafter I've gone'. Invited to her flat by another, he reflects, 'well, it was raining outside, and there are only two things to do when it's raining, and I don't play cards...'Ere'. He regales us with descriptions of the bow-legged dairy-maid, who is 'out on pleasure bent' and who 'can't keep her calves together'. Finally, to the song, often recounting how he 'fell in love with Mary from the dairy', and into the dance — 'goin' rahnd, lidy, goin' rahnd; I don't get giddy, do I?'. No pretension; no message; no sentiment; just wicked unclean fun, delivered with the accuracy of an expert machine gunner. Some comedians, like Max Miller with a London base, adopted a kind of pseudo-Chaplinesque pathos, after the manner of Norman Wisdom

or Charlie Drake, but not 'the Cheeky Chappie'. His presence was always that of the brash, self-assured but essentially likeable rogue; like a good book, you couldn't put him down. Everyone will recall any number of comedians who similarly cracked jokes with enormous *brio*, but few doubt that, from his beginnings in a Brighton concert party to the mournful days when the variety theatres closed, Max Miller was the king of them all.

 SANDY POWELL (Arthur Powell, 1900-1982, born Rotherham)

Amid a host of northern-born comedians, like Frank Randle ('thirty-six burps to the bottle; ah'll sup it if it keeps me up all night) or Albert Modley ('me eyes are goin' funny; I keep runnin' into pubs') let us examine the long career of Sandy Powell as representative of a compound of several variety traditions. A droll stage act for many years, without quite the pulling power of the really top-class names, he contrived to establish himself in differing fashions. He was very much in demand when it came to summer shows, eventually, through year-on-year appearances in what became his adopted home-town, earning the sobriquet 'Mr Eastbourne'. Then he found an outlet in records, and, incredibly, sold seven million of those heavy black discs, having first had the prescience to opt for a small royalty rather then a fee. *The Lost Policeman*, with its constant, sorrowing refrain of 'our Herbert's fallen in the river' was the leading seller among them. Borrowing on years of stage experience, he was a success on radio, where his 'wireless'

cry of 'can you hear me, mother' soon became one of the most famed catch-phrases in entertainment history. He was in a rough-hewn film or two, like the 1948 *Cup-tie Honeymoon,* and ultimately he did television and club work.

Bespectacled, beneficent, unhurried in approach and voice, his face cherubic with that most expansive of smiles, he was, fundamentally, a burlesque comic, more often than not with his wife, Kay White, as his assistant. Before the heady days of Tommy Cooper, Sandy Powell aped the nonchalant, dinner-jacketed magician, with tricks going awry to his barely concealed dismay. Perhaps better remembered, because it was the sketch he did most late on in life, will be his travesty of the ventriloquist. The actual 'vent' he had in his sights was the premier exponent of that minor science, the redoubtable Arthur Prince (1881-1942) who, unusually for a speciality turn, topped the bills before and after the Great War, in music hall and in variety, for some half a century. His dummy was Jim, a somewhat insolent sailor boy, with Arthur Prince in the uniform of a naval officer. He is reputed to be the first ventriloquist to smoke and drink with the dummy 'speaking', and, true to the esoteric nature of that mysterious craft, Jim was buried with him. Other 'vents' of the same era were Fred Russell (Val Parnell's father, incidentally) and Coster Joe, Coram and Jerry, Johnson Clark and Hodge, and Arthur Worsley and Johnny Green. The last is said to have been the most technically proficient and there is an apocryphal story that, when broadcasting, a BBC engineer asked him to move the dummy nearer the mike.

Sandy Powell and his extremely collapsible dummy dressed, not in naval, but in military costume, whilst he wore a large moustache to mask the moving lips. 'And where do you come from, my little man?' he would ask, but, when the dummy found trouble pronouncing Wolverhampton, he would suggest, 'couldn't you make it Leeds?'. Towards the end of his career, especially when abroad or playing some of the tougher 'club' venues, he found that some audience members were either too drunk, too youthful or, one is forced to consider, too unintelligent to realise that he was a 'cod' and not an inefficient ventriloquist. He had a Delphic response to the inebriated hecklers who shouted brusquely, 'I can see your lips moving'. 'Ah yes', he would observe, 'but only when the dummy's talking'.

 ROBB WILTON (Robert Smith, 1881-1957, born Liverpool)

Mention Robb Wilton in practically any group of older people and immediately the right hand of one or two will reach to the face, for the little finger to be reflectively chewed and the other digits to drum a mixed emotional beat on the cheek, prior to the lugubrious announcement of that still durable opening line . . . 'the day war broke out . . .' . A stationary, pale-faced, stolid figure on stage, the flickering fingers and gyrating tongue the sole signs of animation, Robb Wilton soon became an accomplished radio as well as variety star, with his melancholy discourses on petty officialdom, particularly during World War II, bringing much wry solace to the populace.

Over his career, 'the Confidential Comedian', seeking the advantage of his early acting experience and presaging the comic character acting of current TV situation comedy, produced four classic sketches. One was as Mr Muddlecombe J P, fussily adjudicating in *The Court of Not-so-Common Pleas*. Another was as the police sergeant, coping unsurely with the *distrait* self-confessed murderess, played by his wife, Florence Palmer, when, as he can't find the requisite form, he wonders whether she could call back tomorrow. A third is at the fire station, this time with Florence Palmer distraught at his lethargy in mounting an attempt to extinguish her burning home. 'It's a prettier run', he obligingly explains, as she frets over the rather indirect route he plans for the fire engine. Lastly, there is his monologue of the home guardsman, exasperated over the chilly demeanour of his wife, Rita, itself a sidelong peep at the sex-goddess, Rita Hayworth. It is she who, on the outbreak of war, insists he must find work; there is a pregnant pause, followed by the ruminative, 'ee, she's a cru-ell ton-guer, that woman'. It is she who is contemptuous of his capacity to identify the Fuhrer, should Hitler land; 'doesn't she know I've got a ton-guer in me head?', he mutters irritably. It is she who chafes him about the fortuitous martial strategy whereby the home guard are headquartered in a little hut behind the Dog and Pullet. Like Al Read, Robb Wilton made his wife his chief critic, in his case the sniffy demonstrator of his pettifogging inactivity.

All these melancholy proceedings were discussed in a gruffly, deliberate tone, and Robb Wilton deservedly earned the reputation of being the best 'timer' in the business. Listening to him on tape today, one can but marvel that he could dare to contemplate his delivery with such slow-burning composure. As the cocker of snooks at minor bureaucracy, he was in the immediate lineage of Wilkie Bard's policeman, George Robey's mayor and the school-master of his contemporary, Will Hay. Against a larger canvas, he might modestly claim to stand in descent from Shakespeare's watchman, Dogberry, in 'Much Ado about Nothing', Gogol's 'the Inspector General' and Dickensians such as Mr Bumble, the Beadle in *Oliver Twist*. His ghost need not shrink from joining such elevated company.

Unlike several comedians, he was equally droll off-stage. He once stood in the wings of a variety theatre, eyeing a Far Eastern family of acrobats go through their paces. Perspiring freely, they negotiated a series of energetic and torturous routines, leaping, somersaulting, cart-wheeling, pyramid-making, hoop-jumping, hand-standing . . . 'And all because', Robb Wilton murmured, 'the buggers are too lazy to learn a comic song'.

 JIMMY JAMES (James Casey, 1892-1965, born Stockton-on-Tees, Durham)

Jimmy James was the funniest comedian of them all. That is not just a personal opinion. It is a semi-official judgement, for he was widely known as 'the comedian's comedian'. Whenever he appeared, other comics would stand and admire, night after night, in the wings or visit the theatre just to see that one turn. There is little film or television coverage of him, and he did not always play the leading dates. He was an independently-minded man who did not always see eye to eye with lofty impresarios, although, on occasion, he saved London Palladium shows when big names were failing. An inveterate gambler, he also liked to plan his schedule in accordance with local race meetings: bankrupted three times, he wondered aloud, at the third such happening, whether he had won the official receiver outright. Nonetheless, he was one of the seminal artists of the 20th century, for a long line of comedians, as unlike him and as unlike one another as Peter Sellers and Tony Hancock, admitted their debt to him.

He had bemused, doughy features and ruminative spaniel-like eyes; his voice was husky and inquiring; and, eternally, there was his one tiny prop, the swinging arc of his cigarette, the long inhalation and then the peculiar puffing out, like a series of small smoke signals. A 'sketch' comedian, he had three mainstays. The first was a drunk cameo, in effect, three variations on the theme, namely, *The Spare Room; The First Night;* and *Sober as a Judge.* Himself an abstainer, Jimmy James was probably the finest inebriate the theatre has known. He had hit upon a simple devastating truth. Most actors or comics just pretend to be tipsy, but Jimmy James sensed that drunkards are unaware of their alcoholic condition, and his interpretation was based on that premise. The second was *The Shoebox,* where he was accompanied in an exercise in lunatic logic by his stooges, Bretton Woods and Hutton Conyers, variously played by his nephew Jack 'Eli' Casey, his son, Cass James, later a most successful BBC light entertainment producer, the multi-talented Roy Castle, and others. The shoe-box

was full of jungle animals — 'I thought I could hear a rustling', Jimmy James would disarmingly observe — and there followed a conversation-piece which veered, second by second, from the everyday to the bizarre. They would finish with a song, such as *Kisses Sweeter than Wine,* prefaced by a set of yelping 'fah, fah, fahs' as they struggled to find the note. The third, first presented at the 1953 Royal Command Performance, was *The Chipster',* whose vocational hazards, the loss of digits, 'the batterer's elbow', and, the consequence of sizzling fat, 'the permanent wink', eventually led to an exceedingly camp appearance.

From the moment his entrance music, *Three O'clock in the Morning,* played, audiences relaxed to enjoy their connoisseur's treat, for, despite adhering to his major themes, Jimmy James, like the painter with a preponderant style, approached them afresh each evening. There was an alteration here; a *nuance* there; a slowing of tempo; a quickening of response. Robb Wilton and Jimmy James each claimed, in a lovely exchange of compliments, that the other was the best 'waiter' in the business. As Jimmy James so perceptively remarked, the true comedian is 'a man who says things funnily, not a man who says funny things'.

NORMAN EVANS
(Norman Evans, 1901-1962, born Rochdale)

A *protégé* of his fellow-townswoman, Gracie Fields, Norman Evans rose swiftly to become, in the view of many pundits, the best pantomime 'dame' ever. That is a colossal claim when one remembers that the comical genius, Dan Leno, was 'dame' at Drury Lane every Christmas from 1888 to 1903 to critical and popular applause. The male 'dame' convention was sustained by other stars, such as Wilkie Bard (*I Want to Sing in Opera*) and G S Melvin (*I'm Happy when I'm Hiking*), right through to the relishable doom-laden homilies of Les Dawson, in what was an affectionate re-moulding of the Norman Evans 'dame'. They both deployed the prudish device of framing indecorous phrases — 'she's had it all taken away' — without sound, in part a reflection of the mill-girls' need to lip-read over the noise of the looms.

Another lineage of 'dames', including artists like Douglas Byng (*Doris, the Goddess of Wind*) and the dazzling Danny la Rue, opted for a more glamorous approach, but Norman Evans and his ilk were fundamentally northern matriarchs, flexibly gummy, unstoppably gossipy and red-wigged under a mob-cap. To see him baking in the panto kitchen scene was a revelation, especially when, on the unannounced arrival of king or emperor, 'she', in embarrassment, converted unbaked scones and rolling pin into a billiards game. Another famous protagonist of the harridan 'dame' was, of course, Old Mother Riley, that is, Arthur Lucan, with his wife, Kitty McShane, the ever-unpunctual daughter. They made several films which were very popular, particularly at children's matinees, but, unfortunately, their stage sketch, *Bridget's Night Out*, with its furious argument and volley of broken crockery, too closely mirrored their spectacular off-stage rows, leaving it a moot point as to whether or not art imitated nature.

Norman Evans had no such problems, as he maintained his bill-topping grip, with panto dates at all the classiest theatres, including the Palladium and the London Coliseum. He is best known for his 'Over the garden wall' routine, where, as Fanny Fairbottom, he exchanged confidences with an invisible neighbour, with lots of 'ooohs', 'ahhhhs' and ''as she's', and with 'her' jutting bosom — 'that's the third time on the same brick' — constantly damaged as she slipped. A strict watch was kept on the amatory coal-man — 'it doesn't take thirty-five minutes to deliver two sacks of nutty slack' — while the tom-cat — 'I could smell it in t'custard a'Sunday' — was another bane of mill-town existence. Norman Evans had three other comical lines to peddle. He conducted an absorbing solo examination of the tribulations of a visit to the dentist, from fearful wait to agonised extraction. He had a timid panda glove puppet which took a great deal of persuasion to climb from his pocket and play the trumpet. In concert with that diminutive bundle of effervescence, Betty Jumel, he would both embark on a 'cod' brass band performance and, she as the bantam tenor, he as the gigantic soprano, participate in a duet of *The Pipes of Pan*, their sheet-music, under pressure, becoming fish and chip portions.

From Blackpool Central Pier summer shows to Bradford Alhambra pantomimes, as well as plentifully on radio, Norman Evans pursued his tittle-tattling way. What could be more mordant than his constructive advice when sick-visiting a neighbour: 'shouldn't you have yer bed moved downstairs; they'll never get a coffin round this landing'.

BOB HOPE (Leslie Townes Hope, 1903- , born Eltham, London)

Let us celebrate the impact of fast-talking American humour upon our indigenous brand with a pen-picture of its finest protagonist, English-born Bob Hope, who went to the USA aged four, grew up in Cleveland, and was awarded an honorary knighthood in 1998, in chief for years of entertaining troops. The USA navy's second largest ship is named after him, but, despite his long marriage to Dolores and their four adopted children, he also has a less than secret reputation as a serial philanderer.

Discovered by Fatty Arbuckle, he worked his way from being a vaudeville song-and-dance man to radio and Broadway parts, not least when he partnered the leather-lunged Ethel Merman in *It's De-lovely* in Cole Porter's *Red, Hot and Blue* revue. 1938 was his breakthrough year. He was given his own radio show and he made his first feature film, *The Big Broadcast of 1938,* in which he introduced, with the help of Shirley Ross, the tune that was indelibly to become his identity-song, *Thanks for the Memory.* Thereafter it was a non-stop, life-long wealth of radio, film, stage and television extravaganza that made Bob Hope, so it is opined, 'the most wealthy entertainer who has ever lived'. His pleasant, unassuming vocals and uncomplicated dancing meant he was always useful in musical films like *Star-spangled Rhythm* (1942) or *The Seven Little Foys* (1955), while his catchy *Buttons and Bows* in the 1948 movie, *The Paleface* won an Oscar as surely as *Thanks for the Memory* had. His 'Road' films with Bing Crosby, with whom he swapped career-long friendly insults

(although they were not too close off set) and the sarong-clad Dorothy Lamour, made him especially popular in Britain. On radio, as well as on screen, notably in films like the comedy-thriller, *The Cat and the Canary* (1939) or *My Favourite Spy* (1951), he was the blustering coward, over-aware of his ski-slope nose, and always keen to grab the girl. As a comedian, he was the easy master of the wisecrack, the sparkling unbarbed one-liner, rarely risking the complexities of the anecdote. To arm him for this barrage of facetious shellfire, he was surrounded by a regiment of artillery, munitions workers in the guise of script-writers — 88 of them over the last 50 years, the creators of over a million gags. This was the fashion for American radio, with others such as pouch-eyed and cleverly satiric Fred Allen, the durably philosophic, cigar-puffing George Burns with the incorrigible Gracie Allen, and Jack Benny. Jack Benny adopted stinginess as his abiding characteristic and he was a skilled, composed 'timer' of material.

F J Turner, the American historian and purveyor of the concept of 'the Vanishing Frontier' (the way in which American internal colonisation gradually drove the border westward to the Pacific coast) urged that the resultant human melting pot gave rise in American culture to the 'vital entertainer'. Mark Twain was an example of this animated, vigorous style; Bob Hope was another. The British had to respond, and *ITMA* itself was inspired by the quick-fire American mode, while Tommy 'You lucky people' Trinder had some of that knowing flair. Perhaps the key English individual to model himself thus was Ted Ray (1906-1977), who wore, unusually for those days, a lounge suit, crackled away in a mid-Atlantic accent, and hosted the hugely successful *Ray's a Laugh* radio series for twelve years from 1949. A last word, however, from Bob Hope: 'the girls call me Pilgrim, because every time I dance with one, I make a little progress'.

 HYLDA BAKER (Hilda Baker, 1905-1986, born Farnworth, Bolton)

Hylda Baker was probably the hardiest plant among the few women who challenged the comic dominion of men on the variety stage. She forms a link between Nellie Wallace (1870-1948), a grotesque of staggering man-hungry proportions (*My mother said, always look under the bed*) and Beryl Reid (1919-1996), who, after creating the knowing school-girl, Monica, and the Birmingham-based Marlene on radio, flourished as a fine film and theatre actress. Both played 'dame' in panto, Nellie Wallace being one of the first female 'dames', and Hylda Baker normally cast as Widow Twankey. She made her debut at, of all unlikely places, Tunbridge Wells, at the age of ten in the middle of the Great War. She struggled and fought for another 30-odd years, being one of the first women to manage her own touring shows, such as the salaciously-titled *Bearskins and Blushes*, an example of the purportedly exotic revues that marked the end of variety's battle for survival.

It was the 1950s, close to the finish of our period, before Hylda Baker became an established star, with big Christmas and summer dates and with, crucially, an over-night triumph in 1955 on *The Good Old Days*

television programme. For a decade or so she realised all her heart-felt ambitions. Later there followed her long-running TV series as Nelly Pledge in *Nearest and Dearest* (1968-1973), which involved a long-running a feud, one that became a show-biz legend, with her co-star and on-screen brother in their pickle factory, Jimmy Jewel, who for years beforehand had shared with Ben Warriss in a likeable double act. Hylda Baker was also to take cameo roles in films, as, for instance, Aunt Ada in *Saturday Night and Sunday Morning* (1960) and Mrs Sowerberry in *Oliver!* (1968). However, she will be long remembered for her comic routine with the silent, bean-pole friend Cynthia, played over the years by many male actors. Barely five feet in height, but full of determined grit and homespun counsel, Hylda Baker, with her capacious hand-bag and uncontrollable feather boa, would launch bossily into a string of thundering Malapropisms. 'The condescension was running down the walls', she would declare, or, indignantly, 'no one has dallied with my afflictions and I say that without fear of contraception'. These nuggets of wisdom would be confided to the mute, omniscient Cynthia, drawing from Hylda Baker the admiring assessment, a phrase that is enshrined in the lore of variety, 'she knows, y'know'. Next time you see Victoria Wood on television, particularly when she is the grinning, not very intelligent young woman, looking for her friend, Kimberley — ''ave you seen 'er?' — and you will observe some affectionate memorial to Hylda Baker. Some will also recall and note a likeness in the externally prim cockney mum of Rex Jameson's Mrs Shufflewick, with her bedraggled fur ('untouched pussy; practically unobtainable in the West End of London) and with her excuse of 'I've always been weak-willed and easily led'.

It is as well that her memory is preserved in such manner, for, unhappily, Hylda Baker, rendered neurotic by the ceaseless fight to preserve her professional credentials, measuring, for instance, the size of her billing on theatre posters, and the prey to ailments real and imagined, was not well-liked among her colleagues. In a business which tends to laud its heroes and heroines, it is sad to record that only five people attended her funeral.

 ## MURRAY AND MOONEY
(Harry Murray, (1891-1967; Harray Mooney, 1889-1972)

Murray would commence his monologue, 'Jack was a coward, a great big coward with a turned-up nose' or 'It's a funny old world we live in, but the world's not entirely to blame', only to be interrupted by Mooney — 'I say, I say, I say' — with some ludicrous question, such as 'how do you spell Charley?'. Murray would pause and repeat the poser, 'I don't know, how do you spell Charley?'. 'H-A-R-L-E-Y', was the curious response. 'H-A-R-L-E-Y?', quoth the baffled Murray, 'Where's the C?'. 'Just over there', came back the clincher, with a finger pointed beyond the deck-chairs, 'behind those people'. 'I don't wish to know that', cried Murray, struggling pompously to conserve his injured dignity, 'kindly leave the stage'.

Such was the rather laboured but time-honoured formula, mathematical in its exactitude, of the premier double act, for, although no one is certain Murray and Mooney invented that dispensation, everyone is convinced they should have done, in that it was truly their construct. And the oceanic tang of the example cited reminds that it was the seaside pierrot show and concert party where the cross-talk act evolved, largely fuelled by the old-time, black-face minstrel shows in which Massa Bones would wonder aloud as to why the chicken crossed the road and Massa Interlocutor would fall into the trap and invite Massa Bones to elucidate. Scott and Whaley adorned the Kentucky Minstrels in this fashion. The format reaches further back to the Italian, maybe Roman origins, of Punch and Judy, a physical and mental contest already established in Britain by the 1790s. Few approached the challenge with the ritualistic fervour of Murray and Mooney, who, by the 1930s and latterly as Mooney and King, were the leading double act throughout the United Kingdom.

Traditionally, variety shows, on stage or on radio, as in Saturday evening's *Music Hall* would start with such a double act, usually an angry straight man or stooge, tall and thin, ever failing to get the better of the funny man, short and fat. Come panto, they would be the broker's men in *Cinderella*, the Chinese policemen in *Aladdin* or, and here Jewel and Warriss deserve special praise, the Robbers in *Babes in the Wood*. The old music hall preferred the single acts, and there were only a few duos, none of them in the top-class category. Reaching a pinnacle in the potent chemistry of Morecambe and Wise, they then all but vanished, save for vestigial snipings from Cannon and Ball or Little and Large, both pairs ideal illustrations of the old-fashioned mode. In the variety years from 1920 to 1950 there were literally scores of double acts. Older folk will be able to rattle off the comical couplings: Joe and Dave O'Gorman; Naughton and Gold; Nervo and Knox; Bennett and Williams, with their phono-fiddles; Clapham and Dwyer, with Cissie the Cow; Morris and Cowley, usually as Chelsea Pensioners; Syd and Max Harrison; Collinson and Breen ('someone's pinched me pud-ding'); the Two Pirates; Hatton and Manners ('don't yer know there's a warrrr on'); Mike and Bernie Winters; Revnell and West, 'the long and short of it'; Elsie and Doris Waters; Caryll and Mundy; Nat Mills and Bobbie; Claude 'Mrs Gibson' Dampier and Billie Carlyle; Elsie and Renee Houston; Chic Murray and Maidie; Laurie Lupino Lane and George Truzzi; Max and Harry Nesbitt . . .

One last verticle and response: 'why don't elephants like penguins?' — 'because they can't get the silver paper off'. All right, you don't wish to know that, I'll kindly leave the stage.

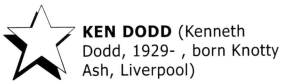 **KEN DODD** (Kenneth Dodd, 1929- , born Knotty Ash, Liverpool)

'Number ten already', one hears the disgrun-tled reader sigh, 'and no mention of Max Wall, master of excruciatingly eccentric motion and linguistics, nor of Sid Field, who, with the help of Jerry Desmonde, etched his exquisite portraitures — 'what a perform-ance!' — of the mayor's photographer or the novice golfer . . . or what about *Cleopatra's Nightmare*, the dead-pan, thin-legged, perfectly disciplined sand dance of Wilson, Keppel and Betty that so completely

captured the soul of variety?' There was such a wealth of comedy on the halls, and yet few would quibble with the choice of Ken Dodd, even if he does only just edge into our period, making his full-time professional debut in Nottingham in 1954. He is, however, the opposite of Tony Hancock, who, through radio and, critically, television, button-holed us on our settees in one and twos and con-fided in us his fears and ambitions. Ken Dodd has not needed the media to boost his fame, nor does he take naturally to it. He is the last and the greatest of the stand-up comedians, who would not be disconcerted to find him-self sharing the bill with Grimaldi or Dan Leno. Even now, he is, with Victoria Wood, the only comic guaranteed to pack the larg-est of halls again and again.

There is a kind of evangelism about his approach; like George Robey, he plays not to but with an audience. They are drawn into his comic thrall, as he hits the stage with explosive glee and unwraps a bewildering assortment of fruity humour. Both audience and performer become ever more involved; the incandescent fire-works crackle and flame; the congregation roars raucously and gasps for breath; they are temporarily eased by the intercession of a sentimental hymnal ballad, like *Tears* or *Love is like a Violin*; then the pyrotechnics begin again; until, at the last, both the customers and the apostle of mirth reach satiation; and they stumble out exhausted to seek their late-night buses. When the charismatic Ken Dodd is on soar-ing song, the epithet 'died laughing' springs to fevered mind. His hero is Al Jolson, another artist who hit the boards running, full of zest and gusto. Thus Ken Dodd's entry, in outrageous rig, tickling sticks at the ready, with hair in abstract shapes and teeth in fang-like leer, is a nuclear incident in itself. His endless material is devoted to observations on the human condition, above all, the human body. He piles absurdity upon incongruity: the mouth on top of the head so that late risers may stick a bacon sandwich in, put their hat on and rush to work; the eye on the end of the finger so that one can read under the clothes in bed — and all touching dangerously on sexual portents. 'What a wonderful day for running down the road, sticking cucumbers through the letter-box and shouting the Martians are coming' is a statement open to three interpretations of differential propriety. Known as 'the slide-rule comedian' for his detailed study of humour, and the effect of locality, weather, dress and other variables on the expectations of an audience, he has, in the Knotty Ash home of his boyhood, a treasure trove of analysis from throughout his career, as he has dedicated his life and princely talent to pressing at the frontiers of comedy.

Optimistic and fervent in his 50 weeks a year mission to spread the gospel of 'happiness', it is not unduly blasphemous to celebrate Ken Dodd as the John the Baptist of British comedy. A last example, rejoicing in his continuous *brio*. We hail him as perhaps the last and certainly one of the very best of a grand tradition: 'would you like a moonlight dip, missus? You'll have to warm your hands first'.

Billy Bennett

Flanagan and Allen

Laurel and Hardy

George Robey

Professor Jimmy Edwards

Ken Dodd

Sandy Powell

Mickey Mouse

MR. AND MRS. RAMSBOTTOM

Archie Andrews

Sexton Blake

Albert, the son of Mr and Mrs Ramsbottom

Larry the Lamb

The Scarlet Pimpernel

Just William

Dick Barton, Special Agent

COW PIE
Medium Size

Desperate Dan, still going strong after 63 years in the *Dandy*, 1938
invented by Dudley D. Watkins, for over 30 years a prolific contributor
to D C Thompson of Dundee, he did *The Broons* and *Oor Willie* for
The Sunday Post as well as pages for the *Topper* and the *Beezer*.
Besides *Lord Snooty*, he did illustrated classics such as *Oliver Twist*
and *Kidnapped*, as serials and in books

Jane one day in 1944, the strip ran in the *Daily Mirror*
from 1932 to 1959

Fictional Fame
Ten Famous Imaginary Characters

The current age needs little introduction to the potency of fictional characters. The rising foam from the 'soaps' has seen to that. The people living down Coronation Street or among the Eastenders make lurid front page headlines in the tabloid press, not with their actors' but with their characters' names being used. The identification by viewers with characters is often total. Tales abound of new babies in 'soaps' being the recipients of gifts, of wreaths being sent to the funeral of a fictional deceased, or of villains in these series being practically forced to leave the country, such is the abuse piled upon them should they be intrepid enough to take to the streets. A favourite story from some years ago tells of a character emigrating from *Coronation Street*: dozens of people wrote in asking whether they could have the tenancy of the house. That leaves a fascinating poser hanging in the air. Did they think, should they become this householder, that they would automatically be on the programme, rubbing shoulders over a pint with Jack Duckworth and Rita Sullivan in 'the Rover's Return'?

It was less intense — or was it? — and we were less gullible — or were we? — in the 1920s, 1930s and 1940s. Nonetheless, fanciful figures did sometimes catch the public imagination in much the same way as did singers or comedians or sportspersons. This section eulogises ten of these, although one or two did have real-life personifications. Some of them made a special appeal to children, but, then, many readers were youngsters during those years.

We are, of course, deliberately addressing the pre-televisual era, but the mechanical apparatus available before the 1950s was obviously making its mark. Were one to retreat in time over a hundred years, rather than just 50 years, one would have found a different order again of fictional characters. The top ten a century and more ago would have been mainly from literature, although one or two stage names — Sweeney Todd or Maria Marten of Red Barn notoriety from the gory world of melodrama or even a character, like *The Mikado's* Lord High Executioner, from the Gilbert and Sullivan *oeuvre*, might have pushed into the frame. Moreover, it is likely that some of them would have been recruited from classical literature. A Dickensian or so, such as Little Nell or Oliver Twist or Scrooge, would have been oft mentioned — and they still carry some symbolic weight in the everyday metaphor of writing and talking at the present time. Sherlock Holmes would have been another and that intellectualised sleuth is a reminder of the potent force of fiction, for there were — and are — many who believed him to be a genuine article.

By the end of the century the integrated culture of the Victorian period — the fashion in which its great communicators, like Charles Dickens, had made a cross-class and inter-generational appeal — was, sadly, lapsing. In literature and in the arts the division was widening between the populist and the *avant-garde*, and so it has continued, with only occasional radio and television entertainments — *ITMA* and *the Morecambe and Wise Show* are, respectively, positive examples — to remind us of a time when middlebrow was all the rage, with both lowbrow and highbrow much more at the margins.

Thus these ten popular illusory figures of the post-1920s phase are less 'classical' than Ebenezer Scrooge, Alice in Wonderland or Long John Silver, while, at the same time, they emanate more from radio, film and the press than from literature *per se*. Four found their chief fame on radio; one on film; three through newspaper or periodical means, and just two principally, but neither by any means exclusively, in book form. It is true that, as with other sections of the book, some thought has been given to choosing representative characters. It is likely that, had there been

some type of referendum about the popular culture at that time, there would have been more than one animated cinematic cartoon character on the voting list, so it might be argued that our list is a more mixed one than mathematical accuracy would have allowed. Basically, an attempt has been made to range over the gamut of fictional characterisation that during this period, and, in the main, solely during this period, urged itself on the public attention. Some, of course, were played by actors on radio, but, with the odd exception, it was not the same as going to the theatre or the cinema to watch a famous star enact the role of a fictional figure. The performer was secondary; not least through the excellence of his or her creation, the character existed integrally in its own right.

These are all fictional personalities taken from fiction, in that they were all in the business of telling stories or making fun. One might have turned to the advertising icons that were beginning to be household names. Sunny Jim of cereal fame or the Ovaltinies spring to mind. Government propaganda, especially during the World War II, created a number of specialist fictitious creatures, such as the nasty Squander Bug, festooned with a swastika, while there were spontaneous Kilroy-like manifestations, like the Chad character that one found chalked peering over a wall, with his 'wot, no . . . beer or petrol or fags'. . . . or whatever the shortage was. Cartoonists provided both political figments, like Low's depiction of the trade union movement as a carthorse or his satirical Colonel Blimp creation, or sporting anti-idols, like Tom Webster's 'great white hope' or the British 'horizontal heavyweight'. However pertinent, these do not quite fall into the category of those fictional characters who were involved in some form of narrative.

Perhaps this section will give rise to more controversy than others. The selections in almost all the other sections were the result of some preliminary and confessedly fairly primitive canvassing of all the hundred names. Of course, people argued that this or that name should have been included among the radio or the stage stars, for that is the nature of the 'reminiscence' game, but, with this list of fictional characters, there was rather more disagreement about the whole shape of the rota, with lots of other characters suggested and with rather more forceful reasons urged for why those included ought to be expelled. Children's literature was, interestingly, the source of several of the suggestions, with A A Milne's Christopher Robin and Arthur Ransome's nautical brood among them, while Sapper's Bulldog Drummond and Leslie Charteris's the Saint were mentioned from the ranks of adventure stories.

Turn, then, to this disputable ten. As Hughie Green was wont to say at the end of *Opportunity Knocks*, 'it's make your mind up time'.

 ## SEXTON BLAKE

To Wilkie Collins goes the honour of producing the first — and, according to T S Eliot, the best — detective novel, with *The Moonstone* in 1868. Sergeant Cuff became the first of hundreds of fictional sleuths, right through to the present day with the television deluged by loners like Dalgleish, Morse and Frost. Sherlock Holmes, of course, was the supreme example. Sir Arthur Conan Doyle's creation of the aloof egghead, violin-strumming and drug-taking, still finds himself featured on TV and film, although the stories themselves were written between 1887 and 1927. Between the wars Dame Agatha Christie (1890-1976) became 'beyond doubt the most famous detective novelist of the century', with the vain Hercule Poirot introduced in 1920 and the perceptive Miss Marple in 1930. Such ingenious plots chiefly appealed to the middle classes and their circulating libraries. The Americans shifted the angle. With Dashiell Hammett's Sam Spade and Raymond Chandler's Philip Marlowe, there was spawned another sort of solitary, the private eye or gumshoe, somehow predestined grittily to walk the mean and perilous streets.

In Britain the mantle of Sherlock Holmes was adopted and popularised by Sexton Blake. There was a sudden flood of comics in the 1890s, and the Alfred C Harmsworth press published several of these, including *Chips; Comic Cuts* (said at the height of its popularity to have had 2.5 million readers); *Wonder; Marvel* and *Union Jack*. As well as the usual school yarns and tales of martial valour, there was also a craze for the detective story, and Sexton Blake solved his first case in the *Marvel* in 1893. His progenitor was Harry Blyth (1852-1898) under his pen-name of Hal Meredith. His criminological elbows were jostled by other "tecs' like Nelson Lee and Dixon Brett, but somehow Sexton Blake was the fittest and survived for 55 years. He proved sturdy enough to stand on his own feet and the Sexton Blake Library was established, for many years with a weekly product, with subscription and postal delivery a major element. It is estimated that 200 million words were scribbled on his cases by a band of hardworking writers. In each tale he demonstrated his investigative genius and complex theorising, along with a ration of violence just a trifle more noticeable than had been found in the decorous annals of Sherlock Holmes. Sexton Blake, ascetic, percipient, his middle-aged but lean frame topped by the high forehead, piercing eyes and lantern jaw of the prototype intellectual, took on an assistant in 1904, the young, enthusiastic, open-faced and uncomplicated Tinker. Doctor Watson planted a family tree as flourishing as Sherlock Holmes'. The number two is always removed from the number one in brain-power and professional or social rank. Tinker slipped neatly into this *niche*, alongside Nelson Lee's Nipper; Dixon Brett's Pat Malone and Bill Slook; Falcon Swift's Chick Conway...and note the preference for the bisyllabic forename and the monosyllabic surname. On, then to Hercule Poirot's inane Captain Hastings; Lord Peter Wimsey's chauffeur-valet, Bunter, the creations of Dorothy L Sayers in 1923, and Morse's unprotesting Sergeant Lewis.

Although he was the subject of a few cheaply made films, Sexton Blake was overwhelmingly known through the periodical format. He rejoiced in the sobriquet of 'the office boy's Sherlock Holmes', a phrase which speaks volumes about the youth culture and employment of the age.

THE SCARLET PIMPERNEL

How we love disguise! From Shakespeare (Rosalind as Ganymede in *As You Like It*, for instance) onwards, the stage is littered with the masks of changed or hidden identity. In *Our Mutual Friend* and in the unfinished *The Mystery of Edwin Drood*, Charles Dickens relies heavily on disguise. Both *The Count of Monte Cristo* and *The Man in the Iron Mask* depend on the mystery of such deception. Moreover, we seem to harbour an especial affection for those pieces of human camouflage where the heroic shell hides an ordinary mortal like ourselves. There is nothing new about Superman, who has been inhabiting the mild frame of Clark Kent, on film and television, since his origins in press strip-cartoons in the 1930s. Danny Kaye, in *The Secret Life of Walter Mitty* (1947) and *Wonder Man* (1945), also fuelled the fantasy we all share of being the hero. It would, for instance, be stupendously satisfying to do what Rudolf Rassendyll did in Anthony Hope's spirited yarn, published in 1894, *The Prisoner of Zenda*: to have the nerve to impersonate the King of Ruritania, outwit Black Michael and Rupert of Hentzau and fall in love with the beautiful Princess Flavia.

This is the point at which Mrs Montague Barstow enters these proceedings. She is better known as Baroness Orczy, although her full roster of forenames is Emma Magdalena Rosalia Marie Josefa Barbara. Born in Hungary in 1865, she came to England at the age of 15 and grew into an admiring Anglophile. She married Montague Barstow, a fellow art student, and took up writing. She wrote *The Scarlet Pimpernel* in 1902 but it was summarily rejected by publishers, so her husband and herself dramatised the tale and it was then triumphantly published in 1905. Beginning with *I Will Repay* (1906), there were umpteen sequels, to say nothing of cinematic and allied spins-off, notably the film of 1934. With Leslie Howard as the Pimpernel, with

Merle Oberon as the delectable Lady Blakeney and with Raymond Massey as the villainous Chauvelin, thoroughly enjoying the Reign of Terror, a critic called it 'one of the most romantic and durable of all swashbucklers'. Earlier there were two silent versions, starring Dustin Farnum in 1917 and Matheson Lang in 1929, whilst David Niven took on the French Revolutionaries in 1950, followed by television interpretations, first by Marius Goring and then by Anthony Andrews. The dandified Sir Percy Blakeney, with his dainty manners and indolent habits, was the perfect pose for the razor-sharp, dedicated rescuer of Guillotine-bound *aristos*. The combine of books and films created a fictional model of sumptuous magnitude, even if, like *a Tale of Two Cities*, it offered the English a one-sided, right-wing view of the French Revolution that remains its popular image. A similar story was told in the several films about Zorro, the black-masked, sword-swishing Diego de Vega, returning from Spain and, behind the masquerade of the bored, unconcerned young fop, valiantly saving Mexican California from fell tyranny. Douglas Fairbanks, silently, in 1920 and, with rather more hullabaloo, Tyrone Power in 1940 have been the leading Zorros. The tale originated in a strip cartoon by Johnson McCullery in 1919, and the 1940 film, *the Mark of Zorro*, has been described as 'an amalgam of the Scarlet Pimpernel and Robin Hood'; Zorro is Spanish for fox.

Baroness Orczy died in 1947. 'That demned elusive' Pimpernel lives on.

MICKEY MOUSE

'The best known and most popular international figure of his day'; thus *The New York Times* on the subject of Mickey Mouse. Actually, he began life in the 1920s as Mortimer Mouse, but both his name and outline were changed so that, by the early 1930s, the sturdy, squeaky little black and white creature was a global phenomenon. He was, of course, the creation of Walt Disney, whose name became synonymous with cinematic animation and made him an icon of world popular culture. Indeed, there are only two or three others — Chaplin, say, for film; Pele for world football and Elvis Presley in the field of popular music — whom you might dare to place in the same category of planet-wide influence. Walt Disney was born in Chicago in 1901 and died in New York in 1966 and packed into those years a great substance of animated invention. He used his own voice for the initial mouse, first filmed in 1928; later Jim MacDonald and Wayne Allwinch provided the twittering vocals, as scores of cartoons came from the Disney Studio. Those short, well-paced, punchy tales amused and bewitched: it is difficult now to re-conjure the magic, even the disbelief, of watching those original essays in moving drawings. Probably Mickey Mouse's most classic performance was in 'the Sorcerer's Apprentice' episode in the excellent *Fantasia*, released in 1940. The affectionately disposed Minnie Mouse was very often by his side, while Donald Duck, irascible and squawking, appeared first in 1934 in *The Wise Little Hen*. He, too, quickly sprang to world-wide fame, as did their farmyard companions, Goofy and Pluto.

Walt Disney then turned to more ambitious projects. His *Flowers and Trees* in 1933 was the first-ever full Technicolor film, but that was but a prelude to the magnificent *Snow White and the Seven Dwarfs* (1937) that entranced public and critics alike. It was the first full-length animated cartoon film and it took 600 artists and two million drawings to produce. It was a smash-hit, second only to *Gone with the Wind* during the 1930s. People can still sing the songs and name the seven dwarfs. There followed *Pinocchio* in 1940, based on Carlo Collodi's 19th century Italian tale of the impetuous puppet, and, in 1942, the charming tear-jerker, *Bambi*, whilst *Cinderella* (1950), from the Charles Perrault fairy-tale was a further triumph. So the flow was to continue, while, in 1950, with *Treasure Island*, in which Robert Newton starred as a succulent Long John Silver, the Disney Studio began another series, this time of live-action films.

It is an incredible story of over 70 years of apparently endless and profitable success, with the Disney label still attractive, especially for the younger film and video fans. No wonder Walt Disney said 'I love Mickey Mouse more than any woman I've ever known', for it all began with the stroke of genius that brought a few minutes of flickering images of a tiny rodent to our screens. After the fashion of small acorns and mighty oaks, it was from this mouse-like venture that an empire of elephantine proportions was eventually constructed. How strange that, nowadays, 'Mickey Mouse' is used to describe something insignificant. Small he may have been, but it would be difficult to find a more significant figure in the history of world popular culture in the 20th century.

DESPERATE DAN

Sometime after the first world war comics, unlike leopards, changed their spots. In the wake of the somewhat moralistic *Boy's Own Paper* (weekly from 1879 to 1913, when it was forced to go monthly, finally expiring in 1967) came periodicals like the more commercial *Gem* and *Magnet*, started in 1907 and 1908 respectively, neither of which, after colossal success, survived the opening years of World War II. Their rationale was the boarding school story, ripping yarns about the likes of Harry Wharton and his 'famous five', although, of course, it was the anti-hero, Billy Bunter, cowardly, greedy, mendacious, who emerged as the major literary figure. His creator was Charles Hamilton, better known as Frank Richards, one of his 25 pseudonyms, the constructor of no less than 105 fictional schools, of which Greyfriars was the best known. Reputed to be the most prolific writer ever, he wrote up to 70 million words, the equivalent of a thousand full-length novels. Gradually overlapping this type and then replacing it were comics of wider scope, several of them from the D C Thompson stable. These included *Adventure* (1921); *Rover* and *Wizard* (both 1922); *Skipper* (1930) and *Hotspur* (1933).

The mood, however, in a more visually conscious age began to favour more pictures and less prose, a concept thus far the province of comics for younger children, like *Twinkle* or *Bubbles* or *Tiny Tots*. Indeed, by the end of our period in the 1950s, 'older' comics like the *New Hotspur* and *Eagle* were making a principally strip cartoon appeal. Again the Thompson company had been in the van, with the *Beano* in 1938 and *Dandy* in 1939. Few of those who were youthful from about that time will fail to recall a character or two. Lord Snooty and his pals, that curious mixture of aristocratic decorum and brattish behaviour, were fielded by the *Beano*, while the *Dandy's* mob-handed equivalent was Our Gang, a replica of the Hollywood film troupe, with Spanky MacFarlane, Alfalfa Switzer, Buckwheat Thomas and co. The *Dandy's* front page was normally the natural habitat of Korky the Cat — research into the place of the cat, from Felix to Tom, in film and comic cartoon would make interesting reading.

Nonetheless, it is probably Desperate Dan who would be most affectionately remembered from those lively pages. The mighty Dan, with his wide-brimmed Stetson, with his mammoth jaw and with bristles on his chin each capable of stabbing a recalcitrant steer, was a cowboy by trade, his diet, fondly prepared by his 'ma', consisting of cow pie, that is, one such bovine sacrifice for each pie. He was something of a Forrest Gump character, a gentle and not overly academic giant of the range, righting minor wrongs or mending small disputes by the pitting against the odds of his massive strength. Despite Goliath's bad publicity, the reliable, loyal, unimaginative Titan seemed to strike a chord with the British school-child. There is something of Desperate Dan in Edgar Rice Burroughs's Tarzan of the Apes or in Little John, Robin Hood's large and stalwart henchman. (Incidentally, Greyfriars and Sherwood have much in common: Bob Cherry is Little John to Harry Wharton's Robin; Mr Quelch is the Sheriff and Billy Bunter, Friar Tuck). Desperate Dan made children laugh and, even now, his name is quick shorthand for big helpful tough guy. The peculiar fact is that Dan

was rarely desperate. Hungry; always: perplexed; frequently; but he was much too sturdy in mind and physique to have ever been frantically hopeless.

ALBERT RAMSBOTTOM

In 1929 Gracie Fields gave some professional advice to Stanley Holloway. Her wise suggestion was that he should include monologues in his variety act. Born in the East End of London, Stanley Holloway (1890-1982) had been a boy soprano and a member of the renowned Co-optimists concert party, before making his living on the halls, singing songs like *The Sergeant Major's on Parade* or *Old Father Thames* in his brisk, hearty baritone. The versatility of his later career must be well-known to all: as a film actor in Ealing comedies like *Passport to Pimlico* and *The Lavender Hill Mob*; as Alfred Doolittle, the dustman, in the Broadway, Drury Lane and Hollywood versions of *My Fair Lady*, and in sundry other triumphs, he delighted all kinds of audiences in all kinds of ways. He took his Mentor's advice in regard of monologues and became probably their most loved purveyor.

The monologue, defined as a piece of publicly declaimed narrative verse, had really begun life as social and political comment, as in *It is Christmas Day in the Workhouse*, George R Sims' assault on the practice of segregating married couples in the workhouse. Later, no music hall bill was complete without some Thespian, like Bransby Williams, reciting the Robert Service/Cuthbert Clarke standard, *The Shooting of Dan McGrew* or the Milton Hayes/Cuthbert Clarke classic, *The Green Eye of the Little Yellow God*. Next came the comic monologues from entertainers like Billy 'Almost a Gentleman' Bennett; Gracie Fields herself, when in comic mode; Cyril Fletcher with his 'odd odes', and, on more serious topics, Nosmo King. For his part, Stanley Holloway adopted the flat vowels and prosaic tenets of the Mersey Valley at a juncture somewhere between Widnes and Stretford. His monologues, most of them written by Marriott Edgar, compiler of most of Will Hay's screen-plays and a half-brother of Edgar Wallace, the thriller writer, fell into three main categories. There were mock history lessons on the Burghers of Calais, the Magna Carta or the Battle of Hastings — 'leaving 'arold alone on the 'ill-top, on 'is 'orse with 'is 'awk in 'is 'and'. There were the exploits of Samuel Small, a stubborn and unsentimental soldier, who famously refused to pick up his musket until personally approached by the Duke of Wellington. There were the diverse experiences of the Ramsbottom family, Ma and Pa and 'Albert, their son'. Their cost-conscious attempt to cross the Mersey by foot, rather than pay the exorbitant charge of 'tuppence per person per trip' on the Runcorn-Widnes ferry, typified their prudence: 'it's the spirit that's made Lancasheer what she is; they'd sooner be drownded than done'. It is otiose to add that it is the saga of the consumption of Albert by Wallace, the Blackpool Tower Zoo lion, that has endured longest. Strike up with 'There's a famous seaside place called Blackpool.' and there's nearly always someone available to recite the whole epic through to the end, where Ma, 'proper blazing' at the condescension of the judge, cries 'what, waste all our

lives raising children to feed ruddy lions? Not me!'. On stage, record and radio, Stanley Holloway brought exactly the right note of cautious, dry, unemotional scepticism to these proceedings, while Albert, tiny, cheerful, resourceful, armed with his 'stick with an 'orse's 'ead 'andle', wears a large cap and a tight waistcoat in the illustrations. When Wallace coughs him up and he returns home, his father, in the sequel, has already collected £9.4s 2d insurance money, from which he — muttering 'I'll never trust lions again' — gives Albert a shilling with the order 'go and see what the tigers can do'.

⭐ JUST WILLIAM

Students of children's literature use 1865 as their BC/AD, Before Carroll/After Dodgson, for it is the publication year of the original *Alice's Adventures in Wonderland* by Lewis Carroll *aka* Charles Dodgson. Before this breakthrough, most children's stories had been improving and moralising or youngsters had had to depend on books aimed at adults like *Gulliver's Travels* or *Robinson Crusoe*. 'Alice' recognised the child-likeness of children and avoided treated them as mini-adults. Soon there was a more specialist market for children's clothes and artefacts, with, for example, John Tenniel, Alice's graphic illustrator, also supplying the pictures for the card game, *Happy Families*, as games and parties became more child-oriented. *Treasure Island, Black Beauty* — there was to be a whole host of children's books after 1865. But there were those who were to move the goal-posts, shifting them further away from children being, by and large, well-conducted, like Alice or Jim on the 'Hispaniola' or Enid Blyton's 'Famous Five', towards a notion of children not just different from but in conflict with adult hegemony. This was not just the jape played on the beak or the illicit midnight feast in the dorm of school-boy fiction. This was more realistic. This was a refusal to submit to adult authority on such elementary matters as school-work, hygiene, the niceties of grammar and sartorial neatness. Of the several subversives who acted in this fashion, the undoubted paramount anti-hero was William Brown.

Richmal Crompton (R C Lamburn, 1890-1969) was teaching classics at Bromley High School when she discovered the 11 year old William in 1917, basing him, it is said, on an argumentative nephew. The first short story was *The Outlaws* and she gathered a collection of these tales together as *Just William* in 1922, the first of over 30 books, which sold more than eight million copies by the time of her death, some of which were transferred, not always satisfactorily, to radio, film and TV. Like Conan Doyle and Sherlock Holmes, she sometimes tired of William, and it is interesting that, because she also aimed them at the adult audience of her higher hopes, she was able to dodge the scolding tone that children's literature still insisted upon should youngsters behave badly. Over the years, William's social circumstances changed, with the disappearance of servants and with changed roles for his elder siblings, Robert and Ethel. His mother remained bewildered throughout and his father never ceased to grizzle, while his companions, Douglas, Ginger and Henry, to say nothing of the emetically challenged Violet Elizabeth Bott, stayed

constant. Hitherto the downright naughty boys of literature had tended to be working class urchins, deserving of grave retribution. William Brown was from high-class suburbia, robed, however scruffily, in the uniform of a respectable, middle-class school. Tousled, ever-inventive but always fractious in the face of grown-up resolve, he was an anti-establishment figure from within the establishment, even if sometimes his troubles were the consequence of botched but laudable efforts.

Like Peter Pan, another candidate for the gallery of fictional notables, he never grew up, for all the 46 years of his outrageous adventures. Even today the sight of a boy with a skewed tie, a torn jacket, an unkempt cap and a scowling expression may still evoke the whispered response: 'Just William'. Let us pray he never reaches his twelfth birthday.

 LARRY THE LAMB

Asked during the London mayoral campaign of 2000 whether he would vote for Ken Livingstone, the one-time miners' leader, Arthur Scargill, declared, 'I wouldn't vote for him as Mayor of Toytown'. Did he vaguely recall in his indignation that there actually had been a Mayor of Toytown? He was the somewhat self-important chief official of the make-believe town, first written about as *Tales of Toytown* in 1928 by Sydney George Hulme Beaman (1886-1932), usually known as S G Hulme Beaman. He wrote some 30-odd episodes for radio before his premature death, which occurred just as his creations were gaining national prominence on *Children's Hour*. These adaptations were broadcast from 1929 to 1963, offering several generations of youngsters a chance to enjoy the cheerful yarns, introduced, as they were, by the lively, gallant tones of *The Parade of the Tin Soldiers*. Hulme Beaman, a toy-maker by craft, built a model of Toytown, and of nearby Arkville, where the Mayor was a much more proletarian fellow, and peopled it with his characters. He contributed the illustrations to his own books based on this prototype. Although he made no attempt to humanise the necessarily wooden appearance of the toys when he translated them to pictures, they proved satisfyingly authentic.

The Mayor of Toytown had his work cut out trying to control these very three-dimensional characters, his only assistance supplied by a lugubrious custodian of the law, one Ernest the Policeman, whose deep, gruff voice was forever heard saying 'I'm afraid I'll have to take your name and address'. A constant thorn in their sides was that inveterate complainant, Mr Grouser, Toytown's answer to 'Disgusted, Tunbridge Wells', with his invariable snorts of 'It's disgraceful' and 'It ought not to be allowed'. There was a wacky Inventor and a Magician, whose articulation defied phonetics as he concentrated on performing 'spwellls at the cwrosss-wroadsss'. There was also the slightly disreputable, slightly caddish figure of Captain Higgins. Then there were the animals, Dennis the Dachshund, guttural and with ponderously Teutonic word-order, and the timid little lamb, Letitia. But they were only foils for Larry the Lamb, bleating with anguish — 'Ohhh, Missssterrr Mayorrr, sirrr' — and somehow combining naiveté and a not negligible slyness, as havoc was created in and around the fair environs of Toytown.

As children, we all knew that Larry the Lamb's voice was provided by Uncle Mac, whereas, as far as we were concerned, Ernest, Dennis and the rest were, well, Ernest, Dennis and the rest. Perhaps this gave a certain edge to Larry's character, although it would be true to add that many of the stories of this model municipality were woven about that ovine creature. Whatever the reason, many would agree that, of all Toytown's cleverly drawn personalities, Larry the Lamb, that anxious yet endearingly obstinate innocent abroad, is the first to spring to mind when the evocative signature tune is heard, or when someone, usually rather contemptuously, it has to be said, refers to Toytown. Let them speak discourteously and dismissively of that fictional urban area. Listening in the cosy shelter of a fire-warmed kitchen, it seems, looking back, that life therein was considerably more sane than in many real-life local authorities.

 JANE

For a long time the British were, and they remain, the world's most voracious newspaper readers, with competition for that readership always very sharp. The appearance of the *Daily Mail* in 1896 was a critical point. Just as new technology was developing wireless, film and gramophones, it acted, through mechanical type-setting, to accelerate and cheapen the production of news-print. The half-penny 'Mail' also met the new desire for general display as opposed to specific small-scale advertising and circulation soared to the unimaginable heights of an average of 750,000 a day. Rivals joined the fray and the total of newspaper readers doubled, then doubled again, before the Great War. The *Daily Mirror* was first to a million readers in 1912; the *Mail* reached that target in 1915. The *Mirror* was the first paper to adopt the regular use of half-tone photographs, another technical breakthrough. Many will recall the circulation wars of the 1918-1939 period, with gifts on offer and with seaside resorts visited by characters such as Colley Cibber or Lobby Ludd, from whom the lucky or discerning might claim a money prize, if brandishing the right newspaper. Soon popular newspapers began to include strip cartoons, some of them for children, like Rupert Bear in the *Daily Express* or Teddy Tail in the *Daily Mail*. Hollywood names were adapted, such as Blondie, who, with her husband, the idiosyncratic sandwich-maker, Dagwood Bumstead, enjoyed light-hearted adventures.

The *Daily Mirror*, appealing to the armed forces and the younger, relatively well-paid working classes, managed, even with wartime restrictions on news-print, to publish a pageful of these cartoons. By far the most famous was the nubile figure of Jane, who, as some sort of secret agent, found herself scantily attired, in lingerie or diaphanous night-wear, even, on rare glorious occasion, naked, to the delight of her many followers. Her dachshund, Fritz, and her boy-friend, George, were her chief companions, as this fair-haired, slender but curvaceous young woman eternally cavorted through bedrooms and bathrooms, but never, such were the mores of the time, sinned. There were other reasons why the *Daily Mirror*, with its hard-hitting campaigns, often led by the vigorous Cassandra (the columnist, William Connor) claimed a goodly proportion of the 16 million newspapers sold each day, but Jane was its top selling-point. She did have a non-fictional counterpart. Chrystabel Leighton-Porter, (born in Hampshire in 1913, died 2000), was the model used by the 'Jane' cartoonist, Norman Pett. He introduced *Jane's Journal or the Diary of a Bright Young Thing* to the 'Mirror' in 1932 and it ran until 1959. With long blonde hair and amply endowed, Chrystabel modelled in the afternoons and played variety in the evenings, complete with Fritz. Like Phyllis Dixey (1914-1964, born in Newport, South Wales), with her decorous Gypsy Rose Lee act, Jane starred in the stationary nude shows that, eventually, betokened the end of variety. They were pruriently naughty and often quite tawdry, their titles — 'Fig-leaves and Apple-sauce'; 'Strip, Strip Hooray'; 'the Bareway to Stardom' — promising more than was delivered. Nonetheless, Jane survives in a part-myth of psephology. Although the notion is scoffed at a little now, there was a belief that soldiers and airmen took the *Mirror* because of Jane's fleshly antics, and because the *Mirror* wholeheartedly backed the Labour Party, they all voted against Winston Churchill and in favour of Clement Attlee. She would certainly enliven the political broadcasts of the present day.

DICK BARTON - SPECIAL AGENT

Special agents who make a career out of single-handedly protecting the nation's security are ten a penny in literature, running a long gamut from Ivanhoe, the eponymous hero of Walter Scott's 1819 novel about saving

Richard Lionheart's realm, to Ian Fleming's James Bond. Bond was first brought to our notice in *Casino Royale* in 1952, although, truth to tell, 007's morals were a tad slacker than Ivanhoe's. Nonetheless, the true-born Brit secret agent, cool yet chivalrous under the stress of his cloak and dagger activities as he thwarts yet another evil foreign plot, does hold a consistent place in fiction. John Buchan's Richard Hannay, first heard of in *The Thirty-nine Steps*, published in 1915, is a significant representative of the line. Another favourite was Sapper's Bulldog Drummond, although, by modern tastes in political correctitude, he may be deemed a trifle sadistic and paranoid.

That could not be said of Dick Barton. Introduced by the urgent strains of *The Devil's Gallop*, composed by Charles Williams, he first took a grip on the nation's consciousness at 6.45 on 7 October 1946. In 15 minute episodes, with three dramatic climaxes in each, it became the paciest show on either American or British radio and, by 1947, it was attracting huge audiences to its weeknight treat of foiling alien miscreants. Snowy White, renowned for his 'quick thinking', and Jock Anderson were his loyal sidekicks, and, true to the mould of gallantry, the BBC issued 12 Rules of Conduct for its brave hero, including his violence being 'restricted to clean socks on the jaw' and a ban on language 'not considered admissible for child usage in middle-class homes'. The background file on Dick Barton's prior biography is amazingly complete. Did you know that he was born at 5.0 pm Tuesday 10 December 1912, or that his father, Robert, was senior partner in a flour-milling business, or that they lived in High Wycombe, or that Dick, commissioned

in the Royal Engineers, having graduated with an appropriate degree from Glasgow University in 1933 and having worked on construction projects in Peru and Persia, had won the Military Cross at Dunkirk, or had later served as Captain with No. 20 Commando Unit? Oh, and it was mild with a little rain on the day he was born.

Noel Johnson, born in Birmingham in 1916 and also in attendance at Dunkirk, where he was wounded, played Dick Barton, although it could have been Bill, Roger, Rex, Pat or Peter Barton, such was the extensive search for the right name. He was the ideal actor, with his decently classless articulation and, technically, his smooth expertise for a fast-moving script. A handsome man, he also looked like Dick Barton, although, of course, that mattered only in so far as publicity was concerned. It was not altogether a joy-ride. He became hideously type-cast and struggled somewhat when he left the programme in 1949. It is said that the reason we were never told the name of the actor who, about the same time, played Dan Dare for Radio Luxembourg, itself a neat link between Flash Gordon on film and *Star Trek* on telly, was to avoid the performer in question suffering the same fate. Duncan Carse took over from Noel Johnson and *Dick Barton — Special Agent*, immensely popular especially among children, ran for two more years. Radio serials were expanding. *The Robinsons* was the fairly cheerful forerunner to the more broad-ranging *Mrs Dale's Diary* and lots of being 'worried about Jim'. That took up the afternoon spot, while Dick Barton was replaced by the legendary Archers of Ambridge.

ARCHIE ANDREWS

In the late 1990s Peter Brough, (born 1916), died. He had been a resident in the Denville Hall actors' care home — and Archie Andrews was still hanging there in his room. The science of ventriloquism — literally, speaking from the stomach — had originally been utilised for awesome religious ceremonies, but few of those primitive rituals could have been as weird as the broadcasting of a ventriloquist. Yet the education of Archie Andrews became a record-breaking BBC subject. *Educating Archie* was first broadcast in June 1950 and was soon drawing audiences of 12 million, as it had protracted runs throughout the 1950s. To be candid, several 'vents' of the time refused to regard Peter Brough, himself the son of one of that breed, namely, Arthur Brough and Tim, as a *bona fide* member of the clan, arguing that his technique was so crude that radio was the best place for it. They viewed him as a 'child impersonator', like Harry Hemsley, with his clutch of Ethel, Johnny and 'what does Horace say, Winnie', but, on the back of his 'wireless' achievement, 'Brough', as that impudent mock fourteen year old, Archie, always called his guardian, also enjoyed outstanding success in variety. Furthermore, Peter Brough, on his father's advice, had, like Kenneth Horne, the fail-safe of a business career which he continued long after his show-biz days were over. In the meanwhile, television has created a new and extremely tough opportunity for ventriloquists; note, incidentally, how Ray Allen's aristocratic dummy, Lord Charles, wears his own mike in the lapel of his dinner jacket — a neat touch from a polished performer.

Educating Archie was the English answer to American radio's Edgar Bergen and Charlie McCarthy, and Archie had had some apprenticeship in *Navy Mixture*. Commercial exploitation followed in the guise of jigsaw puzzles, scarves, painting books, slippers, key-rings and soap tablets, even life-size replicas, to say nothing of the 200,000 members of the Archie Andrews Club, sponsored by the makers of the Archie Andrews lollipop, 15 million of which were sold in the first year.

The cheery notes of *We're Educating Archie* heralded thirty minutes of cosy, formulaic family fun, with as many as 50 catch-phrases, situations and pieces of business crammed into that brief half hour. The script-writers, including famous names such as Eric Sykes and Marty Feldman, helped create this amazing phenomenon, but perhaps the most surprising outcome in retrospect was the number of artists who made or embellished their reputation on the show. Assembled, Archie's tutors and handymen and girl-friends read like a roll-call of top post-war entertainers. Max 'That's a good idea, son'; 'I've arrived and to prove it I'm here' Bygraves and Tony 'Flippin' kids' Hancock lead the motley, but there were also Beryl 'my name's Monica' Reid, Robert Moreton, Hattie Jacques, Alfred Marks, Gilbert Harding, Harry Secombe, Bernard Miles, James Robertson Justice, Warren Mitchell, Sid James, Bruce Forsyth, Bernard Bresslaw, Dick Emery . . . and a 13 year old girl making her radio debut, Julie Andrews.

Possibly the mask of radio actually added to the sense of Archie being somehow 'real'. He was certainly one of the most famous fictional characters of the era and, for anybody over 55, maybe over 35, he remains the one 'vent's' dummy that is best remembered.

Gordon Richards

Cliff Bastin

Tommy Farr

Joe Davis

Henry Cotton

Wally Hammond

Wilf Mannion

Stanley Matthews

Donald Campbell

Denis Compton

This Sporting Life ~ At Home ~ Ten British Sportspersons

The golden age of collective leisure ran from around 1871 to the early 1950s. 1871 is a useful date to choose because it was the year of the Bank Holidays Act, the introduction of national secular holidays, a sign that the general populace was seeking opportunities for leisure. One should not be surprised to learn that the first time turn-stiles were used at a cricket ground was in that same year that Bank Holidays were initiated. And why do Football League games kick off normally at 3.0 pm? Because the welcome half-day Saturday meant that workers toiled from 8.0 am to 2.0 pm, rather than 8.0 pm, and that gave then an hour for a pie and a pint before the match. By the mid-1950s the inroads of television and the private car, of which there were four millions on the roads, compared with under two millions in 1938, were beginning to make enjoyment a much more private process. One began to note that people found more to entertain them in the home or by making visits by car, and there were fewer crowds thronging seaside resorts and, in particular, sporting events. It had been

during that last quarter of the preceding century that sports had become much more organised on a national basis, with leagues, cups and other competitions, and much more beholden to the professional ethic.

For example, the first FA Cup Final was in 1872; the Football League started in 1888; the County Cricket Championship dates officially from 1890, although there were less formal arrangements beforehand; the first Test match in England was in 1880; Jim Corbett defeated John L Sullivan in 1892 to become the first world heavyweight champion under the new Queensberry Rules; the Rugby Union was established in 1871; in 1877 Spencer W Gore became the first Wimbledon open tennis champion; Willie Park of Musselburgh won the first open professional golf championship at Prestwick in 1860; and, in 1875, Captain Matthew Webb became the first person to swim the English Channel.

By the 1920s and through to the 1950s, hordes of people swarmed to watch these and other sports, with their interest enlivened by the spacious coverage of all these activities in the daily press, by the cinema newsreels, by lots of radio commentary and by other devices such as the cigarette card, sets of which were devoted to well-known footballers and cricketers. Nowadays only the top football teams and the international cricket fixtures draw huge 'gates', whereas, pre-1953, it was not uncommon for small-town football teams and local league cricket teams to attract many thousands of spectators. Yet another starting-point for our period might be 1923, for, in April of that year, Wembley Stadium was opened and, four days after its completion, it hosted the first Wembley cup final. 25,000 tons of concrete, 15,000 tons of steel, half a million rivets, and a battalion of infantry marking time for 15 minutes on the terraces to test their durability — they are some of the characteristics of the construction of that now doomed most famed of arenas. A mass of 200,000 people — some estimates put it as high as 250,000 swamped the ground with its 127,000 capacity. Amazingly, there was little panic and the heroic 'policeman on the white horse', G A Storey by modest name, was central to clearing the pitch, although there were odd complaints about speeding footballers being tripped by opposing fans. Bolton Wanderers beat West Ham United amidst those astounding scenes. All-ticket matches were just around the corner.

J B Priestley, in the opening chapter of *The Good Companions*, wrote of 'a tide of cloth caps', the 35,000 men and boys who had paid a shilling to watch Bruddersford United, for 'a man who had missed the last home match of t'united had to enter social life on tip-toe in Bruddersford'. The football team of that size of town would be fortunate to draw an average crowd of a couple of thousand today. Similarly with cricket. 78,617 watched the Lancashire and Yorkshire three-day match at Old Trafford in 1926, while a Lancashire League Worsley Cup-tie, Nelson against Colne, attracted 14,000 in 1934. The glorious summer of 1947 saw nearly three million people watching first-class cricket. There were 14,000 present on the first day of the Oxford and Cambridge Universities game at Lord's that year, a fixture which is now observed by the merest of handfuls. Indeed, the numbers paying to watch county championship cricket in England has slumped to under 200,000 all told over a season, something like a tenth of the spectators in days gone by.

Horse-racing, rugby league, speedway and boxing were other sports that attracted fair-sized crowds in those days, and professional sport was the chief topic of conversation, especially for working men and schoolboys. Everyone seemed to have their favourite sport, their favourite team, and their favourite star. Possibly the hero-worship was more localised than nowadays, particularly as ease of transport, predominantly by plane, and ease of communication, predominantly by television, has increased the order of international sport tremendously. Admittedly, it was more of a masculine activity, both in playing and in spectating, at that time. The only sports involving women that would have touched on the threshold of consciousness of the average sports enthusiast would have been tennis or swimming and, post-war, maybe athletics. Indeed, if one examines a list of main money earners in world sport at the present time, women are far and away down the roster, although, of course, names like

Tessa Sanderson or Olga Korbut have been very familiar to the sporting public

This explains the seemingly male biased selection of British sportspersons profiled in the following ten pages. Spare a thought, then, for Mrs Stokes, a notoriously rough prize-fighter of the early Hanoverian era; young Charlotte Dod who, in 1886, terrorised her opponents at lawn tennis with 'man-like' vigour, and the intrepid Eleonora Sears who, in 1909, was expelled from the polo ground for wearing trousers. It has, and it continues to be, a long haul for the ladies to be allowed to emulate the lads. It really is a scandal that the Football Association, formed in 1863, has only arrived at the decision to do something serious about women's football in England in the year 2000.

That said, it would be fascinating were readers and users of this book able to assemble a case for a British sportswoman being included to the rightful exclusion of one of the ten chosen sportsmen. In fact, here's one extra task you may like to envisage, one not really possible in several of the other fields such as radio, dance bands and the like. Who would be the top ten British sportspersons in terms of popularity and recognisability today — and how many women would be among them?

 **CLIFF BASTIN** (Clifford Stanley Bastin, 1912-1991, born Exeter)

No wonder Cliff Bastin was given the nickname, 'Boy' Bastin. He was quite the youthful prodigy. He was only 17 when he signed for the famous Arsenal club and moved from Exeter — it is rumoured that he signed for Arsenal and moved to London because, in spite of the wages being low, it gave him time to play tennis, a game he loved. He was 18 when he played in his first Cup Final in 1930, the youngest cup finalist until Kendall of Everton broke his record in 1964. He was 19 when he played in a Football League Championship winning side. He was 20 when he first played for England, going on to win 21 caps, quite a few for those days when international matches were strictly limited and chiefly the paradoxically termed 'home' internationals against Scotland, Wales and Ireland.

The nippy fair-haired Bastin was a joyous sight on the football grounds of the day, His blondness made him easily distinguishable as, spring-heeled and swift, he dribbled, swerved and shot. He was an outside-left, and, unlike many wingers of his day, he was a fluent goal-scorer. He scored 33 goals in 42 league matches in the 1932/33 season, and his goal scoring record for Arsenal — 150 league goals — was only overtaken in the late 1990s by Ian Wright. He played in three cup finals, as well as contributing to Arsenal's flurry of championship titles in the pre-war decade. Had not the war years intervened, he would doubtless have added further to these laurels and, for instance, made his goal scoring record unchallengeable.

Arsenal were the trend-setters of the inter-wars seasons, a club of magnificent organisation and playing capacity. They were formed by munitions workers at the Royal Arsenal, Woolwich, in 1886, turned professional in 1891 and entered the Football League in 1893. They moved to Highbury Stadium, then the top of the range venue in regard to facilities, in 1913 and dropped

'Woolwich' from their title the following year. Gradually, they moved upwards and onwards, with their managers, Herbert Chapman (1925-34) and George Allison (1934-47) proving very effective. Just as the club itself was ahead of its time, so were its managers setting the modern agenda of how a big club should be run. It was Herbert Chapman who persuaded Cliff Bastin to join the Arsenal, where his Mentor and left-wing partner was that great Scottish inside forward, the diminutive, twinkle-toed, Alex James. Around this period, Arsenal won the F A Cup in 1930 and 1936, being runners-up in 1927 and 1932, whilst they took the Football League Division I title in 1931, 1933, 1934, 1935 and 1938. Post-war, they won the cup in 1950 and the league in 1948 and 1953.

In 1934 they provided seven of England's 11 against Italy, for it was verily a team of all stars. They fielded, over this time, the highly responsible and impressive full-back, Eddie Hapgood, the strong half-back trio of Crayston, Roberts and Copping, and the dynamic yet cultured forward play of Alex James, Ted Drake, Joe Hulme, David Jack and Charlie Buchan. However, the name that springs to mind when the fabled Arsenal team of pre-1939 vintage is mentioned is that of 'Boy' Bastin. He barely played after the war; off he went to do what lots of ex-footballers used to do — he kept a pub.

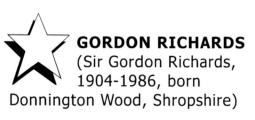

GORDON RICHARDS
(Sir Gordon Richards, 1904-1986, born Donnington Wood, Shropshire)

On nearly 22,000 occasions Gordon Richards

was, as the racing *cognoscenti* say, 'up', and on almost a quarter of those rides, he remorselessly drew away from his competitors, and, the affectionately disposed crowds roaring him on up the straight, made a winning beeline for the finishing post. He was very much the people's jockey in the sport of kings. Not taking kindly to the humdrum jobs on offer in his native Salop, the young Gordon Richards answered an advertisement for apprentice jockeys and was enrolled at the Foxhill Stables in Wiltshire. He was a small but stocky lad, with immensely powerful limbs — ideal material for racing. He was barely six and a half stones when he had his first mount in 1920, and his thick, tousled black hair led him to be nicknamed 'Moppy'. His first winner was Gay Lord in 1921, and, at the end of his apprenticeship in 1924, he moved to the Russley Park stables, also in Wiltshire, where he rode for Capt. Thomas Hogg and Lord Glanely. In 1931 he joined Fred Darling's string at Beckhampton, which was taken over by Noel Murlees in 1947. These were to be the seasons of his unprecedented greatness.

Apart from 1926, when he suffered from the tuberculosis that was to prevent him doing military service, he was the leading jockey for a almost a score of years from 1925, when, with 118 winners, he was Champion Jockey for the first time. In 1930 he won his first classics, with Rose of England in the Oaks and Singapore in the St Leger. In 1931 he beat Fred Archer's long enduring record of 246 winners in 1885 with a shattering sequence of 259 victories — and in 1947 he broke his own record with 269 winning mounts. In 1943, when he won on Scotch Mist at Windsor, he overtook Fred Archer's record total of 2748 winners. In all, he was Champion Jockey no less than 26 times and he ended with the unbelievable catalogue of 4870 winners from 21843 mounts. Like 'the long 'un', Lester Piggott, his successor as most famous jockey, he was an unorthodox jockey, his body skewed unevenly to the left. Nonetheless, it was said that 'horses ran straight as a die for him', and that was, of course, the mystery and the secret of his essential dominance of flat racing for so long. His knighthood was a tribute as much to his integrity — in a sport not always as pure as the driven snow — as to this mastery of his craft. His post-jockey's life was less eventful but he had his moments as a shrewd judge and trainer of horse-flesh, so that his entire life was spent in the service of the flat racing business.

His inability to win the Derby became notorious. Time and time again, he seemed to have the right horse but something went wrong on the run in, notably in 1947 when, after Tudor Minstrel had strolled home comfortably in the 2000 Guineas, it looked like a one-horse race. Then, just as Stan Matthews won his overdue Cup Final medal in Coronation year and Mount Everest was first conquered, Gordon Richards won the 1953 Derby, at his 28th and final attempt, on Sir Victor Sassoon's horse, Pinza. Following in the footsteps, or rather, stirrups, of 'Come on, Steve' Donoghue, Gordon Richards became one of Britain's most popular four or five jockeys ever, and very probably was the most popular of that select group. He joined that exceptionally tiny band of sportsmen and women of whom **everyone** had heard, irrespective of whether he or she was interested in the sport in question.

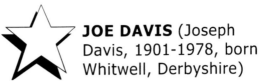

JOE DAVIS (Joseph Davis, 1901-1978, born Whitwell, Derbyshire)

From his youngest years Joe Davis haunted the billiard room of his father's Derbyshire pub, the Queen's Hotel, and, aged 13, he became the proud winner of the Chesterfield and District Billiards Championship. He found employment managing billiard halls, an amenity that even the smallest town then boasted, and this, self-evidently, offered him ample chance to perfect his superb game. Coached by Ernest Rudge, he won the World Billiards title in 1928, 1929, 1930 and 1932, whereafter he was beaten by the patient, skilful Walter Lindrum in the next two years. Indeed, their very mastery killed off billiards as a popular sport, for their total dominion of the green baize became boring. Walter Lindrum once made a break of 4137, whilst Joe Davis had several astronomical breaks to his name, including one of 2501. Joe Davis, however, had the wit to spot the possibilities of snooker. Snooker is that rare game, one that was deliberately invented, like basketball and didn't 'just grew', like cricket or football. Curiously, for what was to be regarded as a working man's pastime, it was devised by Neville Chamberlain — no, not that one, but an officer serving with the Devonshire Regiment in Jubalore in 1875 who, when the rainy season brought *ennui* to the mess, created snooker from the billiards and betting variations, like Life-pool and Black Pool already tried. A 'snooker' was the French-derived slang name given to a first year cadet at the Royal Military Academy, Woolwich which had come to mean a novice, so that, when a visiting second-lieutenant missed a simple pot, he described himself as 'a regular snooker'. Chamberlain assured him that they were all snookers at this game and the label stuck. It was the billiards professional, John Roberts, who brought snooker back to Britain from India in 1885.

Joe Davis and a Birmingham sports equipment trader, Bill Camkin, persuaded the Billiards Association to arrange a snooker competition in 1927 — and Joe Davis walked off with the prize of £6.10s . . . He then proceeded to win the world title every year until 1946 and, indeed, after he relinquished the championship, it languished and was not competed for from 1957 to 1964. Colour television was to be the saviour; the snooker table appears to fit snugly into the televisual frame and modern players certainly earn a shilling or so more than £6.10s. if they win the title. It was Joe Davis, dark, balding, chubbily built and with enormous reserves of mental stamina, who 'virtually ran the game', its chief venue then the Leicester Square Hall which was a kind of Buckingham Palace for the monarch of the cue. It was Joe Davis who innovated the concepts of break building and positional play that are the common strategies of the game today. Needless to say, it was not just the theory but his glint-eyed sharpness and purity of potting control that enabled him to reign so supremely. In 1928 he made the first public snooker break of a hundred, the first of his 687 centuries before he finally retired in 1964, after lots of exhibition matches, war-time charity events and stage appearances, from the game he had established on the world stage. In 1955 he made the coveted 147, the highest possible break. It all but passes belief that, in this lengthy progress from 1927 to 1964, Joe Davis only lost four games on level terms,

all of them to his brother, Fred Davis, another of the 'greats' of the snooker table. Alec Higgins and Stephen Hendry *et al* are Joe Davis' princely heirs and successors.

 HENRY COTTON
(Thomas Henry Cotton, 1907-1987, born Holmes Chapel, Cheshire; knighted posthumously, 1988)

It is said that James IV of Scotland, Mary, Queen of Scots and her son, James VI of Scotland and I of England were avid golfers, keen to perfect their swing among the heather. Scotland, with Royal St Andrews the then and now centre of the game's authority, remained the chief focus for the sport. Clubs were formed and they retained workers to tend the courses, fashion and mend equipment and perhaps offer coaching. Thus, in a rather feudal way was born the golf professional. This paid cadre, led by Alan Robertson, Tom Morris, father and son, and Willie Park Senior, soon began, because of their aptitude for golf, to bring prestige to the clubs that employed them. This obviously was intensified as national and then international tournaments spread. In 1860 Willie Park of the Musselburgh Club won the first Open Professional Championship at Prestwick; it was 1885 before Allan F MacFie won the first Amateur and 1894 before Lady Margaret Scott won the first Ladies' Championships.

Henry Cotton was not just a highly talented golfer. His father enrolled him as a member of the Aquarius Golf Club, London, at a youthful age, and, a gifted scholar, his headmaster was in despair when the 16 year old

Henry opted to become a golf 'pro'. His clubs began with Fulwell, then ranged through Rye, Langley Park, Waterloo (near Brussels), Ashridge, under the influence of the Earl of Rosebery, and finally to Coombe Hill and to Royal Mid-Surrey. It was the Langley Park club which supported him in his golfing safari in 1928/29 to the United States and to Argentina, at a time when the American golfing presence was becoming strong and when few British players had experience of overseas conditions. Apart from this ambitious venture paying off in golfing terms, it also provided Henry Cotton with his fortunate meeting with 'Toots' Estanguet Moss, the lady who, after her divorce, became his wife and life-long lieutenant. A knowledgeable and well-travelled woman, she was of undoubted and dedicated value to Henry Cotton's burgeoning career. He made his global name with the winning of three British Open Championships, at Royal St George in 1934; at Carnoustie in 1937, and at Muirfield in 1948, while he also captained the Ryder Cup teams of 1939, 1947 and 1953. Like so many sportsmen of his generation, the second world war interrupted his career adversely; he served in the RAF until a stomach ulcer led to his being invalided out, whereon he devoted much time to playing golf on behalf of the Red Cross charity. Later he turned advantageously to writing, teaching and, above all, building. He constructed 23 golf courses, the most famous being Penina in the Algarve region of Portugal. However, golf historians agree that his main claim to renown was not just his fine golfing technique but his almost single-handed elevation of the status of the golf professional. Highly intelligent, aloof, self-reliant, strong-willed and capable

of the most intense application, these very virtues that enabled him to master golf also equipped him, with the assistance of the sophisticated 'Toots', to insist on a life of the best clothes, cars, residences and the like. Not for Henry Cotton the role of the forelock-tugging senior caddie that was the prior lot of the golf professional, however talented. He asserted his right to be accepted as a professional in the middle class sense, as if he might have been a lawyer or a surgeon. Today's golf professionals, of all nations, should nightly offer up a silent prayer in thanks for what he did for their vocation.

 STAN MATTHEWS
(Sir Stanley Matthews, 1915-2000, born Hanley, Stoke-on-Trent)

'. . . he draws defenders towards him, the ball a bait./They refuse like a poisoned chocolate, till he slows his gait'. . . thus Alan Ross, famous for his cricketing verse, here capturing 'the wizard of the dribble' in poetic evocation. Not many footballers have odes dedicated to them, but, then, there have not been many footballers like Stan Matthews, for he might fairly claim to have been the United Kingdom's most legendary soccer player. Hanley boasts a statue, a full-sized replica of him, spry and alert, the ball at his feet. You almost expect the statue to dally, to shimmy and then to dart effortlessly away. That was the Matthews magic. He is acknowledged simply as the best dribbler of a football there has been. He liked to receive the ball at his feet on the right wing; then he would draw the opposing full back into juddering uncertainty; then there was the sudden burst — for Stanley Matthews had shattering acceleration over those first few yards — and then there was the perfectly launched cross to his teammates. It was a classic cameo, replayed Saturday after Saturday, season after season.

His father was Jack Matthews, 'the Fighting Barber', a nickname encapsulating his two professions. His prodigally talented son joined Stoke City in 1929, aged 14, and swept the dressing rooms and cleaned 48 pairs of football boots.He made his professional debut, aged 17, against Bury in 1932 and two years later, as a 19 year old, he won the first of his 54 England caps. A fitness fanatic in an age when there was less emphasis on such matters than now, he prolonged his career to great length. He was 42 when he made his last England appearance and 50 when he played the last of his 710 League games. He also played 30 war-time internationals and, of course, World War II, in which he served in the RAF, bit heavily into his overall record. He moved from Stoke to Blackpool in 1948, having guested for the sea-side club, like other footballing airmen, during the war when Blackpool was a major RAF centre. It was there where he created the most abiding memory of his stupendous career. Blackpool had lost two Cup Finals in 1948 and 1951 and, when they again reached the Wembley final in 1953, it was widely felt that this was Stan Matthews' last chance of a coveted Cup Final medal. The game was against Bolton Wanderers. It was a dramatic encounter, ebbing and flowing, and with Bolton appearing to have the edge. In the dying minutes, however, spurred on by the likes of Ernie Taylor and Stan Mortensen, Stanley Matthews crowned Coronation Year with a superlative

show of mesmerising skill — and Blackpool won the cup 4-3. In 1961 he returned to Stoke City when their performances needed lifting and soldiered on a few more seasons.

Dapper, dark hair combed neatly back, a trifle bandy-legged and unassuming to an inordinate degree, he never retaliated or complained, whatever the rough treatment dealt out to him. Colleagues said of him that a referee never once had to speak to him, and he never once spoke to a referee. 'His fame timeless and international' is a phrase from his statue's inscription and he is rightly regarded as one of England's premier sportsmen. One wonders whether he learned the tough lesson of such good attitudes from his father, who never asked him when he returned home, as a youngster, from a match, how he had fared. 'He never asks me', explained 'the Fighting Barber', 'how many hair-cuts I've done'.

 WALLY HAMMOND
(Walter Reginald Hammond, 1903-1965, born Dover, Kent)

Wally Hammond succeeded W G Grace and Jack Hobbs as monarch of English batsmanship. He was sumptuously the greatest home-grown batsman of his generation, crucially in the 1930s, and England's chief batting counter to the unrelenting scourge of Don Bradman in that era. Given the elegant style of his majestic stroke-play, several critics continue to prefer him to Bradman, despite the latter's undeniable statistical record. Even so, Wally Hammond emerges with some challenging arithmetic. Although a trifle slow to reach his full promise with Gloucestershire, he certainly then dominated English county cricket. No one has equalled his achievement of being top of the English batting averages in eight consecutive seasons, that is, 1933-1946, with, of course, six chances of making it a likely sequence of 14 lost because of World War II. He completed a thousand runs, that normal mark of consistency, in 17 English summers and also on five overseas tours. No English batsman remotely approaches his record of 36 double centuries and, in all, he made 167 hundreds, his highest score being 336, not out, for England versus New Zealand at Auckland in the winter of 1932/33. He made over 50,000 first-class runs at an impressive average of just over 50. A most agile slip fieldsman, he took an astounding 819 catches in his career, while his all-round play was such that he also took the goodly total of 732 wickets with his medium paced bowling. The large inter-wars crowds savoured his talent: it combined the mercurial with the assiduous, a rare mix of steadiness and loveliness.

Socially, rather like WG Grace, he fell between the rigidly placed stools of English status. He was the son of a soldier who was commissioned from the ranks, itself an uneasy rite of passage, and he himself went to grammar school. Now this was a time when 'Players', that is, professional cricketers, still usually left their senior schools about 13 or 14 just about the time their 'Gentlemen', that is (not always an accurate label) amateur, colleagues were, more often than not, going to their public schools. Whether his shy, somewhat brusque temperament was shaped by this circumstance, or was inherent, is a moot point, but he does seem to have had difficulties of professional relationship. On the one hand, he was better paid than most cricketers of his time. He earned £450 a year with Gloucestershire, plus bonuses and a healthy benefit in 1934 of £2500, and he was also the first cricketer to get a sponsored car. Along with his contemporary, Herbert Sutcliffe, he did much to raise the social level of the cricket professional. On the other hand, he did not find it easy to sustain the living standards — the posh suits, the expensive golf clubs, the hob-nobbing with the aristocracy — that he felt were his proper due. It is not surprising that, in 1937, he found irresistible the offer of a £2000 a year company directorship, with its in-built opportunity to turn 'amateur' and captain England. This he did, at first successfully, and then, post-war, less so on the doom-laden Australian tour of 1946/47. He soon slipped away to South Africa where, after business failures, he died aged 62, partly in consequence of a severe motor accident five years before. His social diffidence did not extend to the distaff side, for, something of the film-star cliché in being tall, dark and handsome, he was a noted ladies' man. This caused him a problem or two and there are hints that the illness he contracted on the West Indian trip of 1925/26 was what is politely termed 'social'. A Prince Charming he may perhaps have been; what is definite is that he was the Prince of batsmen, one who, sadly, gave more happiness than he himself enjoyed.

 **TOMMY FARR** (Thomas George Farr, 1913-1986, born Blaenclydach, Rhondda, South Wales)

The gruelling poverty of a large miner's

family was the backdrop to Tommy Farr's boxing career, although, unlike some others of his ilk, it also instilled into him a certain prudence about money. For instance, from his early times as 'Kid' Farr, scrapping, sometimes five times a night, in the Joe and Daisy Gess booth at Tylerstown, he managed to save £109 and buy a house in Tonypandy. 'In-fighting was my speciality', grinned the tough Welshman, six foot tall and broad-shouldered, but, in an era that looked for style, he was overshadowed by the more elegant Jack Petersen, who, in 1932, became the first Welshman to win the British Heavyweight Championship. Tommy Farr remained a 'small hall' boxer, but, as a teenager, he had been befriended by the astute Joe Churchill, who remained his career-long adviser. Having won the Welsh Heavyweight title at Mountain Ash in 1935, he moved to Slough and contracted himself to the well-known London manager, Ted Broadribb. Their relationship was almost as stormy as a session in the ring with the hard-hitting boxer, with frequent returns to Tonypandy and with Joe Churchill ceaselessly providing the soothing balm. Tommy Farr's jabbing and spoiling techniques were still not too popular with spectators, but he persevered and, in 1936, he defeated the former champion, the American, Tommy Loughran.

Thus to 1937: Tommy Farr's *annus mirabilis*. First, at the recently opened Harringay Arena, he gained the British and Heavyweight Championships in a somewhat desultory bout with Ben Foord, Jack Petersen's conqueror. Next he out-pointed the brash Max Baer of Nebraska over 12 rounds. Then he knocked out the German contender, the beefy Walter Neusel. All this led to Tommy Farr's impor-

tant trip to the United States to fight the 23 year old Joe Louis, then at the peak of his fabulous career, for the World Heavyweight Championship. This was for a purse of $50,000, whatever the result, a far cry from the annual £150 that had amounted to Tommy Farr's usual earnings until these last one or two years. For 15 grinding rounds, Tommy Farr fought valiantly, never once being knocked down by this most impregnable of opponents, cleverly calling on all his ingrained skills of close-order boxing. Few had expected him to endure for long against the American; as it was, he lost narrowly on points in an epic contest. Millions listened to the fight broadcast in the wee small hours of the morning from the USA. It was the first sporting event to be broadcast by transatlantic cable, a technological triumph that obviously added to the event's lustre. Tommy Farr went on boxing, winning some and losing some, even trying again as late as 1950, having been discharged as unfit from the RAF during wartime. He had had his moment and that really was that, even though his essential Welshness was sufficiently potent for him to cut six records of his singing.

All in all, he accepted that his day had come and gone, leaving him reasonably comfortably off, and he lived out the rest of his life in the happy bosom of his family, with Muriel, his wife, in Sussex. But that hour or so of crackling excited commentary from America sealed his fame in the remembrance of his generation. As the boxing writer, Stan Shipley, concluded, 'Farr's gritty loss was sporting memory's gain'.

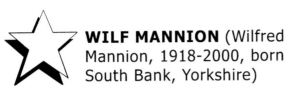

WILF MANNION (Wilfred Mannion, 1918-2000, born South Bank, Yorkshire)

'The Golden Boy' of football, Wilf Mannion, perhaps the most instinctively brilliant footballer of his generation, was one of several top-class sportsman to be robbed of years of grandeur by World War II. He made his debut for Middlesbrough as a teen-ager in 1937 and quickly made a name for himself, before war service in France — he was snatched from the beaches of Dunkirk — and later in the Middle East. Thereafter he soon became something of a legend in possibly one of England's strongest ever teams, partnering both Stanley Matthews and Tom Finney and master-minding a forward line that also included the likes of Jimmy Hagan, Raich Carter and Tommy Lawton. Behind them was the cultured half back line of Cliff Britton, Stan Cullis and Joe Mercer, whilst the full backs were normally Laurie Scott and George Hardwick, with the powerful Frank Swift in goal. Wilf Mannion was capped 26 times for England, a good number for that era, and he score 110 goals in 368 games for Middlesbrough. An inside forward of imaginative vision, he could dribble at disconcerting pace, he could hold the ball with assurance and pass it with equal certainty, and he could crack home goals of superlative quality. He was not tall, perhaps some 5ft 5ins in height, but he was robust enough to withstand the rigours of first division and international football, at a time when tackling was often, as Albert expected lions to be, 'ferocious and wild'.

His blond locks added to the golden image, making him simple to identify on muddy fields. He is one of those footballers one now remembers sorrowfully when one reads of the astronomic sums paid nowadays to sometimes inferior players. His was the feudal age of football, with players tied by strict contract to clubs and restricted to a maximum wage, in Wilf Mannion's case, never more than £10 a week. A man of independent turn of mind, he attempted rebellion, seeking a move to Oldham Athletic in the winter of 1947/48, even selling chicken coops in Oldham to keep the wolf from the door in vain anticipation of a Middlesbrough change of mind. 'Boro' were relegated at the end of the 1953/54 season, and, after moving to Hull City, Wilf Mannion's career foundered rather in desultory non-league soccer and inefficacious management. He ended his working life on building sites and fell towards penury, although, in the 1980s, Middlesbrough did provide him with a testimonial. One of the bitter little tales he told was of sitting on his case in the corridor of a crowded train *en route* for Glasgow where he was selected to play for England against Scotland before a crowd that would include many of those lucky enough to have had comfortable seats on that train: no joint travel arrangements or pre-match assembly; none of the careful preparation of major football today. Wilf Mannion's life is a parable of the sporting culture of his day. There he was, a people's hero, a name on a million lips, still, indeed, adorated on Tees-side, a man of immense talent, hailed by the press and with his countenance impressed on thousands of cigarette cards. Yet, at base, he was a wage-slave, a working class man, limited by a pitifully meagre income and corralled by a contractual system so prohibitive that eventually it would be ruled unlawful.

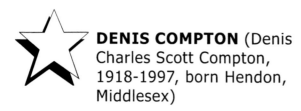

DENIS COMPTON (Denis Charles Scott Compton, 1918-1997, born Hendon, Middlesex)

The evocative memory of the high summer of 1947, recalled by many as the finest of all cricket seasons, is dominated by the vivid wit and audacious exuberance of Denis Compton. The figures are of themselves fabulous. He created new records in 1947 with a gigantic season's total of 3816, at an average of just under 91 an innings, and with a series of 18 centuries. Over his career, he was to score nearly 39,000 runs and 123 centuries and take 622 wickets with his speculative left-hand bowling, plus, for he was a daring fielder, 415 catches. Moreover, he was one of the best of the cricketer-footballers, proving to be a sparkling outside-left for Arsenal, alongside his brother, Leslie, who also played for Middlesex and the Arsenal. In spite of his unruly black hair, he was one of the first sportsman to benefit from advertising monies, as he became the famed Brylcreem model, itself an enduring image. Indeed, it was not just the absolute hegemony over the cricket field that endeared Denis Compton to post-war Britain. It was more the manner of his doing it. His gaiety and invention, his unquenchable enjoyment of his sporting gifts, carried to the rings of crowded spectators and beyond, via radio and press and news-reels, so that a war-torn nation, struggling to come to terms with an arduous peace, found in Denis Compton a sunlit icon to adore and relish.

This genial temper was part and parcel of his other than vocational life. The 'happy' but 'poorish' (his own words) childhood gave rise to an appetite for life that was as legendary as his unique cricketing talent. Tales abound

— and suffer embellishment — of his giddy comings and goings, his Bohemian ways, his unpunctuality, his careless regard of letters and cheques, and a score of other fairly minor *peccadilloes*. These all served to enamour him ever more completely with the British sporting public and the dodgy knee of his later career was to attract the degree of news-coverage usually reserved for a European war or a sensational murder case. It was the discovery of a cache of unopened letters, containing cheques and offers of journalistic work, that led to Denis Compton becoming the first major British sportsman to employ an agent, one Bagenal Harvey. Thrice-married, Denis Compton formed friendships with other high-living cricketers, among them several South Africans, and this appears to have biased his views rather towards the right-wing when the controversies about Apartheid and sporting links with South Africa intensified in later years. He was never forgotten. There were, of course, several cricketers who kept the flame alive just after the second world war, among them Denis Compton's 'Middlesex Twin' and fellow-roisterer, Bill Edrich, to say nothing of the serene and disciplined genius of Yorkshire's Len Hutton; his doughty Lancastrian partner, Cyril Washbrook; that cavalier of wicket-keepers, Godfrey Evans; and indefatigable Alec Bedser, one of the world's best four medium-fast bowlers of all time. Effective as each in his own way was, it was Denis Compton who was showered with magic. Aptly, Bill Edrich and he were batting together at the Oval in 1953, as England regained the Ashes from Australia. On his death, aged 78, the applications for places at his memorial service were the most numerous received by Westminster Abbey for 30 years.

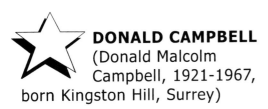

DONALD CAMPBELL
(Donald Malcolm
Campbell, 1921-1967,
born Kingston Hill, Surrey)

The lone quest for some non-functional goal . . . it is strange how tempting that seems to be for some men and women, as they contemplate the towering mountain or the polar ice-cape. Imagine the August of 1875, for instance, when Captain Matthew Webb, that valiant Shropshire soldier, took the chilly plunge and became the first person to swim the English Channel, a feat which somehow manages to combine grandeur with a certain hollowness. Speed, on land or water or in the air, is an aspect of this felt need, and Donald Campbell became obsessed with its conquest. It scarcely helped him in the last analysis that he was the son of Sir Malcolm Campbell who, in 1939, had established the water speed record of 141.74 miles an hour. The son seemed beset by the father's achievement and, initially, matters did not go too well. Donald Campbell had to leave his public school, Uppingham, suffering from rheumatic fever and then, forced out of the RAF through illness, he spent, by his standards and anticipations, a mundane and frustrating war as a special constable. Next he attempted to defend his father's record in his father's boat, only to fail miserably in 1949, 1950 and 1951.

Then the jet engine came to his aid and was his temporary salvation. *Bluebird*, his new boat, an all-metal hydroplane, equipped with two jet engines, stormed across Ullswater in 1955 at an average speed of 202.32 mph. He built up this fine record in a further six forays, the last of which, on New Year's Eve 1964, on Lake Dumbleyoung in Australia,

saw *Bluebird* lift the figure to 276.33 mph. In the meanwhile, and from 1960, Donald Campbell also turned his attention to the land. He had some difficulties, including the salutary experience of sustaining a hair-line fracture to his skull at 365 mph. However, he became the first man to guide a shaft-driven vehicle over 400 mph (his average over two runs was 403.1 mph) and to establish both the land and water records in the same year. In 1966, with the substantial help of a British-Siddeley Orpheus jet engine with a 5000 lb. thrust, he set his heart on taking *Bluebird* over the 300 mph mark. There were problems of a financial, a meteorological and a technical brand and, as had happened during some of his previous projects, there was hostile criticism from the press. It has been said that 'he lived in a world which had outgrown him'. His temperament was touchy and his values remained boyish, so that he was not always the easiest man to counsel. Moreover, science was gazing ahead to a future of space travel and astronauts, and sponsors were finding motor boats a trifle old hat.

Perhaps reacting a little rashly to these circumstances, Donald Campbell decided to try his luck on 4 January 1967 — and luck was not to befriend him. His forebodings and fears were confirmed. He made an outward run of 297 mph, and the return run was said to be faster, possibly tipping the 300 scale. Unfortunately, *Bluebird* somersaulted: boat and driver were destroyed. Donald Campbell's lost boat and body were recovered in 2001, and the memory of his many attempts to live up to his father's exacting criterion — a memory underlined by scores of newsreel pictures and newspaper coverage — lives sadly and nobly on.

Joe Louis

Johnny Carey

Helen Wills Moody

Fanny Blankers-Koen

Emil Zatopek

Keith Miller

Don Bradman

Babe Ruth

Rahmadhin and Valentine

Jesse Owens in the Berlin Olympics in 1936

This Sporting Life ~ Abroad ~ Ten Overseas Sportspersons

In 1844 the USA played Canada at cricket in a sequence that endured for many years. This improbable venture makes it arguably the first true international contest in sporting history, unless one counts the ancient doings of the Greek city-states in the original Olympics. International sport was a long time a'coming. There were the first association and rugby football matches between England and Scotland in 1871 and 1872 respectively, but none of those ambivalently termed 'home' internationals involving parts of the United Kingdom have quite the necessary global ring about them. Countries like the USA were developing their own sports, such as baseball (the National Association of Baseball Players was formed in 1858) and basketball (a rare example of a game invented rather than evolved — in 1891 by the Rev James A Naismith).

In general, however, the initial sport to enjoy a world-wide acclaim from an Anglocentric stance was cricket. Such was the ideal of cricket as 'God's classroom', and its place in the ethics of Empire-building, that first Australia and then many other parts of the Empire engaged themselves in 'the Imperial game'. The so-called Test matches between England and Australia began in 1877 and soon English spectators were eager to learn of the exploits of Australian cricketers, like the 'demon bowler', F R Spofforth. It may safely be averred that W G Grace, 'the great cricketer', is the first genuine international sportsman of prominent stature. Indeed, he remains, along with the old Queen herself, just about the only Victorian personality easily recognisable to many today. He is the begetter of the worldwide phenomenon of professionalised spectator sport that so dominates our newspaper sports pages and television screens today.

The twentieth century had dawned before other sports commanded attention in Britain in respect of their planetary focus. Baron Pierre de Coubertin (1863-1937) re-invented the Olympics Games in 1896 in Athens, but it was a sporadic affair and the idea took a little while to catch fire. Gradually, sports like golf, tennis and boxing adopted a world-wide dimension, with open championships of one kind and another — the first Davis Cup for tennis was competed for in 1900 — and soon most sports had international as well as national boards or associations to control them and organise their various tournaments. Curiously, Britain, the originator of football, was a little shy of international involvement, although FIFA, the world football alliance, was formed as early as 1904, while the first World Cup was in 1930. England did not compete in the World Cup, and then disastrously, until 1950. This insularity meant that foreign footballers were not as well-known then as they are today, with the Brazilian, Pele, the first of the really big names.

On the other hand, and apart from Australian cricketers and some All-Black New Zealand rugby union players, people, especially in the inter-wars period, began to grow familiar with individual sporting stars, many of them of American base. Boxers, golfers, athletes and tennis champions were notable among this group, together with a few continental European names. Naturally enough, this partly arose because of their visits to Britain to compete, particularly in the 'open' tennis and golf tournaments.

The steamship was the key to this increased exposure of sportsmen and sportswomen. The railways had made possible the national breakthrough, with the last quarter of the 19th century being a very fecund period for the beginnings of organised, spectator sport. The cricket County Championship would, for instance, have been impossible without the regularity and rapidity of the new railway system, for teams could not, in earlier times, have realistically guaranteed to maintain the travel implicit in a congested fixture list. Something of the same is true of the Football League programme, whilst it was trains and trams that were on hand to transport the spectators to the venues. Newspapers became increasingly bound up with sport and this conveyed the data about the games to a huge range of interested fans. The steamship did the same for international sport, enabling teams and contestants to make good their commitments, bringing Australian cricketers, New Zealand rugby players and American tennis stars to British shores. In turn, the telegraph quickly brought news of our own heroes when they were visiting foreign parts, while, by the 1920s and 1930s, the 'wireless' was adding yet another dimension to the provision of news about and direct commentary on sporting events.

Soon there were overseas stars whose names were as well-recognised as the home-brewed variety. Occasionally there were was a sporting legend — Babe Ruth is perhaps the best example from those years — whose fame was known to the British public, although his chosen game did not have a local orientation. Of the ten selected here, we find four cricketers, although two are immortally coupled together, three athletes, a boxer, a tennis star, a baseball player and just one footballer — and he is a close call, being born in the Republic of Ireland. There are two women, which is two more than we were able to muster for the list of British sportspersons, but they proffer just a hint that the age-old prejudice against women on the sports-field was beginning to lift. Of the ten, two are Australian, four are American, plus a West Indian twosome, and three are European. It is hoped that it represents a reasonable range of nations and of sports.

After the end of our period there was to be another sea-change in both the transportation of sport and of the conveyance of news about sport. The plane and the television ushered in a further and enormous revolution, with, of course, the motor car and the coach playing an important subsidiary role for spectators and players alike. This opening out of sport on a wide plane of international activity attracted the commercial moguls and the global marketing of sport has now reached phenomenal proportions. Sportsmen, such as boxers, earn as much as £17m annually, while events like that the football World Cup Final might be viewed by a quarter of the world's population. Television rights, commercial sponsorship and widespread advertising amass infinitely more money that actual spectatordom, now that world sport is non-stop and incessant. One could watch it on television 24 hours a day. It affects every country in the world and practically every household. Whereas the cinema cannot manage that degree of penetration, not least because there is often a language problem, and popular music sometimes runs into cultural barriers as it, too, tries to conquer the world, spectator sport is the first and only piece of cultural activity to have achieved world dominion on that astounding scale.

And it all started with W G Grace.

 **BABE RUTH** (George Herman Ruth, 1895-1948, born Baltimore, USA)

During the relevant period, when there was no television coverage and little overseas radio, the foreign sportsmen and women who became well-known to British sports-lovers were invariably engaged in games played at a high level in Britain itself. We knew, for instance, about Don Bradman because he played against England at cricket. The one towering exception to this rule was Babe Ruth, baseball's most popular figure ever, for, of course, baseball was all but unknown in the United Kingdom, and was thought of by many, with gross unfairness, as a kind of swinging version of rounders. What an impact Babe Ruth made that, from a few grainy shots on news-reels and a few mentions on our sports pages, he forced himself into the recesses of our folk-memory. There had been some controversy about the true origins of baseball, some seeing it as an English import along the lines of rounders, some, more patriotically, associating it with the American pastime known as 'old cat'. They gave the credit to Abner Doubleday, a brave hero of Gettysburg, for having developed the modern version at Coopersville in 1839. Whatever the rights and wrongs of that dispute, the initial rules drawn up in mid-19th century by Alexander J Cartwright became the authorised convention, with his New York 'hard ball' mode out-vying the Boston 'soft ball' approach. Soon after the American Civil War almost a hundred clubs joined the first National Convention, and the structure of a number of major national leagues evolved.

Like many American sportsmen, Babe Ruth struggled to survive in deprived conditions and, in fact, was boarded in a Baltimore industrial school, something akin to a refuge for waifs and strays, from the tender age of seven. It did, however, engender in him an interest in sport and in 1914 he began his professional career with the local Baltimore club. Such was his immediate success, he was quickly transferred that very season to the Boston Red Sox, while in 1920 he moved on, at a then exorbitant fee of $125,000 to the New York Yankees. He played his final season of 1935 with the Boston Braves, before acting as a coach for the Brooklyn Dodgers.

It is important for British readers to realise that he was an all-rounder, not only the best batter but one of the best pitchers. It is also of interest that he batted and pitched left-handed, and it is also fair to add that he was a highly competitive character who had an occasional brush with prim authority. He was a big man, weighing in at 15 stones and well over six feet in height. His digestive capacity and gargantuan appetite was alomost as fabled as his big hitting. Like many popular sportmen, he was easily recognisable from the terracing and he built up a tremendous following. It is said that during his Major-league career he broke over 50 records. He hit over 40 home runs in each of 11 seasons, with his finest year being 1927, when he established the astounding record of 60 home runs in a 154 game season. In sum, he struck 714 home runs in 22 big league seasons, whilst he also held records for scoreless pitching. He played in ten World Series, three with the Boston Red Sox and seven with the New York Yankees.

Whether we quite understood the detail of what he attained, of one thing we were certain: 'the Sultan of Swat' was a world-class sportsman and the greatest baseball player of all time.

 HELEN WILLS (Helen Newington Wills Moody Roark, 1905-1998, born Berkeley, California)

Court or Real (that is 'royal', as in Real Madrid football club) tennis has a long history as a pastime of the rich. With its elaborate galleries and complex architecture, it was a game that only the well-to-do could afford, and it had staunch regal support in previous centuries. 'Tenez', the French for 'take it', gives us 'tennis', whilst 'love' for nil derives from the French 'l'oeuf', the round egg of zero or, in cricket, a 'duck'. It was not until 1874 that Major Walter C Wingfield introduced his hour-glass shaped or 'Sphairistike' outdoor court, and the All England Croquet Club, being very short of funds, decided to add some of the new 'lawn tennis' facilities to its Wimbledon base. 22 men, almost all real tennis or rackets players, competed for the first championship in 1887, and 200 watched as Spencer W Gore became the first Wimbledon champion. In 1884 the rectangular dimensions for lawn tennis were agreed; the English Lawn Tennis Association was founded in 1886, and the game rapidly spread across the globe. The modern Wimbledon club was opened in 1922. The Davis Cup, the Wightman Cup and a number of elite open championships proved highly popular and there were the beginnings of the current highly valued professional component of tennis. The Americans began to dominate.

Despite the efforts of Englishmen like Fred Perry, who had a hat-trick of Wimbledon triumphs, 1934 to 1936, there were USA stars like William Tilden, J Donald Budge, Jack Kramer and Pancho Gonzales to capture the imagination. On the distaff side, Suzanne Lenglen, the elegant French player, was a major influence, winning six Wimbledon titles after the first world war, before turning professional, but it is perhaps Helen Wills who may be most clearly remembered by tennis fans among the older generation. It should be recalled that, until the tough teenager, May Sutton, appeared to win the 1904 USA and the 1905 Wimbledon titles (she was the first American to win an English title) ladies' tennis had been decorous rather than competitive. Helen Wills built on this revolutionary approach.

Helen Wills was of medium height and with a well-proportioned figure. She approached her task with the utmost seriousness, giving rise to her sobriquet, 'Little Miss Poker Face.' Although not as speedy as some of her contemporaries, she demonstrated a compelling all-round show of shots, including, crucially, the strong forehand drive, that mark of the prominent tennis player. Thus she came to dominate ladies' world tennis through the late 1920s and the 1930s. Having begun playing at 13, she won her first title at 17, and went on to win eight Wimbledon titles, seven USA titles and four French titles, together with 12 women's and mixed doubles championships, and two gold medals at the only Olympics — Paris in 1924 — in which the USA tennis players have participated. She played in the first Wightman Cup match against Great Britain in 1923 and, in ten Wightman Cup appearances, she won 18 out of 20 singles matches. From 1927 to 1932 she actually won every singles set she played. Later her bitter rivalry with Helen Hull Jacobs added zest to the women's tennis circuit. She owes her lengthy name-count to her two marriages, viz, to F S Moody in 1929 — hence the umpires and commentators called her 'Mrs Moody' in the rather formal *patois* of the tennis court — and to Adrian Roark in 1937. Helen Wills was to have several glorious American female successors, Doris Hart, Louise Brough and 'Little Mo' Connolly among them in the immediate post-war years.

 DON BRADMAN (Sir Donald George Bradman, 1908-2001, born Cootamundra, New South Wales, Australia)

Rarely has a person dominated a sport, in fact, any calling, with the assiduous comprehension of Don Bradman, rightly said to have been 'the most effective batsman the game has yet produced . . . Bradman's achievements remain beyond parallel'. He was but an occasional bowler, while, as a fielder, he was efficient rather than outstanding, so that he was not, like Wally Hammond, an all-rounder. However, the staggering efficacy of his batsmanship is truly bewildering. He scored over 28,000 runs at an average per innings of 95, with a highest score of 452, not out, still the biggest innings ever played on Australian soil. He scored 6996 of those runs in his 52 Test matches at an average of 99.94. Had he not famously succumbed for a duck in his final Test at the Oval in 1948 and instead scratched just four runs, his international average would have been 100. Even the ill-starred 'Bodyline' series of 1932/33 in Australia, when the unbending patrician, Douglas Jardine, organised the controversial fast leg-theory bowling of Harold Larwood and Bill Voce to minimise the Australian's menace, did not see him flag substantially, although it did lead to a political rumpus of some proportion. For once the figures do not lie and, for once, the figures tell much of the story. Don Bradman was the *nonpareil* accumulator of runs. Nimble, sturdily built, hawk-eyed and mentally unwavering, he appeared to be entirely without inhibition or anxiety. It has been said of him that, such was this command and the time he found to decide on his actions, he usually had a choice of shots for each ball, although he cleverly kept the ball on the ground, to avoid giving catching chances, while he was also adept at guiding the ball among the gaps left by fielders. Moreover, he believed thoroughly in the need to score quickly, in order to amass vast totals yet leave plenty of time for one's bowlers to remove the opposition. The old American Civil War general's motto — that the battle goes to those who 'gets thur fustest with the mostest' — might have been coined for Don Bradman.

It was with a mix of apprehension and admiration that thousands flocked to watch him on the four occasions he visited British shores, in 1930, in 1934, in 1938 and in 1948. Never once did he fail, scoring over 2000 runs on each visit, including a Test innings at Leeds in 1930 of 334 — a world record until Len Hutton's famous 364 at the Oval against Bradman's injury-plagued team of 1938 — followed by a 304, also at Leeds in 1934. He may have had a couple of off-field problems.

It seems he did not always see eye-to-eye with some of his colleagues *apropos* social activities, whilst his discerning biographer, Charles Williams, remarks on the personal tension between 'the Don' and some of his teammates, such as Bill 'Tiger' O'Reilly and Jack Fingleton. In turn, this possibly epitomised the Australian rift between the firm monarchical lower middle-class English Protestantism, represented by the former, and the staunch working class Irish roman catholic roots of the latter. These are marginal points. Few of the germane generations will have forgotten the name and what it meant in world sport. The urbane cricket correspondent, Neville Cardus, wrote of a Bradman innings, when, in 1930, he scored 155 in 155 minutes on the Saturday of the Lord's Test, before going on to make that 254 on the Monday, 'Never before this hour has a batsman equalled Bradman's cool deliberate murder or spifflication of all bowling'. Spifflication of all bowling was his life's work. He is widely regarded as Australia's one great hero and his death in 2001 was an occasion of profound national mourning.

 JOE LOUIS (Joseph Louis Barrow, 1914-1981, born Lexington, Alabama)

Joe Louis was the Muhammad Ali of that age, the boxer of whom everyone had heard. A 14 stone six-footer of massive build, he began his boxing career in Detroit and enjoyed huge success as an a amateur. Having won the light-heavyweight amateur championship in 1934, he turned professional and sustained his winning ways, typically by all-consuming knock-outs, for his punch was wholly destructive. In his first year as a paid boxer, he won ten of his 12 fights with such knock-outs. It was a gruelling vocation: in his second year, he fought five times in 25 days. In 1937 he won the World Heavyweight Championship, knocking out the holder, James Braddock, in the eighth round. He proceeded to knock out five other world champions; Primo Carnera, Jack Sharkey, Max Baer, Max Schmeling and Joe Walcott. He successively defended his title no less than 25 times, more in total than his eight predecessors, and retired, undefeated, in 1949, having held the world title longer than anyone. Like so many boxers, he felt obliged to make a come-back; like so many boxers, it ended in failure, at the lethal hands of his successor, Ezzard Charles. Nonetheless, shrewdly managed by the promoter, Mike Jacobs, he made well over $4m and was involved in some of the first $1m receipts for boxing tournaments. Serving as a soldier in World War II, he entertained his fellow-servicemen with exhibition bouts and, in 1954, he was elected to boxing's Hall of Fame.

Bare knuckle bouts had given way to the relatively civilising effects of the Queensberry Rules in mid-19th century, but the trade still remained a rough one. Modern scientific boxing emerged from those bruising days that ended with the battering heroics of John L Sullivan, and witnessed the advent of the adept cleverness of Gentleman Jim Corbett, who was champion from 1892 to 1897. Throughout the 19th century the sport had become, as it was to remain, 'the short cut to riches and social acceptance' for the impoverished, giving rise to the myth that only hungry boxers made the grade. Certainly it was a sport dominated in the USA by oppressed minorities, such as the latest tranche of European immigrants or the Afro-Americans, the sons and grandsons of ex-slaves. Joe Louis was the second black American to win the crown, emulating and then surpassing the achievement of Jack Jackson, champion from 1908 to 1915. Thereafter, black Americans came to the fighting fore, among them Ezzard Charles, but also Ray Robinson, Jersey Joe Walcott, Floyd Patterson and Sonny Liston. Joe Louis did more than take and hold the World Heavyweight Championship, the blue riband of boxing, for a record span. The fact that he did so with enormous dignity and civility was almost equally significant. It was a time when racial relations were, to say the least, uneasy in the United States and when some boxers, among them Jack Dempsey, refused to 'cross the colour line' and fight black opponents. Joe Louis was a model both of powerful skill and decent values, a figure, then, of immeasurable influence in the slow mending of that cruel divide. Unluckily, inefficient management left him with a massive federal tax burden and there was a point where he was reduced to acting as a 'greeter' at Caesar's Palace, Las Vegas. As for older British fans, the potent memory remains of listening to a 1937 wireless commentary, beset by static and whistling echoes, from the United States, as the valiant, tough-hearted Welshman, Tommy Farr, came as close as any 20th century Briton did to wresting the championship for the United Kingdom.

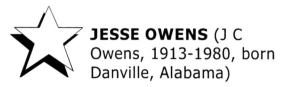

JESSE OWENS (J C Owens, 1913-1980, born Danville, Alabama)

In between the two world wars, there was no more dramatic event of a political-cum-cultural nature than the performance of Jesse Owens at the 1936 Berlin Olympics. Billed by the Nazis as a theatre for Aryan virtue and supremacy, and noted by many modern historians as a diplomatic staging-post on the road to World War II, the whirlwind victories of the black American athlete rocked the Hitlerite regime. The Fuhrer himself stalked from the Olympic Stadium rather than recognise the achievement of the superb black runner. It was a staggering tale of success. Jesse Owens won four gold medals, setting world records in three of the events and an Olympic record in the other one, a 10.3 seconds 100 metres dash. His world records came in the 200 metres, with a run of 20.7 seconds; the running broad jump, that is, long jump, with a leap of over 26 feet, and as anchor-man in the USA 400 metres relay team with a bewildering time of 39.8 seconds. A man of considerable self-respect and nobility of character, as well as of phenomenal physical gifts and the mental discipline to make these physiological advantages count, his life after athletics was one of civic duty and responsibility. He became involved in youth work, in goodwill missions for the American State Department, in public relations and in athletics administration in Illinois.

Jesse Owens had been fortunate enough to find his route through the American schools system, with its marked emphasis on promising athleticism. He attended the Fairview Junior High School at Cleveland, Ohio, where staff and students alike were surprised at his audacious form. He broke the junior high school record for 100 metres with a straight 10 seconds sprint, and he further impressed when he moved on to the Cleveland East Technical High School. In 1933, in a spirited prelude to his Olympic activities, he enjoyed great success at the National Interscholastic Championships at the University of Chicago, whereafter he simply left a burning trail of smashed track and field records everywhere he competed. During this time, and as a member of the University of Ohio State University athletics team, he attended the Western Conference (Big Ten) meeting at the University of Michigan, a competition among strong college teams. Here is what he achieved in a single day, the momentous 25 May 1935. First, he equalled the 100 metres record with a time of 9.4 seconds; secondly, his 22.6 seconds sprint broke the 220 metres world record; next, he did the same for the 220 metres low hurdles, clocking a time of but 22.6 seconds; finally, he managed a record for the long jump of a trifle over 26 feet 8 inches which endured a generation. Talk about one crowded hour of glorious life. It would be difficult to find a similar day in any sport where a man or woman so stated their case for being regarded as the supreme and most versatile practitioner of that sport.

His fame, especially given his Olympian glory, was extensive in Europe. It was such a boost for anti-Nazi morale when the unassuming, but highly tenacious, American athlete found his way past Adolf Hitler's black smut of a moustache and got right up his Fascist hooter.

FANNY BLANKERS-KOEN (Francina Blankers-Koen, 1918-2000, born Baarn, Holland)

Pierre de Coubertin, believing, perhaps naively, that the Grecian ideal could be replicated in a modern Olympiad (possibly not having realised that one of the reasons the ancient Greeks forewent the pleasure was because of political wrangling and intrigue) lit the new Olympic flame in 1896. Twelve nations had been represented at a conference at the Sorbonne in Paris in 1894 and then, under the sponsorship of the King of Greece and in a purpose-built marble stadium in Athens, the first Olympic Games of the modern dispensation was held. James Connolly of Boston became the first champion, winning the hop, skip and jump, while, appropriately enough, a Greek, Spyros Louis, won the Marathon. There were only about 40 events, but the modern games were successfully launched. Yet prejudice against women abounded. Pierre de Coubertin was himself a virulent critic of sportswomen. 'Women have but one task', he opined, 'that of crowning the victor with garlands'. There were other setbacks. At the 1928 Amsterdam Games, for example, the women's 800 metres was a fiasco. Five competitors dropped out; five collapsed; and the eleventh woman, the only finisher, fainted afterwards. The cry was raised that women were too feeble for such exercise, but soon it was realised that it was not gender, but poor preparation and training, that was to blame. Even at the Wembley Games of 1948, with the world looking to cement new-found international friendships in that first post-war athletic celebration, there were ten sportsmen to every one sports-

woman. Fortunately for woman's athletics, one of them was Fanny Blankers-Koen.

Although she came of a sporting family, young Fanny Koen had herself taken little interest in athletics until, aged 16, she met Jan Blankers, who became her trainer and then her husband. At 17, she made her debut, winning an 800 metres race, and then, between 1938 and 1951, she held seven world records in an astonishing period of supremacy. These were in the 100 yards, the 100 metres, the 220 yards, the 80 metres hurdles, the high jump, the long jump and the Pentathlon. In 1946 she won medals in the 80 metres hurdles and the 4 X 100 metres relay, just six weeks after having given birth to her first child. At the London Olympiad of 1948 the British press claimed that she was too old and would show little form. So much for journalistic prophecy. Uniquely, at that time, she proceeded to win four gold medals and became the much-heralded heroine of the games. The 100 metres, the 200 metres, the 80 metres hurdles and the 4 X 100 metres relay race all fell to the smiling but intensely competitive, flaxen-haired Dutchwoman. Her chief threat was from the English hurdler, Maureen Gardner, in the brief exhilaration of the 80 metres. Jan Blankers had the perfect choice of words to sharpen his wife for the battle. 'Don't forget, Fanny', he whispered, as she prepared for the start, 'you're too old'. She did not fare too well at the following Games, at Helsinki, in 1952, but, aged 38 in 1956, she completed a wind-assisted 80 yards hurdles in just 11.3 seconds, very near her own world record time of 11 seconds. At long last the focus was on a woman athlete and, of course, at subsequent games, the strong prowess of East European women came to the fore.

It has been justly said of Fanny Blankers-Koen that she was 'the greatest all-round woman athlete of the century'. It was good to hear of her in 1999, an 82 year old grandmother, attending an international athletics meeting in Monte Carlo.

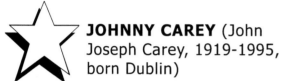 **JOHNNY CAREY** (John Joseph Carey, 1919-1995, born Dublin)

Out of the debris of war stepped a 35 year old army warrant officer. He was destined to create Britain's major footballing phenomenon, the universal triumph of Manchester United. It was Matt Busby. When he took over as manager after World War II, the Old Trafford ground had been bombed, and first team games had to be played at Maine Road, home of Manchester City, rivals whom, before the war, had usually been the premier Mancunian outfit. One advantage Matt Busby did have was the support of a world-class player who, technically, came from overseas, although he had been on active service during the second world war. It was Johnny Carey from Eire.

His positional skill, sharp footballing brain and deft feet were such that he was the complete all-rounder, probably the most comprehensively so of any footballer before or since. His intelligence enabled him to move into high-class management, once his own footballing days were over, and he was also a competent linquist. He played in every position, including goal-keeper, for Manchester United, except for outside-left, in a sport where many players are usually narrow in their specialism. In the grandeur of his post-war years, he normally played right back, then later on at right half. Urbane, unflurried, with a civilised air of composed authority, he was one of the first of the cultured defenders, no hard-booting clogger he, and friend and foe alike admired him respectfully. He was the captain of the first great United team, the one that won the FA Cup against Blackpool in 1948, a game still recalled by critics as the finest of the Wembley finals in its counterpoint of drama and artistry. He captained United in their first post-war Championship season of 1951-52. Voted Footballer of the Year in 1949, he won many international caps and had the unique distinction of captaining the Rest of Europe *versus* Great Britain at Hampden Park, Glasgow, in 1947. It was a time of ability and solidity across the football of the four nations, and the Europeans, sparkling as each was individually, could not match the overall strength of their opponents.

Great Britain won 6-1, but complacency would soon be shattered when, in 1953, England's unbeaten home record was shattered when the brilliant Hungarians romped to confident victory at Wembley — another little curtain descending to bring our period to a formal close. About this time the 'Busby Babes', with Duncan Edwards their titanic inspiration, emerged as the second great United combine, only for them to be mown down before they reached their peak in the icy tragedy of Munich. Out of those ashes then rose the Phoenix of a third splendid team, that of Denis Law, George Best and Bobby Charlton, first English winners of the European Cup. In the modern era, Sir Alex Ferguson has built a side of world-enhancing might. Yet so much of this glamorous history may be traced back to the manager/

captain partnership of Sir Matt Busby and Johnny Carey. Balding, serious in face and manner, Johnny Carey also was, as a citizen of Eire, something of a forerunner of another modern dispensation, and that is the Cantonas, the Zolas and the Bergkamps who bring so much of foreign flair and colour to the British game. Possibly none of them could manage to sing Johnny Carey's party-piece, performed when United were travelling or celebrating, namely, *Paddy M'Ginty's Goat*.

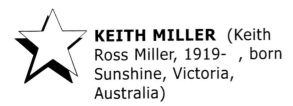 **KEITH MILLER** (Keith Ross Miller, 1919- , born Sunshine, Victoria, Australia)

Occasionally people are born in appropriately-named places. Keith Miller certainly brought lots of sunshine into the lives of cricket watchers in the immediate post-war period. He was, so to say, the Australian Denis Compton — and it should come as no surprise to learn that the two were life-long buddies. An officer and a pilot in the Royal Australian Air Force, he was properly conscious, having seen colleagues, including fellow cricketers, killed in action, of his good fortune in surviving. As a consequence, he was determined to squeeze the zest out of life to the utmost. A brilliantly instinctive player of manifold gifts, he was an all-rounder of dazzling class. Tall, strong, good-looking, and with his quiff of sleek black hair boyishly drifting across his brow, he thought little of defence. In combine with the devastating Ray Lindwall, he formed one of those fast bowling duos, like Trueman and Statham or Tyson and Statham or, pre-war, Larwood and Voce,

that bring such high drama to cricket grounds. He was a very quick but a very unpredictable bowler, ready at less than a moment's notice to forego his lengthy run-up to the crease and bowl something surprising off a two-pace run. A fine athlete, he was a superb catcher and thrower in the field, again always seeking to curtail and cabin the opposing batsman. As for his batting, when on song, he was hugely enterprising. Never happy to be bogged down by bowlers, he sought to assail them at all reasonable times, cracking the ball to all quarters with a sumptuous array of stylish shots. It is true that, by temperament and by inclination, he was not always authority's favourite child, and he found it hard to engage himself in cricket where the challenge was less than spirited and lively. He was rather bored by easy pickings, where many sportsmen are pleased to find comfortable chances to domineer. But this was merely the other side of the medallion of his nonchalant sportsmanship. What is interesting — as with Denis Compton — is the manner in which this mettlesome and chivalrous approach conveyed itself to the bleachers and to the terraces of Australian and English cricket grounds. By some kind of psychological osmosis, spectators picked up the signals of Keith Miller's knightly virtues and, in years of post-war recovery, were only to delighted to find escape from the bleak dullness of their surrounds.

It may seem shameful even to mention the dry feature of statistics when so Lancelot-oriented a cricketing warrior is being profiled, but, for all he was devil-may-care and personally uninterested in the maths of cricket, they are worth at least a mention. His first-class batting average is a sterling 49, and in

Test matches it was 37; he made 41 centuries, the best of them being 281, not out, in 1956; he took 497 first-class wickets at an average of 22, with a 170 of his victims, a substantial proportion, in Test cricket, at an average of 23. He adorned Don Bradman's Australian team of the winter of 1946/47 out in Australia and in the 1948 summer in England. There are knowledgeable commentators who assert that this was the greatest Test team ever. It had Sid Barnes and Arthur Morris as its obdurate opening pair; there was the youthful Neil Harvey, brimming over with talent, and the shining stroke-play of dapper Lindsay Hassett; while Don Tallon was the extremely competent wicket-keeper, the focus for tight and efficient fielding. Keith Miller became a respected journalist after his cricketing days were ended, leaving behind sparkling memories of his sporting adventures, as something of a Robin Hood among cricketers.

 **ZATOPEK** (Emil Zatopek, 1922- 2000 , born Koprivnice, Czechoslovakia, as was)

Emil Zatopek began his life in the sphere of athletics in the 1940s. He first came to notice in 1946 and for two reasons. He cycled from Prague to Berlin in 1946 to participate in the Allied Occupation Forces athletics meeting there — and he romped home in the 5000 metres. That duality of the slightly off-beat and the rigorously combatant was to mark the course of his athletic contributions. At that time he was a private in the Czech army and that, in itself, was characteristic of the form sport in the east of Europe would take.

Although it was not an entirely new phenomenon, the armed forces acted as the occupational host for many athletes in the pro-Soviet regimes of post-war Europe. Moreover, the Olympic Games had increasingly become the focus for international politicking and grandstanding, however pure the original ideal. Gradually, the nationalist trappings had been added. Even the 1896 Games had been marred by the rage of the defeated Greeks, to say nothing of the Americans squabbling among themselves and the Germans being a trifle insufferable. The 1908 Americans left London, disgusted by 'such cruel and unsportsmanlike treatment' of what they regarded as the grossly unfair British judges and they vowed never to compete again. By 1932, in Los Angeles, each country had its own hamlet, the triple victory rostrum was introduced and national anthems were played. National medal league tables, not the assembling of the world's youth, became the tawdry criterion of success. Practically every Games has had a political agenda of one kind or another, with some — the murder of eleven Israeli athletes at Munich in 1972 is a particularly dreadful illustration — spoilt irrevocably by political incidents.

In the Cold War period, the highly disciplined and regimented Soviet bloc competitors strove mightily to demonstrate the efficacy of their new order. To many in the west, it all seemed too grey and unremittingly stern. Emil Zatopek, the consummate long distance runner, contrived to make many people question those preconceptions. He was the surprising star of the 1952 Helsinki Games, where he won three gold medals, in the 5000 metres, the 10,000 metres and the Marathon. He broke the 5000 and 10,000 metres Olympic records in so doing, while his was the fastest Marathon ever run at that juncture. During his career he held 18 world records in a variety of events, including the 5000 metres, the 10 miles, the one hour (that is, the distance covered in that time), the 20,000 metres, the 15 miles, the 25,000 metres and the 30,000 metres. He held the 10,000 metres record from 1949 to 1954, his best time being 28 minutes 54.2 seconds. However, it was the manner of his accomplishment that also attracted admiration. Against the strict and uniform canvas of Iron Curtain certitude, he conveyed a very genuine spirit of individualism. Chatty and gleeful, his only problem in the Marathon — a race more or less unknown to him until he ran and won it — was losing contact with his rivals and having no one with whom to converse. Rangy in build and craggy of countenance, he belied the ease of his victories with grotesque facial expressions of endeavour, and this all helped to personalise him. It should surprise no one that this very independently-minded soul was deprived of his colonelcy in the Czech Army for speaking out against the 1968 Russian take-over of Czechoslovakia when that nation tried, in the expression of the time, to put a 'smile' on the face of Soviet rule. Happily, he was soon restored to official activity, working, energetically and cheerfully, with Czech athletes of the next generation.

RAMADHIN AND VALENTINE (Sonny Ramadhin, 1929- , born Trinidad, and Alfred Lewis Valentine, 1930- , born Jamaica)

The stately authority of Lord's was shocked, then mildly beguiled, by the rhythmic tones of calypso echoing around cricket's headquarters as, in the summer of 1950, the West Indies recorded their first Test win in England. It was by the very convincing margin of 326 runs. Having lost the first match of the rubber badly, they won this the second, then the next, by ten wickets, and the fourth and last by an innings and 56 runs. The Caribbean stanza that, courtesy of Lord Kitchener and his *confrères*, resounded around Lord's in that carnival atmosphere praised 'those two little pals of mine, Ramadhin and Valentine'. They were unknowns, literally pressed into service after but a brief introduction into first-class cricket at home, and jettisoned into the international arena. They were not similar. Sonny Ramadhin was from Trinidad, and he was a diminutive right handed off-spinner, who, sleeves fluttering, could bowl the leg break without discernible change of grip and action. Alf Valentine was from Jamaica, a tall and rangy orthodox left hand spin bowler with a perilous tweak of turn. Each was barely twenty-one and genuine innocents abroad, as they bamboozled England with their befuddling slow bowling. 'Ram' took 135 wickets, average 14.88, of which 26 were Test victims, whilst 'Val' took 123 wickets, average 17.94, of which 33 — a record for a four match Test series — were in Test matches. In that 1950 Test series they bowled 69% of the West Indian overs and took 70% of the wickets, that is, 59 of the 77 that fell to bowlers.

They were never quite to repeat such sensational feats but they have gone down in cricketing lore as one of the most famed of spinning partnerships ever, just as their near contemporaries, Jim Laker and Tony Lock, the Surrey 'twins', were to have something of a major impact on English and world cricket. It was the more astonishing in that the West Indies had relied in the past more on pace bowling, in the exhilarating hands, for instance, of Learie Constantine, also a whirlwind bat and superhuman fielder, and 'Manny' Martindale, both well-known in northern cricket league circles. Indeed, after the brief Ramadhin/Valentine dominion, the West Indies were to unleash sweep after sweep of terrifyingly quick bowlers that made them, for many years, the most feared of international cricket teams. One thinks of Wes Hall and Charlie Griffith, through to Courtney Walsh and Curtly Ambrose. As for batting,

the West Indies have been blessed with such outstanding talents as George Headley, in the pre-war years; the three 'Ws', Frank Worrell, Everton Weekes and Clyde Walcott of the Ramadhin and Valentine generation, to be followed by such world-class swashbucklers as Gary Sobers, thought by many critics to be the best all-rounder ever, Clive Lloyd, Viv Richards and, currently, Brian Lara. The surprise of the success of Sonny Ramadhin and Alf Valentine came just as the West Indian wave of migration to this country began. Those contemplating the move must have been encouraged by learning of their achievement and by hearing their compatriots' voices raised in the calypso hymn of 'Cricket, Lovely Cricket'. Furthermore, they endeared themselves to English hearts and there are a lot of English cricket-lovers, as well, of course, as thousands of West Indian supporters, who could carol a few lines of that most exuberant and most popular of cricketing lyrics.

NOSTALGIASKING ~ THE BEST-REMEMBERED QUIZ

. . . a hundred questions based on the hundred famous figures profiled in this book.

(Nb. each of the ten stars in each of the ten sections is involved with one question and one question only)

Round One: American Film Stars

Who was the main star in the following USA films?

1. Objective Burma

2. Flesh and the Devil

3. Gilda

4. The Jazz Singer

5. Horse Feathers

6. The Hunchback of Notre Dame

7. Top Hat

8. Key Largo

9. The Littlest Rebel

10. Meet Me in St Louis

Round Two: British Film Stars

1. Who was the odd man out?

2. Who exorcised the ghost of St Michael's?

3. Who were chumps at Oxford?

4. Who was the wicked lady?

5. Who was the Mr Chips they wished goodbye?

6. Who was the tramp?

7. Who was the colourful girl who went with the wind?

8. Who was the lady who had a brief encounter?

9. Who found trouble brewing?

10. Who realised that green was for danger?

Round three: Radio Personalities

With which radio personality would you associate the following catch-phrases?

1. It all depends on what you mean by. . .

2. and this is me . . . at the BBC theatre organ

3. Good night children, everywhere

4. 'Ow do and 'ow are yer?

5. It's That Man Again

6. Right, Monkey

7. Aithangyow

8. Wake up at the back there!

9. Mind my bike

10. This is the nine o'clock news...

Round four: Dance Band Leaders

With which of the following tunes would you mainly associate which band leader?

1. 'You can't do that there 'ere'
2. 'I bring you sweet music'
3. 'Here's to the next time'
4. 'When day is done'
5. 'In the mood'
6. 'Moonlight Serenade'
7. 'On the air'
8. 'Opus One'
9. 'Somebody stole my girl'
10. 'You're dancing on my heart'

Round Five: British Theatre Stars

Who?

1. Was The Prime Minister of Mirth
2. Stole his heart away
3. Asserted there was always tomorrow
4. Stood up and sang with Jack Buchanan
5. Offered negative career advice to Mrs Worthington
6. Thought she would find him someday
7. Kept the home fires burning
8. Firstly, was The Entertainer
9. Threw cares over her shoulder
10. Was Boo

Round Six: Popular Singers

Which singers are most associated with each of the following songs?

1. 'Love is the sweetest thing'
2. 'Only a rose'
3. 'Sweet Rosie O'Grady'
4. 'Wish me luck as you wave me good-bye'
5. 'Down Forget-me-not Lane'
6. 'The blue of the night'
7. 'The Boogie-woogie Bugle Boy'
8. 'Powder Your Face with Sunshine'
9. 'I'll pray for you'
10. 'Whispering grass'

Round Seven: Comedians

Identify the comics from their catch-phrases or bill-matter

1. The Confidential Comedian
2. She knows, yer know
3. The Cheeky Chappie
4. Over the garden wall
5. Almost a Gentleman
6. We are the Diddy-men who come from Knotty Ash
7. The Comedian's Comedian
8. I say, I say, I say...
9. Thanks for the Memory
10. Can you hear me, mother?

Round Eight: Fictitious Characters

1. Who was known as 'the office boy's Sherlock Holmes'?

2. Who proved elusive in a revolutionary era?

3. Which tiny rodent was almost a Mortimer?

4. Which dandified westerner ate voraciously?

5. Which juvenile Lancastrian was fit for a leonine feast?

6. Who joined Henry, Douglas and Ginger in the Outlaws?

7. What ovine creature was requested to proffer his name and address to the constabulary?

8. Which girl was bare-faced enough to give her pet a Teutonic name?

9. Which agent had 'snowy' support?

10. Which model son had a good idea?

Round Nine: British Sportspersons

1. What was Cliff Bastin's nickname?

2. On what horse did Gordon Richards win the 1953 Derby?

3. What was the venue for world snooker championships in the Joe Davis era?

4. Where did Henry Cotton win the third and last of his British Open Golf Championships?

5. In what year did Stanley Matthews famously win his only Cup Final medal?

6. For which county did Wally Hammond play cricket?

7. Who beat Tommy Farr in 1937 to retain the World Heavyweight boxing title?

8. For which football team did Wilf Mannion play?

9. Who was, with Denis Compton, the other 'Middlesex Twin'?

10. What was the name of Donald Campbell's speed-boat?

Round Ten: Overseas Sportspersons

1. Who was baseball's 'Sultan of Swat'?

2. On what English cricket ground did Don Bradman score two Test Match 300s?

3. From whom did Joe Louis wrest the World Heavyweight boxing title?

4. For which football team did Johnny Carey play?

5. What tennis star was known as 'Little Miss Poker-face'?

6. Who was Keith Miller's fast bowling partner for Australia in the post-war years?

7. What nationality was Emil Zatopek?

8. Jesse Owens won four gold medals in the 1936 Olympics - in which city?

9. Fanny Blankers-Koen won four gold medals in the London Olympics — in what year?

10. Who were 'those two little pals of mine'?

Answers on page 158

ANSWERS

Round One:
1. Errol Flynn 2.Greta Garbo
3. Rita Hayworth 4. Al Jolson
5. the Marx Brothers 6. Charles Laughton
7. Ginger Rogers and Fred Astaire
8. Humphrey Bogart 9. Shirley Temple
10. Judy Garland

Round Two:
1. James Mason 2. Will Hay
3. Laurel and Hardy 4. Margaret Lockwood
5. Robert Donat 6. Charlie Chaplin
7. Vivien Leigh 8. Celia Johnson
9. George Formby 10. Alastair Sim

Round Three:
1. Professor Joad 2. Sandy Macpherson
3. Uncle Mac 4. Wilfred Pickles
5. Tommy Handley 6. Al Read
7. Arthur Askey 8. Jimmy Edwards
9. Jack Warner 10. Alvar Liddell

Round Four:
1. Jack Payne 2. Geraldo
3. Henry Hall 4. Ambrose 5. Joe Loss
5. Glenn Miller 7. Carroll Gibbons
8. Ted Heath 9. Billy Cotton
10. Victor Silvester

Round Five:
1. George Robey 2. Binnie Hale
3. Jack Buchanan 4. Anna Neagle
5. Noel Coward 6. Gertrude Lawrence
7. Ivor Novello 8. Laurence Olivier
9. Jessie Matthews 10. Evelyn Laye

Round Six:
1. Al Bowlly 2. Anne Ziegler and Webster
Booth 3. Betty Grable 4. Gracie Fields
5. Flanagan and Allen 6. Bing Crosby
7. the Andrew Sisters 8. Donald Peers
9. Vera Lynn 10. the Inkspots

Round Seven:
1. Robb Wilton 2. Hylda Baker
3. Max Miller 4. Norman Evans
5. Billy Bennett 6. Ken Dodd
7. Jimmy James 8. Murray and Mooney
9. Bob Hope 10. Sandy Powell

Round Eight:
1. Sexton Blake 2. The Scarlet Pimpernel
3. Mickey Mouse 4. Desperate Dan
5. Albert Ramsbottom 6. Just William
7. Larry the Lamb 8. Jane 9. Dick Barton
10. Archie Andrews

Round Nine:
1. 'Boy' Bastin 2. Pinza
3. Leicester Square Hall 4. Muirfield
5. 1953 6. Gloucestershire 7. Joe Louis
8. Middlesborough 9. Bill Edrich
10. Bluebird

Round Ten:
1. Babe Ruth 2. Headingley, Leeds
3. James Braddock 4. Manchester United
5. Helen Wills 6. Ray Lindwall
7. Czechoslovak 8. Berlin
9. 1948 10. Ramadhin and Valentine

THIRD AGE PRESS
. . . *a unique publishing company*
inspired by older people

. . . an independent
publishing company which recognizes that the
period of life after full-time employment and family
responsibility can be a time of fulfilment and
continuing development
. . . a time of regeneration

Third Age Press

...books are available by direct mail order from
Third Age Press or on order from good bookshops.

All direct mail order prices include UK p & p.
Please add 20% for other countries.
UK Sterling cheques payable to *Third Age Press.*

6 Parkside Gardens London SW19 5EY
Phone 020 8947 0401   Fax 020 8944 9316
e-mail: dnort@globalnet.co.uk

Website: www.thirdagepress.co.uk

Dianne Norton ~ Managing Editor
Registered in England Company Number 2678599
VAT registered 627 9627 01

Third Age Press has published the following four books by Eric Midwinter

Lifelines

. . . is a series that focuses on the presentation of your unique life. These booklets seek to stimulate and guide your thoughts and words in what is acknowledged to be not only a process of value to future generations but also a personally beneficial exercise.

A Voyage of Rediscovery: a guide to writing your life story

A Voyage of Rediscovery is a 'sea chart' to guide your reminiscence. It offers 'triggers' to set your memory to full steam ahead (although backwards might be more appropriate) and provides practical advice about the business of writing or recording your story.

1993 2nd Edition 2001   36pages   ISBN 1 898576 00 9   £4.50

Encore: a guide to planning a celebration of your life

An unusual and useful booklet that encourages you to think about the ways you would like to be remembered, hopefully in the distant future.

1993   20pages ISBN 1 898576 02 5   £2.50

The Rhubarb People . . . Eric Midwinter's own witty and poignant story of growing up in Manchester in the 1930s . . .published as a booklet but also as a 90-minute **talking book** read by the author. The talking book includes useful tips on writing or recording your story.

1993 32pages ISBN 1 898576 01 7   £4.50
Talking Book   £5.00

Getting To Know Me . . . is aimed at carers and families of people in care. It provides the opportunity to create a profile of an older person ~ their background and relationships, likes and dislikes, as well as record the practical information needed to make the caring process a positive experience for all concerned. The end result should be a valuable tool for any carer.

1996   24pages   ISBN 1 898576 07 6   £4.50

Lifescapes: the landscapes of a lifetime by Enid Irving

. . . introduces a whole new art form . . . a **Lifescape** is a collage of memories. Make one just for fun or as a very special family heirloom. *Lifescapes* can be made by individuals, in groups, as a family or as an intergenerational activity. This latter approach is particularly recommended for people in care working with students or young helpers. The resulting *Lifescape* is not only decorative but serves to increase understanding of the whole person and stimulate memory.

1996 24pages   ISBN 1 898576 08 4   £4.50

For Carers

Voyage of Redicovery has been particularly popular with individuals wanting to get started on their own life stories but the comprehensive guidelines can equally well be used by people working together. For those working with more frail people, *Getting to know me* is especially designed to create a profile of an individual in care or about to go in to care.

To create a more visual record of a life and, at the same time, stimulate memory and communication, Enid Irving has developed the unique concept of the *Lifescape*. The guidelines can be used by an individual, by two generations working together, by a carer or artist working with a frail older person, or by a group. *Getting to know me* and *Lifescape* work very well together to create a comprehensive picture of an individual.

The Rhubarb People makes an excellent reading-aloud book and stimulates reminiscence ~ or hear the author read his own story on the **90-minute audio cassette**.

perspectives

. . . *offers a comprehensive publishing service for people wanting to produce a memoir for sale or distribution to friends and interested parties, or one beautiful heirloom book for your family. We do not undertake marketing ~ that's up to you (should you wish to distribute to a wider public).*

For clubs or associations, **Third Age Press** *also offers advise and comprehensive publishing services for the production of books, booklets, pamphlets or newsletters. Every project is individually priced and given our expert, personal attention. Please write for details.*

Rufus Segar has illustrated the following two books as well as
Getting to know me **and** *Lifescapes*

On the Tip of Your Tongue: your memory in later life

by Dr H B Gibson . . . explores memory's history and examines
what an 'ordinary' person can expect of their memory. He reveals
the truth behind myths about memory and demonstrates how you
can manage your large stock of memories and your life.
Wittily illustrated by Rufus Segar.

Includes:

• *What is memory?* The four memory
systems. Different sorts of memory.
• *How is your memory changing?*
Meeting people. Mistaking physical
for mental change. Remembering to do
things.
• *The 'Tip-of-the-tongue'
phenomenon* - Breaking the blockage.
The puzzle of blocked recall. The
Freudian explanation.
• *Gimmicks for remembering:*
Mnemonics - Place method - Pegwords
- learning foreign words - 'chunking' -
list of memory aids.
• *Improving your memory* - Memory
training. A practical training course.
What kind of memory have you got?
• *Will you continue to make progress
all your life?* Memory at different
stages of life. Enemies of progress.
Reminiscence.
• *Derangements, diseases and injuries
that effect memory.* Brain damage,
amnesia, depression, senility,
Alzheimer-type conditions.

1995 160pages ISBN 1 898576 05X   £7.00

Buy this book together with *A little of what you fancy* for only £13.00

A Little of What You Fancy Does You Good: your health in later life

by Dr H B Gibson ~ illustrated by Rufus Segar

'Managing an older body is like running a very old car - as the years go by you get to know its tricks and how to get the best out of it, so that you may keep it running sweetly for years and years' . . . so says Dr H B Gibson in his sensible and practical book which respects your intelligence and, above all, appreciates the need to enjoy later life. It explains the whys, hows and wherefores of exercise, diet and sex ~ discusses 'You and your doctor' and deals with some of the pitfalls and disabilities of later life. But the overall message is positive and Rufus Segar's illustrations once again bring whimsy and insight to a very readable text. Dr H B Gibson gives due cause for optimism.

Includes:

• *How much exercise do you take?* - Determinants of fitness. How fitness can be regained in later life.

• *What about diet?* - The constituents of food. Miraculous food & food additives. Can diet increase your life span?

• *What about sex?* Myths about sex in later life. What sexuality means in later life. Shyness.

• *You and your doctor* - Different types of patients. The doctors' dilemmas with older patients.

• *Some pitfalls in later life* - Eating - drinking - smoking. Personality types.

• *Disability in later life* - phyical conditions, sensory loss, dementias, depression, bereavement, loneliness etc.

1997   256pages ISBN 1 898576   £8.50

Third Age Press has published the following two books on social history topics

Our Grandmothers
Our Mothers
Ourselves
A CENTURY OF WOMEN'S LIVES

Charmian Cannon (Editor)
Eleven women who met through a U3A group exploring women's hidden social history talked, and then wrote, about their grandmothers, their mothers and their own lives. Their stories spanned the whole 20th Century, encompassed two world wars and many social and political changes affecting women. Through their discussions they crossed class and ethnic boundaries and exchanged their experiences of education, work and home life.

They shared intimate family recollections honestly ~ uncovering affectionate as well as painful memories.

This book is the result of that journey which has absorbed them for five years. As well as chronicling their individual life histories and setting them in the wider context of social change, the book describes how the work evolved and what they learned about themselves and their memories in the process.

The book includes a section on the increasing use of life histories as a way of linking personal lives and public events, and a list of sources and further reading.

Of interest to:
• anyone who likes a 'good read'
• adult education students
• anyone interested in family history
• women of any age
• teachers of social and/or women's history
• historians

May 2001 200pages ISBN 1 898576 27 0   £9.95

No Thanks to Lloyd George
The forgotten story ~ how the old age pension was won

by Dave Goodman   Foreword by Jack Jones

. . . a new edition of this popular book ~ *No Thanks to Lloyd George* tells a story of passion, dedication, determination and grit. From 1898 old people, living in fear of the work house, thronged to packed meetings all over the country to hear how their lives could be transformed by the introduction of a pension. But it took more than ten years of struggle and disappointment before the first British old people collected five shillings from their post offices.

1998 96pp ISBN 1 898576 12 2   £3.60

An experiment in living: sharing a house in later life

by June Green, Jenny Betts & Greta Wilson

A new lifestyle for a new millennium's thirdagers? Truthful, humorous, thought-provoking, considered and practical . . . . this book is an introduction to a potential new lifestyle by three wise women. With 39% of women between the ages of 65 and 74, and 58% of those over 75 living alone, June, Jenny and Greta asked themselves some searching questions about how they wanted to face the future and came up with a sensible and exciting answer.

Starting with — ***Do you really want to share a house?*** — they take the reader through all the practicalities (sometime worked out the hard way!) involved in finding the right house and turning it into a home where they could all pursue their own interests while, at the same time, providing each other with support and friendship.

But the book is more than just a guide to how to set up house together. Interspersed with the practicalities the three authors have each reflected on *What's in it for them* and their individual attitudes to retirement. Candid friends and young relatives give their views of the arrangements and other options for shared living are also considered.

Maggie Guillon's cartoons cleverly pick up the delights and dilemmas of shared living.

1999 132pages   ISBN 1 898576 14 9   £9.25

Just in case . . . Making a home for elderly people

by Pat Howard.   Illustrated by Maggie Guillon

. . . refreshingly free from professional jargon . . . the language used communicates the dynamics, frustrations and humour of life in a residential home and fires the imagination . . . . the author skilfully weaves her own experiences of managing a care home to research related to older people's experience of living in one . . . one of the relatively few books written by a practitioner in the field, it is a refreshing attempt to help prospective residents glimpse the world of residential care. [Hilary Cox, Head of Care, Abbeyfield Medway Valley Society. Journal of the British Society of Gerontology, Dec 2000]

This is a book to . . .

• inspire and encourage anyone working with older people
• offer advice and reassurance to any one considering moving into a home or looking for a home for someone else.

June 2000 196pages ISBN 1 898576 22 X   £9.25

Consider the Alternatives:
healthy strategies for later life

by Dr Caroline Lindsay Nash   Illustrated by Maggie Guillon

This book offers a clear and unbiased
explanation of the nature and uses
of a wide range of alternative
therapies . . . what you can
expect of complementary
medicine . . . and why
yoga, pets, music and humour can contribute to your personal strategy for
a healthy thirdage. There are also contributions from Dr Michael Lloyd, a
psychologist specialising in the management of pain, and from pensioner,
Tony Carter, on how and why he thinks you should take control of your
own health.
Maggie Guillon's cartoons add a delightful touch.

Includes:
• *Alternative techniques of diagnosis*
• *Physical therapies - external body* - Back pain, chiropractic,
          cranio-sacral, physiotherapy, acupuncture, zero-balancing,
          Alexander technique
• *Physical therapies - internal body* - Nutrition, macrobiotics,
          herbalism, colonic irrigation
• *Mind over matter* - Psychoanalysis, psychodynamic counselling,
          humanistic approaches, psychosynthesis, counselling, group
          therapy, family therapy, transactional analysis, hypnotherapy
• *Something for the spirit* - Past life therapy, meditation, spiritual coun
          selling, spiritual healing, reiki, psychics and mediums
• *A holistic view of health* - Homoeopathy, anthroposophical medicine,
          traditional Chinese medicine, Ayurveda
• *Exercise and relaxation* - Exercise, dance, yoga, tai chi, massage,
          tragerwork, shiatsu, aromatherapy, pets
• *The strange, rare and fun* - Flower remedies, crystal healing, colour
          therapy, feng shui, drama, art and music therapy, laughter

1998 160pages ISBN 1 898576 11 4   £7.00

Changes and Challenges in Later Life: learning from experience

Edited by Yvonne Craig

Foreword by Claire Rayner ~ illustrated by Maggie Guillon

Older people share with those of all ages the desire for fulfilment - a need to transform surviving into thriving. This book brings together experts from Britain's major caring organisations to share their wealth of experience and practical advice on the sometimes difficult situations of later life. The wealth of experience concentrated in this book shows how changes and challenges can lead to positive attitudes and action.

Contents and authors

- *Legal rights and remedies* Barbara Beaton, Age Concern Legal Unit
- *Neighbours* Yvonne Joan Craig, Elder Mediation Project of Mediation UK & Archana Srivastava, Stirling University
- *A good ending* Gillian Dalley, Centre for Policy on Ageing
- *Mistreatment and neglect* Frank Glendenning, Centre for Social Gerontology, Keele University
- *Making the most of change* Mervyn Kohler, Help the Aged
- *Who cares?* Jill Pitkeathley, Carers National Association
- *The right retirement home* Rudi Reeves, Advisory, Information & Mediation Service for Retirement Housing
- *Care homes, residents and relatives* Jenny Stiles, Residents and Relatives Association

Maggie Guillon's drawings give a humourous perspective to each chapter.

1997 160pages ISBN 1 898576 10 6   £7.00

Europe at Walking Pace

by Ben & Betty Whitwell   . . . inspiring **and** practical . . .

can be used as a guide
for long or short walks
or put your feet up and
enjoy the wonderful
descriptions of the off
the beaten track places
that these adventurous
walkers reached and the
detailed observation of
the countryside that you
only get at walking
pace.

Ben and Betty Whitwell
retired early, rented out
their home, loaded up
their backpacks and set
off to walk through France, Spain and Portugal — following
some of the Grand Radonné routes and the Santiago de
Compestela Pilgrim's Way and sometimes just getting lost!

Their imagery is strong enough to rouse the most dormant
wanderlust. The ordinary and extraordinary people they
encountered, the pitfalls and the pleasures, are related with
frankness and humour.

1998 264pages ISBN 1 898576 13 0   £9.25